MW01005477

Rising Powers and Foreign Policy Revisionism

In *Rising Powers and Foreign Policy Revisionism*, Cameron Thies and Mark Nieman examine the identity and behavior of the BRICS (Brazil, Russia, India, China, and South Africa) over time in light of academic and policy-maker concerns that rising powers may become more aggressive and conflict-prone. They develop a theoretical framework that encapsulates pressures for revisionism through the mechanism of competition and pressures for accommodation and assimilation through the mechanism of socialization. The identity and behavior of the BRICS should be a product of the push and pull of these two forces as mediated by their domestic foreign policy processes. State identity is investigated qualitatively through the use of role theory and the identification of national role conceptions. Both economic and militarized conflict behavior are examined using Bayesian change-point modeling, which identifies structural breaks in time series data, revealing potential wholesale revision of foreign policy. Using this innovative approach to show that the behavior of rising powers is governed not simply by the structural dynamics of power but also by the roles that these rising powers define for themselves, the authors assert that this process is likely to lead to a much more evolutionary approach to foreign policy and will not necessarily generate international conflict.

Cameron G. Thies is Professor and Director of the School of Politics and Global Studies at Arizona State University.

Mark David Nieman is Assistant Professor of Political Science at Iowa State University.

Rising Powers and Foreign Policy Revisionism

Understanding BRICS Identity and Behavior Through Time

CAMERON G. THIES AND MARK DAVID NIEMAN

University of Michigan Press
Ann Arbor

Copyright © 2017 by Cameron G. Thies and Mark David Nieman
All rights reserved

This book may not be reproduced, in whole or in part, including illustrations, in any form
(beyond that copying permitted by Sections 107 and 108 of the U.S. Copyright Law and
except by reviewers for the public press), without written permission from the publisher.

Published in the United States of America by the
University of Michigan Press
Manufactured in the United States of America
♾ Printed on acid-free paper

2020   2019   2018   2017   4   3   2   1

A CIP catalog record for this book is available from the British Library.

Library of Congress Cataloging-in-Publication Data

Names: Thies, Cameron G., author. | Nieman, Mark David, author.
Title: Rising powers and foreign policy revisionism : understanding BRICS identity
    and behavior through time / Cameron G Thies and Mark David Nieman.
Description: Ann Arbor : University of Michigan Press, 2018. | Includes
    bibliographical references and index.
Identifiers: LCCN 2017020433| ISBN 9780472130566 (hardback : alk. paper) |
    ISBN 9780472123285 (e-book)
Subjects: LCSH: BRIC countries—Foreign relations. | BRIC countries—Foreign
    economic relations. | World politics—21st century. | BISAC: POLITICAL
    SCIENCE / International Relations / General. | POLITICAL SCIENCE /
    Government / Comparative.
Classification: LCC D887 .T43   2018 | DDC 327.09172/4—dc23
LC record available at https://lccn.loc.gov/2017020433

Cover credit © TinaFields/istockphoto.com

For José Ludwig—Cameron

For David and Ivalene Robbins—Mark

CONTENTS

PREFACE

We began working on this book when Mark was a graduate student and Cameron was a professor at the University of Iowa. We had overlapping interests in international relations theory, hierarchy, and methodological sophistication in testing grand theory. These general themes crystallized in a discussion of the China threat—the belief held by some in U.S. policy-making circles that China was actively seeking to overtake the United States as a kind of global hegemon, regardless of its leaders' stated intentions or behavior. We thought the China case offered a chance to examine both words and deeds to see how China described its identity and how it behaved economically and militarily as a rising power potentially engaged in foreign policy revisionism. We presented our first conference paper on the Chinese case at the 2012 American Political Science Association annual meeting. That would mark the beginning of our work to refine our theory, our combination of qualitative and quantitative methods, and the substantive examination of rising powers.

We have presented various portions of this book at conferences, seminars, and workshops around the world. Much of the theoretical discussion of rising powers was developed for the *Chinese Journal of International Politics* Research Workshop, "Managing Power and Identity in World Politics: The Political Psychology of China's Rise," held at Tsinghua University, Beijing, in June 2014. Many thanks to Kai He for inviting our participation in that workshop and to the editor, Yan Xuetong, and reviewers for the feedback that ultimately produced the 2015 article "China's Rise and the Socialization of Rising Powers." Cameron also received feedback on this work from public talks at the School of Public Affairs at Boise State University in 2016, the National University of Singapore in 2015, and the German Institute of Global and Area Studies (GIGA) in Hamburg, Germany, in 2013.

Nele Noesselt, Detlef Nolte, Leslie Wehner, and others all provided exceptional feedback at GIGA.

We have also presented versions of the substantive chapters as conference papers at the American Political Science Association in 2012 and 2013; International Studies Association in 2015; International Studies Association–Midwest in 2012, 2013, and 2014; International Studies Association–West in 2014; Midwest Political Science Association in 2014; European Political Science Association in Barcelona, Spain, in 2013 and in Edinburgh, Scotland, in 2014; the International Studies Association–Facultad Latinoamericana de Ciencias Sociales meeting in Buenos Aires, Argentina, in 2014; the World International Studies Committee Fourth Global International Studies Conference in Frankfurt, Germany, in 2014; the European Consortium for Political Research General Conference in Glasgow, Scotland, in 2014; and the European International Studies Association, Ninth Pan-European Conference on International Relations in Sicily, Italy, in 2015. We thank our many discussants and fellow panelists at these conferences for their insight and constructive criticism.

Two research stays were also critical in pushing the manuscript along toward completion. Cameron would like to thank the European University Institute in Florence, Italy, for the Fernand Braudel Senior Fellowship, which provided time to help fashion the various conference papers into a working book manuscript in 2015. In particular, Ulrich Krotz was especially generous with his support and feedback. Cameron would also like to thank Ravi Bhavnani and the faculty and students of the Graduate Institute of International and Development Studies in Geneva, Switzerland, for the 2016 visiting professorship that provided feedback on material from the book as it neared completion.

Melody Herr at the University of Michigan Press expressed great interest in the project as well as provided useful ideas that we incorporated in the research, and she ultimately convinced us to submit our work to the press. We also thank Mary Francis and Meredith Norwich, who helped shepherd the manuscript through the final stages. The anonymous reviewers were also very helpful in forcing us to clarify our theory and empirical evidence. Finally, Cameron would like to thank Arizona State University, particularly Dean Pat Kenney, for supporting the project. Mark would like to thank Olga Chyzh and the Departments of Political Science at the University of Missouri-Columbia, University of Alabama, and Iowa State University for their support and encouragement.

CHAPTER 1

Introduction: The "Problem" of Emerging Powers

Nearly two decades has passed since the language of emerging powers or rising powers entered into the business, academic, policymaking, and media discourses. The promise of emerging powers as safe sites for investment that offered large returns with little risk may not have played out exactly as proponents suggested, but forecasting is often difficult in economics and politics. The potential perils associated with emerging powers also quickly entered into the academic and policymaking discourses. In particular, with the increasing decentering and dispersion of power in the international system, were we headed toward some kind of systemic war? Most of our academic theories related to power transitions expected that the kind of economic growth that produces rising power would ultimately lead to demands for political revisionism that could be settled only by force. Challengers, revisionist powers, rising powers, or whatever term you prefer—these states, much like their predecessors in the early 20th century and before, would ultimately engage in war in the attempt to gain their preferred division of global economic benefits and their rightful status as a great power or even hegemon.

The promises and perils of emerging powers have thus occupied academic inquiry to a great extent across a variety of disciplines, but the perils are most frequently discussed within international relations and political science. Scholars have probed the meaning of the concept of emerging power and its relationship to nearby concepts like regional power or great power. Others have discussed whether the emerging powers most commonly identified—the BRICS (Brazil, Russia, India, China, and South Africa)—share enough in common to be considered members of the same category. Many have looked at these specific countries to examine their economic and political development trajectories over time and to assess whether they are in fact rising toward great power or some other status. Theoretical development concerning emerging powers, however, has been sparse. Most scholars are satisfied to review the literature on power transitions among great powers that experienced its heyday in the 1990s and then say either that the new crop of emerging powers fits with the theories or that they do not.

Emerging powers are increasingly self-aware of their perceived status as emerging powers. In other words, this phenomenon is not limited to academics, business, or the media creating a category of states; rather, policymakers within these countries now take this status as a social fact. Cooperation among emerging powers is now institutionalized in a number of ways, including the BRICS Forum and the IBSA Trilateral Forum. These institutions, though hampered by the differences among the members, seem to be able to engage in cooperation on some fronts. As emerging powers, these countries clearly would like changes in the global order, but it is not clear if this will amount to simply tinkering with the rules or eventually lead to a wholesale revision of the global economic, financial, and political order. Policymakers in the existing set of satisfied great powers see this as a particular problem. How should those who benefit most from the current order adjust to accommodate rising powers, or *can* they given their own particular constellation of domestic and international constraints? For academics, the problem of emerging powers is that our old theories on great power transitions may simply no longer apply in the contemporary world.

This book explores the phenomenon of emerging or rising powers. We develop a theoretical framework that encompasses existing knowledge about material competition in the international system. To this horizontal dimension of politics, we add a vertical dimension by taking into account socialization processes that govern ideational components of interstate interaction, including identity construction. While materialist theories of competition tend to be mechanistic in expecting that rising power produces conflict, our incorporation of ideational factors and socialization adds the possibility that agents, too, influence events. Decisions about political revisionism are, after all, decisions made by agents reacting to and shaping structural forces. The idea that agents and structures coact is not new, having been introduced to the discipline by constructivists like Alexander Wendt (1999). And those focused on emerging powers have also begun to consider not just the material bases of power but also the identity of these states. We bring together theorizing about structure at the international level, which makes us very interested as a discipline in emerging powers, with theorizing about agents at the foreign policy level, which helps us to understand their actual behavior.

If materialist theories of competition are right, then increased power should produce conflict behavior. It should also produce foreign policy orientations and identities that are more aggressive and status seeking over time to match the growth in power. Realism, with its belief that everything (interests, identity, beliefs) is reducible to power, becomes the baseline for our analysis. If our more nuanced approach considering both material competition and ideational socialization is correct, then we are unlikely to see shifts in behavior and identity matching power in any lockstep way. In fact, a variety of domestic and international factors may work to shift foreign policy orientations, meaning that dramatic changes in power may not be the only such factor. If anything, we may see socialization working to smooth out rough changes, so that identity and behavior appear more evolutionary.

Our goal is therefore to help academics and policymakers understand the potential for peril connected with emerging powers. Will shifts in power associated with the rising process lead automatically to conflict, or might other factors constrain emerging power behavior? We do not claim to have "solved" the problem of emerging powers for academics or policymakers, but we believe we have provided a more solid theoretical and empirical foundation to evaluate these claims. We combine both qualitative and quantitative empirical analysis in this book—something that has never been done in the study of emerging powers in political science. Statistical analyses of the matter are also rare. In the end, we believe we have elevated the discussion of emerging powers to a new level of theoretical and empirical sophistication.

We begin by reviewing some of the literature on emerging powers. In particular, we are interested in how others have defined them and in laying out our own focus on the BRICS. We then review the importance attached to emerging powers through a discussion of the expectations associated with them in the literature. The rest of the chapter is devoted to laying out the plan of the book, so that the reader understands how we plan to tackle the problem of emerging powers.

What Is an Emerging Power?

Emerging powers, like other categories of states (e.g., great power, middle power, rogue, ally) have important material and social/ideational dimensions. One might imagine the importance of the material and ideational aspects as varying by category, such that some states require a certain level of material capabilities to achieve a designation, even as they may also need some degree of social acceptance that the categorization is correct. Great powers, for example, require a high degree of material capabilities—and those great capabilities may force other states to socially acknowledge them in that status (e.g., U.S. achievement of great power status after the Spanish-American War). Conversely, one can imagine a declining great power ascribed the same status even as the material foundations for that status crumble (e.g., transition from USSR to Russia).[1] An emerging power or rising power (we use these terms interchangeably) clearly requires some shared acknowledgment that increasing material capabilities are consonant with a change in social recognition of the state's status.

Our focus is on the BRICS, the acronym given by an economist at Goldman Sachs to Brazil, Russia, India, and China, with the later addition of South Africa by the BRICS themselves in 2010 (O'Neill 2001). Goldman Sachs drew attention to this group of states because of their economic growth and potential to become sites for global investment. Tracing the process whereby the BRICS became a social category in the lexicon of not just investment professionals but the media, academics, and ultimately policymakers is beyond the scope of this book. Yet the BRICS are now widely accepted as a category of emerging or rising powers. The leaders of these countries have even begun to institutionalize themselves by holding annual summits since 2009 at different locations in the member states. This effort built on previous institutional efforts among subsets of the group, such as the Shanghai Cooperation Organization involving Russia and China (with India as an observer); the IBSA Trilateral Forum (India, Brazil, and South Africa); the BASIC group, which includes all of the members except Russia, and their interactions as members of other clubs like the G20. The BRICS Forum was created as a formal international organization in 2011. The organization has created a development bank that is still in the process of sorting out its operations and has on occasion taken common policy stances. Academics have even founded a number of centers to study the

BRICS phenomenon. By and large, the BRICS are equated with emerging or rising powers.

Many other developing countries are not included in the BRICS group of emerging powers. Mexico and South Korea, for example, are also economically quite developed and already members of the Organization for Economic Cooperation and Development (OECD). The BRICS acronym has led to the proliferation of other such acronyms designed to highlight countries with large and growing economies, such as MINT (Mexico, Indonesia, Nigeria, and Turkey) or CIVETS (Colombia, Indonesia, Vietnam, Egypt, Turkey, and South Africa). A great deal of heterogeneity exists in the countries included in the BRICS designation (Armijo 2007; Hart and Jones 2010). As Cooper and Flemes (2013: 945) suggest, Russia's claim to rising power is mostly a holdover of its status from the Soviet Union in the heyday of bipolarity. Materially, it has a smaller territory and a shrinking population, and it is succumbing to the resource course—it may best be described as a declining power (MacFarlane 2006). South Africa is probably the least likely to have the capabilities for a grab at the brass ring of great power status. Brazil, India, and China all have their own particular issues, with China as the standout on a pure material basis. At the same time, these are all developing countries with large segments of their populations in poverty.

What about these emerging powers as an economic classification? Indeed, Goldman Sachs's interests were not about political power per se but more about the potential for growth and investment in a group of large emerging markets. Armijo's (2007) review of the literature suggests that the BRICS group does not make much sense from a neoclassical economics perspective. They are quite heterogeneous in terms of their growth potential, their current state of development, and so on. Fourcade (2013) argues that each has followed a very different development strategy, leading the BRICS label to have nice symbolic and political resonance but not much economic substance.

We also are often reminded what these states are not. They are not great powers—at least, not yet. Many, such as China and India, have great power aspirations. Some such as Russia, were great powers (and perhaps still are). All emerging powers seem to be assumed to be rising in material power and social status such that one day they might well be great powers. They are also not, according to most observers, traditional middle powers. According to Jordaan (2003), traditional middle powers are wealthy, stable, democratic, egalitarian, and not regionally influential. Conversely, emerging powers are semiperipheral, inegalitarian, recently democratized, or still autocracies that have a great deal of regional influence. Emerging powers are thus almost always regional powers, even if their regional leadership is challenged. They are clearly not the average, small state that populates the international system. Despite their increased power, they are ardent defenders of state sovereignty (Laïdi 2012). Yet it is still difficult to come up with a precise coding scheme that would map emerging powers onto BRICS perfectly.

Yet this categorization has stuck in our collective mind, making it truly a social category of states. BRICS evokes something in our minds that makes these states similar enough to be considered together. As Hurrell (2006: 1) suggests, "They all seem to possess a range of economic, military and political power resources; some capacity to contribute to the production of international order, regionally or globally, and some degree of internal cohesion and capacity for effective state action." Mielniczuk (2013) even suggests that the changes in their identities have led to their common interests. It is enough for our purposes that the BRICS states are seen by most people—including their leaders, who have created a formal international organization—as a recognized social category of actors comprised of emerging powers.[2] This certainly does not mean that each of the BRICS agrees in principle with the others or with the role of the BRICS Forum, but there is at least some element of symbolic and political resonance in the concept (Grosny 2010; Roberts 2010; Tudoroiu 2012). Our task is to determine what this means for international relations.

We are certainly not the first to think about rising powers. A number of works have focused on the regional level of analysis in the aftermath of the Cold War. Much of this literature is devoted to how regions have evolved into more peaceful or more conflict prone zones. Buzan and Waever (2003) expanded Regional Security Complex (RSC) theory based on Buzan's (1991) original work to better understand the variation in regional peace and conflict. Buzan and Waever (2003: 34) put the BRICS on the major power spectrum, with Russia and China considered great powers (but not superpowers with global reach). Russia qualifies because of its recent exit from superpower status and China qualifies because it is talked about and treated as a potential challenger to the one remaining superpower, the United States. India lacks the capabilities, formal recognition, or a place in the strategic calculations of others to occupy the great power role. Instead, this framework positions India, Brazil, and South Africa as regional powers since they help define the polarity of their regional security complexes.

Work by Doug Lemke (2002) extends the power transition model to understand local hierarchies operating within the global hierarchy. The expectations about peace and conflict are the much the same as within the overall global hierarchy: when the local dominant power exercises a predominance of power, then the likelihood of peace within the local hierarchy is high. However, as a dissatisfied state achieves parity with the local dominant state, then the probability of war increases. While Lemke identifies four local hierarchies within South America prior to 1970, including an "Atlantic Coast" local hierarchy (Argentina, Brazil, and Uruguay), after 1970 he identifies a single hierarchy for all of South America dominated by Brazil (82). Lemke identifies an "East Asian" hierarchy dominated by China that includes Japan, Mongolia, North Korea, South Korea, and Taiwan (86) as well as a "South Asian" hierarchy dominated by India that includes Bangladesh, Bhutan, and Pakistan (86), and a "Southern Africa" hierarchy dominated by South Africa that includes Botswana, Lesotho, Malawi, Mozambique, Swaziland, Zambia, and Zimbabwe (89). Since his work focuses on the Third World, Lemke does not analyze Russia.

Several contributions to this literature focus more on the role of great power management of security dynamics and thus do not explicitly discuss emerging powers as regional powers. Contributions to the edited volume by Lake and Morgan (1997) also attempted to uncover the security dynamics of regions based on Buzan's (1991) RSC theory. Mares (1997) focuses mainly on the United States as a great power manager of regional security without focusing on Brazil as a regional power per se. Roeder (1997) notes that the hierarchical post-Soviet RSC quickly turned to one of Russian hegemonic dominance. Shirk (1997) is cautious in the analysis of East Asia and does not identify any of the major powers involved in the region (China, Japan, Russia, United States) as dominant; rather, she explores both balancing and concert opportunities for managing this RSC. Keller (1997) argues for a Southern Africa RSC but does not analyze it in detail or identify a special role for South Africa. Moreover, he also does not analyze India and South Asia.

Benjamin Miller (2007) explains the variation among regions' conflict propensities as a result of the congruence between nations and territorially defined states in a region (more congruence means less conflict) and great powers' involvement in the region (whether a region becomes a site of cold war or cold peace). While his focus is both above (great power) and below (state-to-nation congruence), the level of regional power, Miller credits Brazil with helping to shepherd the region to a normal peace because it has been status-quo-oriented even though the region experiences "partial US hegemony" (326). Miller does not examine any of the other regions considered in our project.

Stewart-Ingersoll and Frazier (2012) build on previous work by Buzan and Waever (2003) and Lake and Morgan (1997) to focus specifically on the importance of regional powers in defining the structure of their regional systems and the production of order. They develop a regional powers and security framework (RPSF) that considers the regional structure, regional power roles, and regional power orientations (e.g., status quo versus revisionist). They identify Russia, Brazil, and India as the regional powers for Central Eurasia, South America, and South Asia, respectively. What connects this work most closely with our own is that they identify foreign policy roles that regional powers play, including regional leadership, regional custodianship, and regional protection. While their identification of roles is largely theoretical—assuming that regional powers must also adopt what we would call the auxiliary roles of leader, custodian, and protector—our approach to emerging powers examines whether they adopt these specific roles and others. We often find the regional leader role and to a lesser extent regional custodian and regional protector in the BRICS states we analyze.

What Should We Expect from Rising Powers?

Those who have written about the rising power phenomenon, including specifically those who write on BRICS, see two general trajectories: either the BRICS behave similarly to rising powers of previous centuries, or they behave differently. So much for prediction. As we explain in the next chapter, most international relations theory expects a fairly close link between rising economic power or economic growth and political revisionism. Much of this theory essentially suggests that as states develop economically, economic power is translated into increased military capabilities as well as a desire to change the rules of the game. Thus, rising powers on their way to great power status typically challenged the international order led by whatever hegemon or dominant great power was in place at the time. The primary mechanism for that challenge was war. The U.S. discussion of the

"China threat" is couched primarily in these terms: China's economic rise will eventually lead it to develop more sophisticated military capabilities and force projection that will be directed against the United States. A war between the two is inevitable in this scenario, with China potentially emerging as the dominant great power at the apex of the international system.

One strand of the current literature has emerged to explore the implications of rising powers for global governance. Much of the debate revolves around whether these states' emphases on sovereignty and autonomy will unravel the global institutions developed since World War II. Gaskarth's (2015) edited volume addresses the issue of identifying rising powers and their interest and effects on global governance as well as the ethical dimensions associated with such potential changes. It also analyzes the BRICS as the central contenders for rising power status while acknowledging the obvious problems associated with each state. Alexandroff and Cooper's (2010) edited volume examines the way in which purported rising powers (i.e., China, India, Brazil, and Europe) interact in current global institutions, such as the G20 and the International Energy Agency, respond to global problems like the Great Recession and the War on Terror. The general tenor of the volume suggests that the world is undergoing a shift in the status quo, though it is tempered by the continued privileged position of the United States in global politics.

The BRICS development bank, these countries' demands for reform of the International Monetary Fund (IMF), and some of their common positions in the World Trade Organization (WTO) seem to confirm their desire to change the rules of the game. While BRICS members have obviously benefited enormously from their participation in a U.S. or Western-led liberal international economic order (LIEO) since the end of World War II and the establishment of the Bretton Woods system, their growing economic clout leads them to desire to alter the system to bring them more input into how it operates and how the gains are distributed. Some of the BRICS' conflict behaviors also seem to initially confirm the notion that as they have grown economically, they have become more prone to conflict. Russia's invasions of Georgia in 2008 and Ukraine in 2014 seem to signal a much more belligerent rising power. Russia's actions and intentions in Syria in 2015 also provoke much suspicion. China's confrontations with Japan over the Senkaku Islands and with many neighbors over the Spratley Islands also seems to represent an ongoing shift in bellicosity that many "China threat" analysts trace back to the Taiwan Straits Crisis of 1995–96.

The other possibility is that the international system has changed in some way, making the past no longer a good guide to the future. The rise of previous great powers took place without the potential constraining effects of formal international organizations. In fact, the rise of Germany and the multiple devastating regional and global wars that accompanied that rise led to the formation of the League of Nations, the United Nations, the European Union, and other international organizations. The institutionalization and legalization of world affairs has reached a high point in the post–World War II era that may have limited the kind of bellicosity often seen with rising powers of the past. We also live in a world where positions of central importance are occupied by democracies, including the United States and European Union states, which still largely control the global economy through the web of post–World War II institutions and have the largest concentration of military power through their overlapping military alliances. Three of the BRICS are themselves full-fledged democracies, with Russia having become much less democratic in recent years and China the only fully autocratic state in the group. If joint democracy is a primary contributor to pacific relations, then many of these BRICS are likely to seek nonmilitary forms of confrontation as they rise in power. Finally, economic interdependence is greater now than at any time since the eve of World War I. While such interdependence did not prevent World War I, the dramatic onset of globalization in the 1990s means that interdependence is not just economic but also social. All of these webs of constraint are likely to lead to more pacific relations (Oneal and Russett 2001). We can also add to these constraints the evolution of norms that may have led to both a situation of largely fixed international borders (Thies 2009; Atzili 2012) and a norm against great power war (Mueller 1989).[3]

While emergence has been associated with regional dominance or hegemony in the past, this may not necessarily be true for the current crop of rising powers. For example, Acharya (2014) lays out a number of future scenarios for Asia's regional security order, including anarchy, hegemony, hierarchy, concert/condominium, and community. Ultimately, he advocates for a consociational security order (CSO), defined as "a relationship of mutual accommodation among unequal and culturally diverse groups that preserves each group's relative autonomy and prevents the hegemony of any particular group/s" (59). While this would not provide for a hegemonic role or even a hierarchical system with China at the center, the CSO does seem to fit with much of Chinese rhetoric about a peaceful rise with China acting as a responsible stakeholder that respects state sovereignty. Similarly, Stewart-Ingersoll and Frazier (2010) consider hegemonic, collective security, power-restraining power, concert, and unstructured regional security complexes for the case of India within South Asia. They argue that India is in a unipolar situation, but the reality is a power-restraining power regional security complex without hegemonic dominance. Wehner (2015) notes that while Brazil's regional power is widely accepted, there are varying degrees of acceptance of its regional leadership role in South America. South Africa similarly suffers from varying perceptions that it is just a "deputy sheriff" in a sub-imperialist role or that it is truly a regional or even continental leader. Russia occupies a very complicated post-Soviet regional space that leads many of its neighbors to cooperate as a consequence of both mutual gains and fear of military or other forms of intervention. Thus, none of the BRICS offers a simple case of regional hegemony.

Even if the constraints posed by international institutions, joint democracy, and economic interdependence were not enough, currently rising states may learn from the rising periods of the current great powers. Buzan and Cox (2013) compare the rise of China to that of the United States and find many similarities in the two countries' foreign policy orientations. Both pursued economic engagement with the rest of the world, internal economic development, and isolationist policies to avoid engaging in global balance of power politics. Both were incredibly reluctant to take on global leadership roles, but once they did, they took firm positions. As a result of the comparison, Buzan and Cox suggest that a peaceful rise for China is possible if it avoids direct confrontation with the hegemon. They argue that the United States pursued this strategy vis-à-vis the United Kingdom. Thus, China may learn about its rising trajectory and possibilities from the U.S. comparison. Wolf (2014) also suggests that China might learn from Germany's rise. In particular, Wolf argues that Imperial Germany and contemporary China are too fixated on their national status, and such lack of recognition of status was one reason that Germany's relationship with the United Kingdom deteriorated prior to 1914. China should also be careful in recognizing the feedback effects of its maritime and territorial conflicts that seem related to status and seek settlement rather than confrontation if it wishes to have a peaceful rise.

On the economic front, Kahler (2013) notes the BRICS' convergence with the developed economies but suggests that their success in the current LIEO will likely lead them to negotiate changes to the rules without undoing the foundations of their success. Ban and Blyth (2013) and Stuenkel (2013) point out that the BRICS not only survived the global financial crisis (GFC) but actually helped the existing great powers through it by increasing their contributions to the IMF. And while the BRICS might be interested in revising the rules of the global economic game, they do not represent a fundamental challenge to the capitalist order (Apeldoorn, de Graaf, and Overbeek 2012), nor are they some kind of counterhegemonic bloc (Bremmer 2009). Instead, all of the BRICS engaged in some form of hybridization of the fundamental tenets of the Washington Consensus. According to Stephen (2014), this hybridization is producing both a more transnationally integrated and less liberal global order. Armijo, Mühlich, and Tirone (2014) demonstrate that the BRICS' systemic financial importance grew during the GFC but did so largely at the expense of Japan rather than the United States. Nel (2010) challenges these views by arguing that the BRICS want redistribution of global wealth and recognition of their new status. Sharma (2012) and Pant (2013) argue that the BRICS group has lost its sheen with growth rates that did not match projections and an inability to translate economic power into political-diplomatic clout. Thus, the BRICS have inspired a variety of reactions to their economic aims and outcomes.

As a result, status recognition has emerged as an important area of inquiry within international relations in the aftermath of the Cold War, including the decline of the Soviet Union/Russia and the emergence of rising powers (Volgy et al. 2011; Wolf 2011). Larson and Shevchenko (2003) draw on social identity theory (SIT) to explore how Gorbachev altered Soviet identity between 1985 and 1991. They argue that the "new thinking" allowed the Soviet Union to enhance its international status while preserving a distinct identity. The use of soft power to reposition the USSR as a moral leader of a new international order was used as a way to achieve great power status vis-à-vis its social group without needing to attain the same level of economic and technological development as the United States—a strategy the authors' term a "shortcut to greatness." SIT expects that states in low-status groups will attempt to improve their position through social mobility, social competition, or social creativity, with Gorbachev pursuing social creativity.

Larson and Shevchenko (2010) update their analysis of Russia and add China as they consider how these states interact in a U.S.-led global governance system in which the support of these countries is important to tackling global challenges such as weapons proliferation, terrorism, and rogue states. These authors argue that Russian and Chinese foreign policy since the end of the Cold War has sought primarily to restore their global power status through social mobility, competition, and creativity. Thus, if the United States wants their cooperation, the best strategy is to figure out how to recognize their status and identity. Larson and Shevchenko (2014) articulate the downsides of failure to recognize such status for Russia, which include humiliation, anger, vengefulness, and shame and produce foreign policy outcomes like the Ukrainian Crisis and Snowden Affair that the United States does not understand or appreciate. These themes are echoed by other analyses of Russia from a status perspective, such as Forsberg (2014).

Paul, Larson, and Wohlforth's (2014) edited volume tackles the issues associated with status inconsistency for rising powers and how existing powers may attempt to manage the rising powers. Contributors wrestle with problems associated with signaling attempts to change status and the kinds of security dilemmas this may provoke as well as with how status may be accommodated through international institutions. The volume adopts the same framework found in Larson's previous work to manage status inconsistency (social mobility, social competition, or social creativity) and applies it to understand India's, Brazil's, and Turkey's aspirations for higher-level status and their strategies for pursuing it. The authors are clear that status inconsistency need not lead to conflict between rising powers and the United States. If the United States pursues a policy of status enhancement that involves the BRICS in elite global clubs, deference on some regional issues, and pursuit of a global division of labor, then accommodation without conflict is a likely outcome. As Bezerra et al. (2015) and Miller et al. (2015) note, status attribution rests not just on capabilities but also on compliance/deviance with global norms, and the status of those norms is more or less accepted in the international system. Thus, attempts at accommodation may be reinforced or undermined by adherence to system norms that are widely accepted.

In general, there is no clear consensus about our expectations for the BRICS as emerging powers. Do they want to maintain the capitalist global economic system as it is, alter some of its rules and institutions, or replace it with something else? Do they want to increase their political power; if so, what would that look like? Even if we could agree on what they want, can they obtain what they want? What means will they use? Will they work through existing institutions to alter rules? Or will they eschew the slow creep of institutional change and diplomacy and adopt more confrontational economic and military tactics? In many ways, these questions can be reduced to a question posed by Brütsch and Papa (2013: 300): Can these alignments of emerging powers transform international relations as a result of their economic growth, or will they be remembered only as a "geopolitical fad"?

Our Argument and Evidence

We argue that previous analyses of emerging powers have focused too exclusively on the material dimension of politics. This is to be expected in international relations, since the analysis of power politics was at the heart of realism and the foundation of the field. The only way realists can predict change is as a result of shifts in power. Power transitions resulting from economic growth and their resulting global wars are thus a mainstay of realist theorizing. It is why so many were left scratching their heads when the Cold War between the United States and Soviet Union ended peacefully. Much of the movement to understand the social aspect of the international system can be dated to that event and activities preceding it, including constructivism and the reinvigoration of the English School. Thus, while it is understandable that rising powers prompt realists to hearken back to the literature on great power transitions, we should be careful to learn the other lessons of our academic discipline that the international system is also a social system. Thus, we combine material and social dimensions in our analysis, both theoretically and empirically.

Our theoretical approach is grounded in role theory, which has seen a resurgence of interest in foreign policy analysis in recent years (e.g., Thies 2010b; Harnisch, Frank, and Maull 2011; Thies and Breuning 2012; McCourt 2014). As role theorists have argued, roles are properties of both agents and structures and thus nicely tie together structural international relations theory and foreign policy analysis (Thies 2010b; Breuning 2011; McCourt 2014). We draw explicitly on a model originally developed by Thies (2001a, 2012, 2013, 2015a) to analyze the interplay of materialistic competition and ideational socialization and the resulting master statuses that states occupy. We add to this analysis a status of emerging or rising power and consider how competition and socialization pressures affect it. Within the socialization dimension we are able to consider the process of making foreign policy that leads states to adopt different national role conceptions, which reflect both past behavior as well as expectations of future behavior. Our behavioral approach to identity does not rule out the functional nature of some positions in international society; in addition, it has the benefit of matching nicely with our analysis of actual conflict events.

We have two primary competing hypotheses: (1) that identities and behavior change purely as a function of growth in material capabilities, and we consequently expect sharp breaks in them during rising periods, and (2) that identities and behavior change more gradually, in response to a variety of domestic and international factors but not solely in response to power shifts. We see these hypotheses as reflecting not only our theory but probably also the general notions in the larger literature. Our novel approach to mixed methods allows us to assess these hypotheses using qualitative analysis of the roles that states select for themselves as well as a quantitative analysis of their actual economic and militarized conflict behavior. We then conduct analyses of each of the foreign policy histories of the BRICS countries to identify the roles they select and examine their economic and militarized conflict history for patterns that match either hypothesis. Our goal is to balance depth in the analysis of each case with the breadth of cross-case comparison in response to theory.

Ultimately, we do not find convincing cross-case evidence that the BRICS identities or behaviors are knee-jerk responses to rising power. We identify foreign policy reorientations represented by roles and find some breaks in the economic and militarized conflict data. Yet these fit with more traditional notions of the domestic and international sources of foreign policy reorientation and less with the notion that rising power drives these changes. At least thus far in their histories, we might side with the notion that the BRICS as emerging powers are a "geopolitical fad."

Plan of the Book

We develop the theoretical framework that guides our inquiry in chapter 2. We draw on existing theories about change in international relations and foreign policy as well as the materialist theories of great power transition to think about the horizontal dimension of global politics associated with emerging powers. We also develop a vertical dimension of politics grounded in a role-theory-based approach to socialization. The interaction of the competition and socialization dimensions allows us to understand the variety of master statuses that states may occupy in the international system as well as some sense of the auxiliary roles they select to represent their identities and the kinds of behavior that may be associated with them. The socialization dimension in particular allows us to think more carefully about how the processes by which foreign policy is made are linked with the structure of the international system. It allows for more contingency and agency than a purely mechanistic material account of emerging powers. We end the chapter with our two primary hypotheses.

Chapter 3 outlines our mixed-method approach to investigating these two hypotheses. We develop a qualitative approach to understanding state identity grounded in role theory. Roles represent patterns of behavior—congealed, historical patterns of behavior that both tell us who a state thinks it is and what it does or is likely to do. Roles are thus a nice way to think about identity from a behavioral perspective. We draw on scholarly research to identify the roles that states select for themselves over time. The collection of these roles that are salient is known as the role set. We examine these role sets for shifts associated with growth in material power as well as other potential foreign policy reorientations identified in the literature arising from various domestic and international factors considered in making foreign policy. We also examine behavior as events that occur over time using Bayesian change-point modeling. This approach to statistical analysis allows us to investigate structural breaks that occur in the data-generating process—meaning changes in the direction and significance of effects of key explanatory variables. The data itself reveal such breaks, and we do not need to impose our theoretical beliefs on the modeling process (other than identifying the endogenous explanatory variables) to identify such breaks. We look to see if the breaks in the conflict behavior match predictions of rising material power, whether they match the kinds of foreign policy reorientations described previously, or even whether there are any changes in conflict behavior over time at all. We do this for data on both economic and militarized conflict. Our mixed-methods approach is unique to the emerging powers literature, as are each of the qualitative and quantitative methods separately.

We begin our analysis in chapter 4 by looking at Brazil. We examine the foreign policy literature to identify the roles adopted by Brazilian leaders on behalf of the state over time as well as the patterns identified in the economic and militarized conflict behavior by the statistical analysis. We then piece together the qualitative and quantitative evidence to analyze Brazil's rise and its association with conflict and a more aggressive foreign policy orientation. Similarly, chapters 5–8 examine Russia, India, China, and South Africa in succession. In each case, we examine the quantitative and qualitative evidence in light of our theoretical expectations.

Our concluding chapter 9 pulls together the analyses across all of the BRICS, something that is rarely done in the existing literature. We ultimately suggest that the brute materialist hypothesis that rising power produces conflict and foreign policy revisionism is not supported in either the qualitative or quantitative evidence for the states under consideration in this project. We see some changes in identity and behavior, but they tend to be more evolutionary and often match other foreign policy reorientations rooted in domestic factors. Thus far, the rise of the BRICS has not produced the kind of economic or political revisionism that proponents of the "China threat" and other realist theories would expect.

CHAPTER 2

Explaining Change in the International System: A Role-Theoretic Approach to Emerging Powers

Anyone interested in the phenomenon of rising powers must come to grips with essentially two interrelated issues. First, how should we conceptualize rising powers as a category of states that is somehow distinct from neighboring categories of states? There is a sense that these states are not great powers yet, but they may be someday. They might be regional powers with associated responsibilities for the maintenance of order within specific geographical or functional regions. Yet all regional powers are not necessarily rising powers on the way to great power status. Thus, we must define the thing we wish to study relative to other classes of similar things. Second, how should we understand the "rising" or "emerging" description of power associated with these states? Rising power refers to an increase in economic performance that is usually thought to spill over into increased military capabilities *over time*. The notion of a rise is thus more than just a quantitative increase; it is an increase over a period of time. Similarly, "emerging" signifies a state somehow being elevated above others. In the contemporary era, an emerging power has developed a certain level of competency in the economy and polity that allows it to stand apart from the vast majority of developing countries that populate the globe. Emergence is also a process that unfolds over time. Much like the next popular actor or singer, the "discovery" of such a state usually marks the accumulation of many years of development leading to a qualitative disjuncture between the past and present perceived performance of the individual.

Our approach to understanding emerging powers is grounded in role theory, which originally developed in sociology and family studies. Role theory was imported into foreign policy and international relations through K. J. Holsti's (1970) seminal study on national role conceptions (NRCs). As

19

Thies (2010a) noted in his review of the literature, role theory's use in foreign policy analysis went through multiple waves of popularity in the 1980s and 1990s. The most recent revival can be traced to developments on both sides of the Atlantic, including work that ultimately produced the Harnisch, Frank, and Maull (2011) edited volume and the Thies and Breuning (2012) special issue of *Foreign Policy Analysis*. The volume and quality of work that has developed since that time might also be considered an emergence of sorts in the theoretical literature attempting to span foreign policy analysis and international relations.[1]

What is most appealing about role theory as it has been used in foreign policy analysis is that it already contains the central insight of constructivist international relations theory—the mutual co-constitution of agents and structures. Agents in the form of states (or leaders acting on behalf of states) interact with each other through foreign policy. These social interactions help to establish who states are—that is, their social identities in the form of roles enacted within role relationships. Agent interaction and practice thus help to form the distribution of ideas that constitutes the social structure, even as the cultural material contained in that structure constrains and enables agents. Stated more simply, individuals or corporate actors like states cannot simply be whomever they want to be—such roles must already exist in the distribution of ideas to allow for the possibility of role taking and enactment. This does not preclude the creation of new roles, but innovations in roles or in their enactment often meet resistance in any culture. While interstate culture is thin relative to that contained within domestic society, it is nonetheless a persistent feature of the interstate system and one that has thickened considerably over time as documented by the world society or world polity approaches in sociology associated with the Stanford School (e.g., Meyer et al. 1997). The creation of new roles or the enactment of roles in different ways often requires cultural power. The form such power has historically taken in a rather thin interstate culture is material power. As Thies (2013) has argued, states can attempt to adopt any role they choose, but they are more likely to be successful the more material power they can muster to defend such choices.

Thus, the perceived increase in power associated with rising or emerging powers that is thought to be the source of new identities and behaviors is perfectly consistent with foreign policy role theory. Rising powers have experienced economic success that then allows them to develop a variety of other capacities, including military capabilities. Their interactions with other states may change as they shed old roles more appropriate for smaller, developing states and take on new roles that reflect their increased status and capacity for action in the region and potentially the world. These role transitions can offer the potential for conflict with other states. Every role requires a counterrole to form a meaningful social relationship. Thus, to be a regional leader, a state needs regional followers. Those followers may have their own ideas about how a leader should behave, thus necessitating mutual accommodation between the leader's self-conceived role identities and those of the followers. If accommodation fails, then the role relationship becomes strained, and this strain can result in militarized or economic conflict (Nieman 2013, 2016b). What heightens the possibility of conflict is that rising powers are by definition more powerful than their neighbors. Thies (2013) has argued that great powers are largely able to adopt roles they choose even if others do not socially ratify or approve of such roles. This observation is also likely to apply to rising powers, which may or may not be constrained by the socialization attempts of existing great powers.

In this chapter, we begin by exploring how previous contributions to international relations theory have thought about change. This is because the "rise" or "emergence" of new powers is a change that not only is relevant to the geographic region such a state inhabits but also has international system-wide consequences. As we will see, previous contributions to the literature that examine historical cases of the rise of great powers tend to see a strong connection between economic growth and political revisionism. Most of that earlier literature grounded in realism tends to view the apex of the system as a confrontation between challengers/revisionists and status quo powers. Such challenges are usually thought to produce conflict and war.

We then draw on an existing role theory framework to understand the contending forces of competition and socialization on states as they occupy various status positions in the international system and adopt associated auxiliary roles. The framework developed by Thies (2001a, 2012, 2013) is modified to include a status for emerging powers. This framework develops a general model of the global political order and the associated mechanisms that drive changes in state identity and behavior. We do not test all of the possible implications from this general model in this book. Instead, we focus on transitions between statuses and their associated auxiliary roles contained in a state's role set—in particular, to the emerging power status and the related potential for conflict. The last section of the chapter develops our understanding about these role transitions and produces two testable hypotheses that are assessed in each empirical chapter using qualitative data on roles and quantitative data on economic and militarized behavior.

Understanding Change in Foreign Policy and International Relations

The problem of understanding change in foreign policy and international relations has bedeviled scholars since the origin of the field and in particular since the theoretically unanticipated peaceful end of the Cold War (Rosati, Sampson, and Hagan 1994).[2] The fact is that foreign policy for most states, most of the time, demonstrates remarkable continuity. Scholars tend to be taken off guard when major changes occur in the international system and in the foreign policy orientations of states. The reasons for this tend to be that the underlying structural characteristics of most states are stable. Rising powers, however, tap into a long-established source of change: economic growth that changes their own capabilities and alters the global distribution of power, thereby encouraging revisionist foreign policy goals that disrupt the international political order.

In most international relations approaches to understanding change, the relationship between rising powers and changes in the international political order is relatively deterministic. For example, Gilpin's (1981) well-known realist argument is based on five key assumptions. First, the international system is in equilibrium if no state believes it is profitable to try to change it. Second, a state will attempt to change the system if it believes that the benefits exceed the costs. Third, a state will engage in territorial, economic, or political expansion until the marginal costs are equal to or exceed the marginal benefits. Fourth, once equilibrium is reached, the economic costs of maintaining the status quo tend to rise faster than the economic capacity to support it. Finally, if this disequilibrium is not resolved, then the system must change to reflect a new distribution of power. The differential growth of power is the primary driver of change, and war is the typical mechanism that leads to movement from one equilibrium to another. Thus, the great powers of yesteryear and their challengers moved through this war-driven system of rise and decline.

Many of Gilpin's ideas about the role of uneven economic growth were derived from Organski's (1958) and Organski and Kugler's (1980) work on power transition theory (see also Levy 2008). In this approach, the international system changes as states rise and fall. Uneven economic growth drives this dynamic and is itself a product of changes in population, economic productivity, and the state's ability to extract resources from society. The dominant power in any system sets up the political order. Other great powers, middle powers, and smaller states that benefit from the existing system are considered satisfied states that ally with the dominant power, bandwagon, and work to support and reinforce the international political order. Dissatisfied great powers pose the greatest threat to this system, as they believe the institutions, rules, and division of benefits in the system are unfair. Dissatisfied great powers are most problematic when their power continues to grow relative to the dominant state. The key proposition that emerges from this theoretical approach is that war is most likely to occur when the dissatisfied challenger begins to achieve power parity with the dominant state. Once war occurs and the challenger has overtaken the dominant state, then a new international system with new rules and political order is established.

Structural theories like these abound to account for the dynamic of systemic leadership, including additional work on long cycle leadership theory (Modelski 1987), power-cycle theory (Doran 1989, 1991), hegemonic stability theory (Kindleberger 1973), and others (see Lake 1993 for a review). Of these, Doran's (1989) relative power-cycle theory perhaps shares the most affinity with the model we develop in this book since he considers both material power and national role conceptions. Despite the consideration of both material and ideational factors, his model still is rather deterministic, though not in the largely linear way of the other structural approaches. Doran argues that great powers follow a cyclical path of growth, maturation, and decline, even though the highs/lows and length of time that these phases last will differ for each state. The unevenness of the cycle is largely attributed to the uneven growth rates of the states in question, just as with the other structural approaches. In Doran's model, war is most likely during two inflection and two turning points in the cycle. The lower turning point is where most states enter the great power system when their relative position changes from a declining to a rising power as capabilities begin to increase. The first inflection point occurs when the state's relative capabilities are still rising but slow down to a more normal rate. The upper turning point is when the state's relative capabilities decline and it changes from a rising to a declining power. The second inflection point occurs when the state's relative decline slows down and the future appears brighter. Since each point is unpredictable, decision-maker planning based on the trend of the current phase can be dangerous. For example, the state's national role conception is in part a function of where it is in the relative power cycle, but once it proceeds through a critical point, difficult role transitions must occur. These critical points are marked by uncertainty, overreaction, and misperceptions, which is why war is much more likely. Carranza (2016) recently applied this approach to both Brazil and India to suggest they have not yet reached the first inflection point.

Despite the increased nuance of Doran's theory, it, like the other structural theories, presumes that underlying changes in economic growth will typically lead to political revisionism, war, and ultimately a new international system with new leadership. Implicitly, economic growth must also then be responsible for reordering domestic political priorities, including the foreign policy orientations of the rising powers. It is not surprising that these structural theories black-box this domestic process, especially given that some scholars argue that theories of international relations cannot also be theories of foreign policy (Waltz 1979; cf. Elman 1996). This is true of even Doran's approach, in which the origin and understanding of national role conceptions is not clearly articulated.

Classical realists have often turned to typologies of states, such as "revisionist" versus "status quo" states (Wolfers 1962) to explain foreign policy orientations in the international system. Schweller's (1997) neoclassical realism expands the typology to wolves, lions, lambs, jackals, owls, hawks, doves, foxes, and ostriches, each of which is thought to engage in different foreign policy behavior based on its interests and capabilities. Yet decisions to engage in foreign policy revisionism are still decisions, even if they are driven by structural imperatives (Hermann 1990: 20; Carlsnaes 1993; Welch 2005; Fordham 2011; Braumoeller 2012). Leaders of rising powers must still work within their cultural and institutional milieus to reorient foreign policy in service of new global goals (Sprout and Sprout 1965). We turn to the foreign policy literature for further insight into the potential for change in foreign policy.

Much of the study of foreign policy change is rooted in the notion analogous to the structural international relations theories that a stable foreign policy equilibrium exists until it is disrupted by some internal or external shock that provides leaders a window of opportunity to reorient policy (Barnett 1999; Gustavsson 1999). Rosenau's (1981) early work treated the state and its foreign policy decision makers as "adaptive entities" that work to minimize costs and maximize opportunities in the environment, much like Gilpin's states in the international system. Decision makers adapt to the domestic and international environments, resulting in policy stasis until some shock occurs. Goldmann's (1988) approach similarly identifies "policy stabilizers" that work to make foreign policy sticky even as destabilizers in the environment lead policymakers to want to change course to adapt. Volgy and Schwarz (1994) describe the various "webs of constraint" that work to maintain policy continuity, while Kleistra and Mayer (2001) discuss "carriers and barriers" for change. Consistent with these accounts, Nieman (2016a) finds that, within the European system, state leaders operated under a common culture that shaped their foreign policy decisions and their expectations of their neighbors' foreign policies until a structural break just prior to World War II. Thereafter, a new, distinct culture emerged, emphasizing a new and different set of constraints in shaping foreign policy behavior and expectations.

Not all change is presumed to be abrupt and dramatic, however. Hermann (1990) identifies four levels of possible foreign policy change: adjustment changes (in effort and scope), program changes (means and instruments), problem/goal changes (ends and purposes), and international orientation change (global role and activities). While the first level is somewhat incremental and even routine, a "major foreign policy redirection" includes the last three levels of change. According to Hermann, these changes can be leader-driven or can result from bureaucratic advocacy, domestic restructuring, or external shocks. From this perspective, internal and external shocks are again most likely responsible for major shifts in foreign policy orientation.

Skidmore (1994) proposes a more general model of foreign policy response rooted in the notion that change can be sporadic or evolutionary. The two familiar variables are once again the degree of external compulsion and the degree of domestic constraint. When external compulsion is high, we are likely to see policy adaptation; when it is low, we are likely to see rigidity. Domestically, a strong, centralized state that is autonomous from society can institute policy change with relatively low costs, while a weak, decentralized state may be unable to institute policy change. Skidmore suggests that this combination of variables underlies traditional realist and institutionalist interpretations of foreign policy change.

According to his argument, realism can best explain the behavior of middle powers that have modest international power yet a great deal of domestic autonomy. Their sensitivity to external compulsion and flexibility to act in the domestic arena provide an opportunity for foreign policy change. This view fits quite nicely with structural theories' views on rising powers as well our approach. Conversely, high degrees of sensitivity and flexibility thus produce more evolutionary foreign policy change. Institutional approaches are better suited to explaining the behavior of states with high levels of international power and low levels of domestic autonomy, such as hegemons. The United States, for example, has a high degree of international capabilities and is therefore less sensitive to external compulsion, yet it is relatively constrained on the domestic level. Foreign policy rigidity is more likely in this scenario. Low degrees of sensitivity and flexibility thus produce only sporadic change in foreign policy. This argument is also consistent with structural theories of international relations that tend to view hegemons or great powers as prisoners of their own successes, destined to decline as a consequence of internal institutional rigidities that lead them to fail to innovate and keep pace with rising challengers.

The kind of nuance introduced by Skidmore into the notion of foreign policy response to external shocks inducing major change is further explored in the some of the early literature grounded in role theory. Holsti (1982: 2) distinguished between normal foreign policy change, which is "slow, incremental and typified by low linkages between different sectors" of functional activity, and "foreign policy restructuring," which "takes place more quickly, expresses an intent for fundamental change, is nonincremental and usually involves the conscious linking of different sectors." Foreign policy restructuring thus constitutes "the dramatic, wholesale alteration of a nation's pattern of external relations" (ix). Holsti concluded that foreign policy restructuring was more likely in small, developing states, including China, which he argued moved from national role conceptions highlighting dependence to self-reliance to isolation to diversity between 1959 and 1976. Although Holsti (198) was somewhat skeptical that we could explain why some countries engage in foreign policy restructuring while others do not, he ultimately suggested that countries that did restructure were mainly attempting to reassert autonomy. Yet the attempt to restructure foreign policy did not always produce the desired results. In general, Holsti argued that success is more likely when states choose foreign policy roles that do not threaten the hegemon or its strategic interests. They are therefore less likely to end up in conflict over their new roles that would result in "coercive, violent, and punitive actions" (218).

Overall, the structural approaches to change recognize that the international system is comprised of a dominant state that largely structures the international order to its own liking. As its relative economic and political preponderance declines and others' power increases, the likelihood of a challenge and major war increases. Economic growth within rising powers is likely to produce political revisionism as these states attempt to alter the international order to produce a greater flow of its benefits to them at the expense of the dominant state and it status quo supporters. Transitions—of power and identity—are difficult and fraught with the potential for conflict. Yet these structural theories were built on historical cases of great powers and their wars centered on Europe. It is possible that the contemporary international system has moved away from major power war (e.g., Mueller 1989). Concerns about the "China threat" may be overblown in terms of a coming military confrontation between the United States and China— China's rise need not be a threat (Chih-yu and Jiwu 2013). Other mechanisms may lead to the transition from one dominant state to another, or perhaps we have entered an era in which such hegemonic-led configurations of international order no longer exist. Moreover, the singular focus on the power transitions of existing great powers may be inappropriate for states that, while rising, may not yet have reached great power status. States at a lower relative power position—such as Brazil, India, South Africa, and other major powers—may have different short-term goals and exhibit different behavior than a rising state that is already recognized as a great power, even if the different categories of states are experiencing similar rates of economic growth. That is, it is not just the rate of the rise but the initial relative position vis-à-vis the hegemon that affects conflict behavior and rhetoric (see, e.g., Kadera 2001). In the end, these systemic theories are suggestive but unsatisfying for understanding emerging powers. Their primary focus on material factors locks them into a very mechanistic relationship between economic growth and political revisionism.

Foreign policy approaches offer a more nuanced consideration of both the international and domestic structures that condition choices to alter foreign policy orientations. There is no doubt that economic growth—and relative economic growth in particular—affects the way a rising power makes calculations about its own roles and behaviors vis-à-vis the rest of the world. The rest of the world is also aware of such changes in relative economic growth. Yet, these structural changes must be filtered through the processes of making domestic policy that lead to choices about political revisionism or mutual accommodation with potential rivals induced by changes in economic and political power. What is needed is an approach that combines both the emphasis on structure contained in traditional international relations theory and the agency associated with foreign policy analyses. Luckily, role theory provides the perfect vehicle to accommodate these two approaches to understanding rising powers within the global political order.

A Role-Theoretic Framework
for Understanding Emerging Powers

At the level of international relations theory, we need a framework that can locate emerging powers within the hierarchy of states. We also need a sense of the mechanisms that are operating at a structural level to move states up and down this hierarchy over time. Drawing on Thies's (2001a, 2003, 2010b, 2012, 2013, 2015a) work on state socialization, we develop a positional picture of the structure of the international system that contains a number of statuses occupied by states. The primary mechanisms driving movement from status to status are competition and socialization, which Waltz (1979) identified as the mechanisms that help bring units into conformity with structure. Thies (2001a, 2010b, 2012, 2013) rehabilitated the socialization mechanism, which had largely been ignored in subsequent neorealist theory and application focused on competition as the primary driver of international politics.

Once we consider the effects of socialization and competition on the major statuses in the international system, we also can get a sense of the types and number of auxiliary roles that states adopt through the foreign policy process as a part of their role sets over time. In this book, we focus specifically on the emerging power status, though the more general model of global political order has been explored through in-depth case studies for the United States and Israel as they transitioned through many of these statuses over their histories (Thies 2013). The empirical chapters in this book detail the auxiliary roles adopted by states over time as they transition to the emerging power status but do not examine the foreign policy decision-making processes at the same level of detail. Our goal is to assess whether foreign policy change has been rather abrupt and pronounced in the revisionist way that one might expect from structural materialist approaches to international relations theory or whether such change has been more gradual, in keeping with the foreign policy approaches outlined earlier. We observe this by examining both the contents of the states' role sets and major shifts in their revealed economic and militarized conflict behavior.

Our role theory framework sets emerging powers within a larger social structural view of the international political order. By virtue of their relative power, emerging powers are likely to become rivals with existing great powers. Existing international relations theory assumes that emerging powers will challenge the status quo as their growth catches up with the dominant power in the system. Thinking about them as rivals softens this mechanistic approach a bit, since rivalry describes an ongoing hostile relationship with periods of cold and warm peace in addition to conflict. As Thompson (1995) argued, there are two general types of rivalries: spatial and positional. Spatial rivalries tend to focus on disputes over territory between minor states with relatively equal capabilities in their region. Positional rivalries, much like those described in the systemic theories, require some rough symmetry in capabilities. The substance of positional rivalry revolves around relative position at or near the apex of the international system. Both types of rivalries are competitions. Thies (2001a, 699) argues that two mechanisms account for competition among states: organizational competency and rational imitation.

Organizational competency refers to the notion that states have developed a certain level of organization that allows them to appropriate benefits from legitimate activities such as trade and to be free of liability for any damage caused in the pursuit of such benefits. The flow of benefits thus allows states to maintain their rank or status in the system. Any innovation in appropriation by other states is quickly adopted by other states to maintain relative status. Rational imitation is a second mechanism that does not rely on a notion of social conformity; rather, imitation is a useful strategy in the pursuit of resources and position.[3] Rivalries conditioned by mechanisms of competition are likely to occur between great powers and between great powers and major powers, according to Thies's, argument, which we can extend to emerging powers since they are somewhere in between major and great powers. These states are likely to have the kind of organizational competency to make the fullest use of their capabilities, and if they imitate, they imitate each other. Thies (2001a, 699) previously compared this way of thinking about competition among powerful states to power transition theory.

Yet competition between highly capable states is not the end of the story. Thies adds to this horizontal dimension of politics a vertical dimension focused on socialization. Great powers are the chief socializers in any international system, and they socialize new states into the rules of the game and attempt to enforce those rules on existing states (see also Nieman 2013, 2016b). Socialization can occur through the direct internalization of communicated normative expectations (through direct instruction or altercasting) or through the indirect assimilation of norms through identification with socializing agents (through imitation or modeling). The two mechanisms associated with socialization in this approach are the social proof heuristic and dissonance reduction.

The social proof heuristic essentially holds that when individuals are unclear about what to do, they observe what others are doing for clues about how to behave—that is, imitation or modeling of similar actors. Dissonance reduction occurs when an actor's beliefs and perceptions appear inconsistent with those of other actors and the first actor moves to reduce the cognitive dissonance. Rivalries grounded in socialization are therefore likely to occur between states of different status, with higher-status states directly communicating norms or indirectly being imitated by states of lower status. Rivalries emerge when lower-status states fail to pick up on cues or resist attempts to bring their behavior into conformity with system norms. Thies (2012, 2013) developed a socialization game drawing on dissonance theory in which states could force or play dissonant roles with resolve, allow them to fizzle, or self-consciously reject them.

Thies's (2001a, 712) framework for the study of emerging powers is useful because he considers how competition and socialization interact on states occupying a master status, which can be thought of as a role/position that is salient in every social situation (i.e., great power, major member, minor member, novice). Table 2.1 reviews the terminology of these master statuses along with terms frequently used in the literature on emerging powers. Figure 2.1 shows an adapted version of Thies's visual representation of these master statuses, and in this discussion, we focus on the transition from the major power master status to the emerging power master status on the way to great power status. Major members have relatively high capabilities and thus have a greater number and type of roles in the international system than minor members or novices. On balance, more of these roles are self-selected and achieved in the system than are ascribed to them by great powers (though this still will occur). On balance, more of the roles will be active rather than passive in nature.[4] Major members who act as regional powers are thought to be responsible for socializing novice and minor members in their geographic subsystem but cannot act with impunity given that they are still subject to socializing activities by the great powers. Thies (2001a, 710) generates a number of testable propositions from this framework; however, the expectations for an acknowledged emerging power are somewhat different than for a major member that may be satisfied with the status quo.

Thies (2001a, 710) predicted that great powers socialize major members and that major members were primarily engaged in competition with other major members. Nieman (2013, 2016b) extends this framework to account for great powers' efforts to socialize all major and minor members, and the degree of success of the efforts conditions how states engage with one another. He argues that states identify how close other states are to a particular great power based on which policies and institutions are imitated and are careful to account for this when interacting with one another. As the number and material strength of rival great powers increases, Nieman finds that

Table 2.1. Terminology of Statuses

Novice: a newcomer in any social system, such as a newly created state with relatively low or uncertain capabilities and few roles, and a state that is subject to high degrees of socialization pressure.

Minor Member: a small state in terms of capabilities, and one that has mostly roles ascribed to it and is subject to medium socialization pressure. Most states in the international system fall into this category.

Major Member: a larger state in terms of capabilities, and one that is able to achieve more roles than are typically ascribed to it. It is subject to medium socialization pressure.

Regional Power: a subset of the major member status that refers to states with higher capabilities than most of their regional peers; those capabilities are thought to imbue such states with special responsibilities for the management of the regional order.

Emerging Power (aka **Rising Power**):   a major member that has begun to move toward great power status. Its growing capabilities allow it to achieve more roles even as it is subject to high degrees of socialization pressure.

Great Power: the status with the highest degree of capabilities in the system and the most roles. It is generally not subject to socialization pressure, but it will be engaged in competition with other great powers as well as major members (and the emerging power subset).

Hegemon: a status above the great powers, reserved for states that dominate the international system via capabilities and socialization efforts to ensure acceptance of the normative order they generate.

Note: Not all of these statuses are represented in the Thies 2001a model, though the others are defined relative to the four that are included (i.e., novice, minor member, major member, and great power).

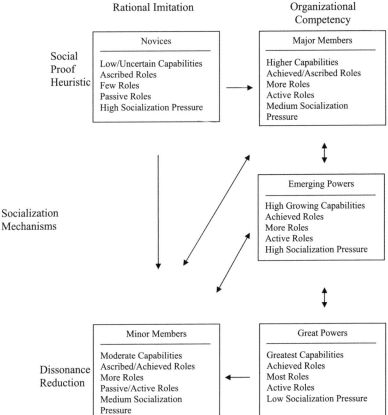

Fig. 2.1. Master Statuses in the International System. (*Note:* Adapted from Thies 2001a.)

they are more likely to act as third-party interveners, competing with one another for member state influence.

What is different in the rivalry context for emerging powers is that they are simultaneously engaged in competition with and socialized by great powers. Thus, there is not only stiff competition as a result of the fact that both are organizationally competent and adopting novel strategies for enhancing their benefits derived from legitimate appropriation as well as a high degree of socialization pressure from the great power to an emerging power. But the emerging power's higher degree of capabilities can also mean that it can demand accommodation by the great power and other member states.

In Thies's (2001a, 713) analysis, the United States was attempting to socialize China in its interstate rivalry—obviously, the socialization process was slow, China did not acquiesce to the U.S. view of the normative order and a rivalry formed. The only other case of a great power socializing a major member identified in his analysis was the United Kingdom socializing the United States. The United States could also be identified as an emerging power, which represents another case of a state with major member status under conditions of rivalry that was also an emerging power.

Thies (2001a, 705) also suggests that rivalries conditioned by the social proof heuristic mechanism of socialization form under several conditions. First, the speed of socialization is affected by the socializee's level of commitment to the socializer and the larger group represented by the latter. If the level of commitment is low, then the process can be long and fraught with conflict. Second, the extent of differences between the socializee and socializer affect the speed of socialization—greater differences reduce the speed. Thus, the level of commitment and extent of difference are likely to affect the pace and outcome of the process of socialization. In the case of the current group of emerging powers, the main issues seem to be their level of commitment to the current global order and the extent of differences between them and the United States and other satisfied great powers.

Given that emerging powers are moving toward great power status, it is likely that dissonance reduction mechanisms also come into play. The emerging power may choose to adopt roles that are commensurate with its new capabilities but that are not accepted by members of the great power rank. Emerging powers may also attempt to enact roles that are inconsistent with their underlying capabilities, thus necessitating socializing pressure to abandon those roles. Positive socialization outcomes (from the perspective of the great power) occur when the emerging power abandons a role judged inappropriate—allowing it to fizzle even if the emerging power still believes the role is appropriate or changing its view altogether (Thies 2012, 2013). Rivalries occur in this circumstance when the great powers are unable to convince the emerging power that it is playing an inappropriate role and the state "resolves" to continue pursuit of the role or enacts it by "force" (Thies 2012, 2013).

We can largely set aside the competition mechanisms for analytical focus, since the organizational competency mechanism is common to all emerging powers. We can therefore focus largely focus on the socialization mechanisms. This model is primarily concerned with the *process* of socialization, such that emerging powers with relatively high capabilities are attempting to achieve more roles for themselves (as opposed to having those roles ascribed to them) and face high socialization pressure. Our knowledge of the social proof and dissonance reduction mechanisms operating on behalf of the socialization process also helps guide our expectations about emerging power behavior. At the same time, these mechanisms contain guidance about the possible *outcome* of the socialization process. The model suggests that with their relatively high capabilities paired with aspects of the socialization mechanisms, emerging powers that have an uncertain level of commitment and great differences with its socializers are likely to resist socialization efforts to produce an outcome that is suboptimal for the great power engaged in the socialization process.[5]

Role Transitions and Foreign Policy Change

Dropping out of the level of structural international relations theory, we can now focus on the foreign policy dimension of roles adopted by emerging powers. In this book, we consider the foreign policy orientations of states to be comprised of the role sets they have developed. A role set consists of any number of auxiliary roles attached to a single status (Thies 2001a). The major power status, for example, might also contain auxiliary roles such as mediator of conflict, internal developer, international developer, peacekeeper, and the like.[6] Stability in foreign policy and associated behaviors is likely when a role set contains the same primary roles over long periods of time. Auxiliary roles may come and go in the role set, but such change is incremental and represents normal foreign policy change. Foreign policy restructuring occurs when the primary roles and their associated auxiliary roles change dramatically at any point in time. Such restructuring normally results from some major internal or external shock, which may cause a realignment of domestic political priorities that either activate latent aspects of identity or call for new identities represented by roles as constructed by political actors. We rely on the existing foreign policy literatures of the BRICS countries to give us indications of the kinds of internal and external shocks that may have brought about foreign policy restructuring. Yet even such shocks may not bring about wholesale foreign policy restructuring, thus requiring the documentation of such roles over time. We carefully examine the role sets of our states before and after purported shocks to see if such restructuring is evident.

For example, Germany's foreign policy role conception as a civilian power underwent scrutiny as a result of a dramatic external/internal shock in the 1990s posed by reunification (Harnisch 2001). Structural realists would suggest that Germany's rising power should lead to the remilitarization of the state and its foreign policy, institutionalists would suggest continuity in the civilian power role as a consequence of Germany's embeddedness in a variety of international institutions, and constructivists would also expect continuity based on the stability of German foreign policy culture. Harnisch (2001) suggests that a role-theoretic approach better explains the aspects of change and continuity of German foreign policy than any of the existing theoretical paradigms. He finds that Germany has, by and large, kept its traditional civilian power role conception, though changes to that role conception thought to be induced by relative changes in power and institutions were actually mediated through the existing civilian power role conception. Thus, the end of the Cold War may have caused significant reflection on Germany's primary role conception and enactment but was not determinative in changing its foreign policy orientation. This example offers a strong caution to structural determinism and leads us to adopt a foreign policy orientation toward rising powers that considers the "carriers and barriers" to change in foreign policy orientation and behavior represented by roles.

Allen and Van de Vliert (1984: 9–16) sketch out a general model of the role transition process. The model begins with antecedent conditions, which include potential causes for role transition, such as chance events, social systemic forces, changes in role senders, or changes in the capabilities or motivations of the agent itself. Chance events that may affect the role transition process for state actors could include a natural disaster or unexpected foreign policy crisis. Social systemic forces would include a change in the distribution of material power in the international system or a change in prevailing values, beliefs, norms, or other forms of ideas. Since roles require counterroles, role senders (those in complementary positions) may change their roles—an existing actor may drop out of a role, a new actor could fill that role, or no actor may step forward from the audience to perform the counterrole. Finally, characteristics of the actor itself may change as it acquires more power or domestic-level beliefs about identity change.

Any of these types of antecedent conditions that generate internal and external shocks may result in the emergence of a new power in the international system.

The next step in the model is role transition itself. The role transition process has three key features: the degree of discontinuity between the two successive roles, the ability to anticipate the change, and the degree of normative governance of the change. The degree of discontinuity refers to the changes and contrasts in the content of the new role compared to the old, how active or passive the behavioral expectations are for the new role, and the mandatory nature of the performance of the new role. In all cases, the behavioral expectations of the old role often bleed into the new role. Further, the more that the actor can anticipate the new role and manage the transition, the easier the process is for that actor (and significant others). If the actor can correctly anticipate a new role and associate behavioral expectations, then the likelihood of role shock or role strain is lessened. Finally, some role transitions may be seen as rites of passage for actors and are therefore governed by norms. For states, this might include emergence from colonial status to newly independent states, the transition from empire to declining great power, and so on.

Some role transitions proceed with ease, especially those in which a clear demarcation between roles exists, with unambiguous expectations accompanied by consensual responses from others. Role strain, which refers to the difficulty felt by the actor in adjusting to a new role, is unlikely when a role has little overall importance to an actor's social identity. However, most role transitions are more problematic and involve some degree of role strain—even if the actor desires the transition and the most optimal conditions are in place for the transition. Role strain can be moderated by a number of factors intrinsic to the actor or found in the external environment, including an actor's sense of control over the situation, the consistency of the role with underlying social identity, and the consistency of the role with the structure of the international system and supportive significant others.[7]

The next step in the model is the reaction of the actor to role strain. Actors might attempt to resolve role strain by changing aspects of role expectations or enactment internally or by attempting to alter aspects of the international system that produce the strain. In the case of states as actors, this might involve domestic political processes that revisit the content of the role or attempts to force the new role on other actors in the international system (Thies 2013). The possibility of conflictual behavior emanating from role strain is what is most interesting when considering the emergence of a new power in the international system, since existing great powers or even smaller states in a home region may not welcome such a transition. These relate to the last step in the model, which is the consequences for the actor and the larger social system.

Transitions from one role to another are difficult even when the actor in question desires a change in identity. As corporate actors, states must somehow aggregate the preferences of society and political elites to select a role among many potential competing roles (Cantir and Kaarbo 2012; Brummer and Thies 2015). Once such a role is selected, it must then be acknowledged and accepted by significant others in the role relationships formed by the state. If the role is not accepted by significant others, then the state must reconsider and decide whether to continue pursuing the role. Its ability to do so will often be a function of its relative power and position in the regional or international system (Thies 2013).

We are interested in the role set developed by the various BRICS, whose status is now widely regarded as that of rising powers within the existing international hierarchy. The role set at any point in time represents a snapshot of these states' self-conceived identity.[8] There have been some previous attempts to classify BRICS states' role set over time, though the literature we review in the empirical chapters frequently refers to roles as well as critical junctures when foreign policy undergoes redirection or restructuring. Are there internal or external shocks that may cause a reorientation of these emerging powers' role sets? Will any of these changes coincide with observable, behavioral changes, especially in conflict behavior? The structural theories of IR would expect that emerging powers' behavior would become more conflictual as their power grows, though our foreign policy approach suggests that "webs of constraint" and the socializing activities of the great powers may restrain such behavior.

We propose two hypotheses relating previous structural international relations theories and foreign policy analyses with conflict behavior. Our first hypothesis is that major foreign policy breaks associated with the changes in BRICS states' material power will produce sporadic and dramatic NRC changes and conflict behavior. Essentially, if major changes in BRICS' state power occur, then the state's self-conceived identity and behavior will change abruptly as well, representing foreign policy restructuring. If this hypothesis receives confirmation, then structural materialist theories of international relations grounded solely in the notion of compe-

tition driving state behavior may gain some support for their view that
BRICS states' rise, like that of rising powers in earlier eras, will lead to more
aggressive foreign policy orientations and increased conflict.

H1:   *Increases in a BRICS state's relative material power are directly
and positively correlated with the adoption of revisionist NRCs and
increases in militarized and economically conflictual behavior as a
result of interstate competition (structural materialist hypothesis).*

Yet if we observe incremental changes in NRCs that comprise a BRICS
state's role set over time and no major changes in conflict behavior, then
traditional structural international relations theories may be incorrect. Instead, our foreign policy approach, emphasizing the web of domestic constraints and international socialization pressures that work to maintain
continuity and incremental change in identity and behavior, is correct.
Rather than being carried along by underlying structural shifts in power
grounded solely in competition, the makers of the BRICS' foreign policies
may exert their agency to determine their national identity and foreign
policy behavior in the face of strong socialization pressure from the great
powers.

H2:   *Domestic political processes within BRICS states alongside socialization pressure from great powers mediate changes in relative material power, leading to more deliberate changes in NRCs and militarized and economically conflictual behavior (foreign policy
hypothesis).*

In the next chapter, we explain how we generate the qualitative and
quantitative evidence that allows us to assess these hypotheses. Rather than
assume that the qualitative evidence feeds into the quantitative analysis, or
vice versa, we allow each type of evidence to stand on its own and offer insight about the material and ideational nature of foreign policy change in an
international system with rising powers.

CHAPTER 3

A Mixed-Methods Approach
to Observing Identity and Behavior

The use of mixed methods to strengthen the kinds of causal inferences we make in political science has made great strides in the last decade or so. Advocates of more systematic approaches to qualitative evidence initially began to push the idea of mixed methods as a way for quantitative researchers to take them more seriously. The result produced many dissertations consisting of a large-n statistical analysis designed to test hypotheses that was followed by several case studies to allow for the more detailed tracing of causal chains. Further developments in this approach then began to take the actual case selection more seriously, so that cherry-picking a case or two to fit the causal story and the statistical results was called into question. A variety of approaches now exist to consider how to select cases based on a large-n statistical analysis (Lieberman 2005; Fearon and Laitin 2008).

Yet in reality, this kind of attempt to integrate qualitative and quantitative analysis is rarely used. Often, the problem is that we learn different things from the two types of evidence. A specific case may or may not conform to theoretical expectations because of its unique features. The findings from a large-n statistical analysis may not be observed in any single case. Today, the division remains as strong as ever between those who advocate for knowing the cases and the causal process that appears to be at work in them versus those who are interested in the average treatment effect of an independent variable on a dependent variable over many cases.

We believe we have surpassed this divide in the way we combine our qualitative and quantitative analyses in this book. We examine the same cases using both qualitative and quantitative approaches. We conduct multiple observations on our cases over time in both a qualitative and quantitative manner. In the qualitative approach, we observe the national role conceptions (NRCs) selected to represent our cases over time. We combine these NRCs into role sets that generally represent the state's identity at any given point in time. We then examine these role sets for evidence of dramatic or more evolutionary role transitions that would be consistent with structural theories or the foreign policy approach described in chapter 2. We compare the role sets of our BRICS countries before and after purported internal and external shocks identified in the foreign policy literatures to see whether dramatic shifts in roles occur. We ask whether we observe role transitions occurring abruptly as a result solely of material competition or more evolutionary changes as socialization and competition work to allow states to locate their appropriate roles during the policymaking process in the international system? This analysis of NRCs and role transition becomes one form of evidence to assess the rising power phenomenon.

The second form of evidence is found in the quantitative analysis of economic and militarized conflict behavior. Using Bayesian change-point modeling, we examine the data-generating processes associated with economic and militarized conflict to see whether any structural breaks occur in the data. In other words, are there periods of time when the variables most likely to predict conflict operate differently? Rather than assume, as many analyses do, that the variables that predict conflict operate the same across countries and across time, we examine our cases and allow the data to tell us whether changes take place over time in the main explanatory factors associated with economic or militarized conflict. Do structural breaks match existing purported internal and external shocks that are thought to have realigned foreign policy? If structural breaks found in the data are associated with dramatic changes in material competition, then we find evidence for structural IR approaches. If we do not observe these structural breaks, then the more nuanced foreign policy approach we advocate may be better at explaining the more evolutionary rise of these countries.

The two forms of evidence—one qualitative, one quantitative—are allowed to stand on their own merits. We do not derive the NRCs to plug them into the quantitative analysis. We do not conduct the statistical analysis to figure out where changes in NRCs are likely to occur. As we explain, there are strong theoretical and empirical reasons to avoid attempting to subsume one under the other. Instead, each analysis provides information on its own, and all of this information can be usefully combined to get an overall picture of rising power identity and behavior. Our approach to mixed methods is therefore to allow qualitative and quantitative evidence to provide independent yet complementary evidence as we test our two primary hypotheses about rising powers. Any overlap in the results from the two approaches increases our confidence in our inferences and provides the strongest evidence either to support or refute our hypotheses.

Observing Identity as Patterns of Behavior Using National Role Conceptions

Our qualitative approach to understanding rising power behavior is based on the analysis of NRCs. What is a national role conception? A role refers to "repertoires of behavior, inferred from others' expectations and one's own conceptions, selected at least partly in response to cues and demands" (Walker 1992: 23). Stryker and Statham (1985: 223) suggest that a role can refer to both a position in a society or group as well as any socially recognized category of actor (i.e., the kind of actor it is possible to be in a society). Thus, roles are an interbehavioral phenomenon, comprised of expectations of the Self and Other as well as cues and demands from others about the appropriateness of the individual in the role. Role conceptions therefore refer to the expectations about the role as held by the Self and are often also referred to as role identities. A national role conception is therefore the beliefs and expectations about a role held by a country (or at least its leaders). NRCs are a form of identity in this sense, since they are rooted in normative beliefs about the appropriateness of a position or social category and its associated behaviors.

Consistent with much of the foreign policy analysis literature using role theory, we focus our analysis here on the NRC or role identity rather than the role relationship (Thies 2010a: 6339). We wish to observe the kinds of NRCs that states adopt for themselves over time as a reflection of their beliefs about their identity. Social theory would normally push us further to understand whether the role identities that states adopt are enacted in meaningful role relationships, since every role implies a counterrole. For example, the role of teacher is meaningless without someone in the role of a student. Yet much of the literature in foreign policy analysis (e.g., Holsti's [1970] original investigation of NRCs) has invested time in discovering what roles states adopt and, most recently, the contestation processes within states that ultimately produce the NRC that represents the state (e.g., Cantir and Kaarbo 2012; Brummer and Thies 2015). Studies that examine the process of forming role relationships are comparatively rare (for an exception, see McCourt 2014).

In this book, we focus on the NRC for a number of reasons. First, simply documenting the NRCs and the associated role sets for the BRICS has not yet been done in any comprehensive manner. We draw on the existing literature to flesh out the major role identities that comprise the role sets of these states. Second, we believe that as rising powers, states can adopt NRCs even when others do not join to form role relationships. Thies (2013) made this argument about great powers in particular. The increased capabilities of great powers allowed them to adopt roles even if others did not provide social ratification. The same is likely true of rising powers that may be transiting to great power status. Third, we are interested in the self-conceived identities of these states as a form of evidence for shifts related to rising power. The acceptance of these role identities is ultimately important if they are to be seen as legitimate in the international order, but it is less important for our more limited goal of examining whether these self-conceived identities change abruptly or more evolutionarily. Finally, NRCs are derived from patterns of behavior. Role theorists' views of identity are probably more grounded in behavior than are constructivist notions, though at heart who you are is often a function of what you do. As the old adage says, if you steal too much, you may become a thief. In this sense, NRCs become a qualitative way of observing general, congealed historical behavior that can stand alongside the quantitative indicators of behavior in the form of specific contemporary events.

Since NRCs represent patterns of behavior, we cannot include them in quantitative analyses of behavior observed as events for fear of introducing endogeneity to a statistical analysis. Since NRCs are congealed general behavior, then using them to predict specific events as behavior is at one level just behavior predicting behavior. This problem is rarely addressed in the conflict literature, though roles such as major power or great power are often included as control variables in analyses of conflict behavior. Yet if one of the behaviors associated with a great power is that great powers intervene in the affairs of smaller states, then it would not be a surprise that these "variables" would be positively associated, and they typically are statistically significant. We seek to avoid this endogeneity problem by keeping our NRC analysis separate from the statistical analysis of economic and militarized conflict behavior.

This is also an unacknowledged problem in the foreign policy role theory literature, as roles may be deduced from foreign policy behaviors but then are treated as independent of such behaviors and used to predict them in a case study. This is the same endogeneity problem. Elevating a pattern of behavior to an identity does not fully insulate one from this problem, nor does variation in the temporal scope of the analysis. It is often difficult to precisely identify the adoption of a NRC, since it is a reflection of a pattern of behavior (which necessarily precedes the adoption of the role identity). It is also often difficult to precisely identify when an NRC is an active part of the role set, when it becomes latent, and when it falls out of the role set entirely. Thus, using a NRC to predict future behavior is also difficult. We therefore do not use our NRCs to predict behavior in the qualitative analysis; rather, we are looking for role transitions that seem to correspond to expected changes based on the previously developed hypotheses.

Surveying the Possibilities for Observing NRCs

There is no definitive methodological account of the best way to identify roles.[1] Generally speaking, scholars have combined two main sources of information, primary and secondary, in many ways to determine NRCs. While role theorists have yet to produce a handbook on methodology for the analysis of NRCs, one can easily find examples of the fruitful use of many different approaches to deriving NRCs. One might think of role theory scholarship as falling on a continuum from purely primary to purely secondary source material, with many gradations in between.

On the purely primary source material end of the continuum we find Holsti's (1970: 255–60) seminal article. Holsti derived his NRCs from coding primary sources such as speeches, parliamentary debates, and press conferences of foreign policy officials of seventy-one governments between 1965 and 1967. Wish (1980) also used elite interviews, speeches, and articles produced by twenty-nine political elites from seventeen states between 1959 and 1968. In both of these examples, the researchers coded for roles as structural positions (e.g., ally or regional leader) or the "kinds of state it is possible to be" (e.g., defender of the faith or anti-imperialist agent). Even though both studies used primary sources, there is still a fair amount of interpretation in determining the roles, especially coding for roles as social categories.

In the middle of the continuum are studies like that of Hermann (1987), who coded elite interviews of African leaders for personality traits that she then combined to code for the presence of NRCs based on her own rules about how combinations of traits match up to role orientations. Walker (1981) analyzed the dataset of NRCs produced by Holsti (1970) in conjunction with a second dataset produced by McGowan and O'Leary (1975) on cooperative and conflictual actions by states. In this case, previous coding of primary sources forms a secondary source of data for analysis, much like quantitative data produced by the Correlates of War or Polity projects. A number of scholars have used the roles identified by Holsti (1970) as a starting point in their examinations of historical cases, often confirming the existence of the same roles (or variations on those roles) outside of the sample of countries and time period originally investigated (e.g., Brummer and Thies 2015).

Finally, on the other end of the continuum are studies that use purely secondary source materials. For example, Walker and Simon (1987) draw on scholarly accounts of events in Southeast Asia to identify roles for their analysis. In fact, this approach to the use of scholarly accounts to identify NRCs has been used quite frequently in recent scholarship. Harnisch (2012) drew on scholarly accounts of U.S., Chinese, and German foreign policy episodes to illustrate his typology of role learning. Thies (2012, 2013) used historians' accounts of Israeli and U.S. diplomatic history to identify socialization efforts over various NRCs. Shih (2012) similarly uses scholarly accounts to interpret and understand China's contemporary role conceptions. Bengtsson and Elgström (2012) also draw on scholarly treatments to understand the interplay of the European Union's role conceptions and role expectations held by others illustrated in two brief case studies. Thies (2016) drew on scholarly accounts to understand the types of roles adopted by former Venezuelan president Hugo Chávez to represent both himself and the state. Finally, Thies (2015a) used the results of an expert survey of fifty-eight Chinese watchers of America and American watchers of China to infer the patterns of behavior that comprised roles invoked on both sides during the Taiwan Straits Crisis. Thies then matched roles observed in the survey responses to those identified in existing scholarly work to provide a check on the validity of this method.

Thus, roles have been observed based on combinations of psychological traits, the expressed statements of elites, and the analysis of history through previously defined roles as well as based on secondary source material in the form of scholarly accounts of historical events. In this book, we pursue purely secondary source materials and use scholarly accounts as the basis for observing NRCs. In this approach, other scholars, even though they are not using role theory, serve as the catalogers of identities and behaviors articulated by leaders on behalf of the states we are observing. We have the opportunity to draw on the "database" of existing scholarly work on the BRICS as coding material for NRCs.

This approach has many benefits. First, none of us can hope to be experts on all countries, let alone even the handful of states represented in the BRICS group. Thus, we can rely on the identities and behaviors already identified by experts on these countries for our source material to code NRCs. Second, this material is largely available in English and is less subject to the well-known problems associated with relying on English-language newspaper coverage of speeches of foreign leaders. The scholars on whose material we draw have already done the hard work of combing through source material in the language of the country in question, and they are familiar with the full range of source material associated with that country. Third, scholars who talk about identities and patterns of behavior are already identifying roles in a naive way, thus simplifying our observation of roles in their analysis. Finally, our identification of NRCs and role sets for each country should therefore resonate with country experts. Nothing that we have to say about role identities and role sets should strike these experts as unusual or strange. Yet the cataloging of role identities and the examination of their transitions over time should add something new to understandings of the BRICS countries.

One of the potential drawbacks of the use of secondary source materials is that they always contain the possibility of bias and selectivity (Lustick 1996; Thies 2002). When using secondary sources, the best one can attain is to minimize the sources of bias and selectivity. The worst case scenario is when the researcher selects secondary sources based on some shared underlying theoretical understanding that means the theory is being tested by observations generated by the theory itself. Lustick's (1996) example of this phenomenon is an international relations scholar developing a realist theory that is then tested using diplomatic historians' accounts of an event that likely shares an underlying realist theoretical orientation. Most of the secondary literature on which we draw to code roles may have used the language of roles, but most have not incorporated the theoretical notions of role theory into their analyses. It seems unlikely that these sources generated for other purposes and this study share a theoretical perspective, thus minimizing potential bias. The selection of source material was also not limited in any particular way—we searched for all articles and scholarly books published on the foreign policy of the BRICS. It is likely that this approach may miss the articulation of some NRCs, but this is equally possible using primary sources.

Our qualitative analysis therefore involves the coding of NRCs, conceived as "repertoires of behavior" that represent positions or social categories of states that may be occupied by BRICS countries. We generate these NRCs from the existing scholarly literature on the foreign policies of BRICS that analyzes their identities and behaviors. Table 3.1 lists the NRCs observed across the BRICS ranked according to a revised and updated version of Holsti's activity-passivity scale. Holsti (1970: 286) developed a scale of activity-passivity in national role conceptions that ranges from 0 to 5 (low to high). We build on his original scale using the roles he identified to anchor each score, then adding observed roles from the BRICS that seem to match the degree of activity or passivity indicated by his original categorization.[2] This scale will be used to indicate which role conceptions require more foreign policy activity in a given time period. Obviously, this ordinal level measurement of activity levels is somewhat rough and is certainly subject to debate, but it gives us another way to categorize the underlying qualitative information. We will explore aspects of these NRCs in more detail for each country. These NRCs are then combined into role sets to examine changes over time for each of the BRICS. These changes—whether dramatic or evolutionary—are essential to understanding what sorts of processes are occurring with regard to rising powers.

From NRCs to Role Sets

Once we have observed NRCs for our BRICS over time, we generate role sets to further help make sense of the various role identities that states have adopted. Since we cannot know with certainty a state's role set because it includes both active and latent roles, we artificially impose a temporal delimitation on NRCs to create a role set. It seems most meaningful in political time to use the decade as the temporal delimitation that creates the role set for a state. Thus, for each decade (e.g., 1970s, 1980s, 1990s), we identify the active roles (in the sense that they are in use) adopted by the state, and that becomes the role set. These decade-long role sets serve as a snapshot of identity over time that we can then observe for changes or transitions.

Policymakers use active roles to guide foreign policy choices and behav-

Table 3.1. NRCs Identified for the BRICS by Level of Activity-Passivity

Level 5 (Most Active)

Bastion (of revolution-liberator, of world revolution, and of socialism)
Colonizer
Defender of the Peace
Enemy
Great power (African, Asian, normal, nonaggressive, responsible)
Hegemon (African, consensual, regional)
Integrator (regional, of Russia with the West/into the Western World)
Leader (regional, of the African continent, trilateral)
Patron
Peacekeeper (regional)
Peacemaker
Pivotal state
Power (Eurasian, leading, major Asian, regional, revolutionary, status quo)
Promoter of a Regional Geopolitical Order
Regional Crisis Manager
Regional Liberator
Regional Protector
Regional Reconciler
Responsible Stakeholder
Superpower (regional, of the South)
Stabilizer of the Eurasian Geopolitical Environment
Swing State
Unifier of Sinic World

Level 4

Active Independent
Active Promoter of a United Front against the Hegemony of the Two Superpowers
Advocate of Developing Nations
Anti-hegemony
Anti-imperialist Agent
Anti-revisionist/Zionist/Communist Agent
Anti-Soviet Hegemony
Balancer (and guardian of global stability)
Deputy Sheriff
Independent and Influential Player
Liberator-Supporter/Supporter of National Liberation
Opponent (of hegemonism, of Soviet social imperialism, of Soviet expansionism)
Power (autonomous, bridging, emerging, intermediate, rising, major, Third World)
Protector of the Russian State and Independent Player
Promoter of a New International Order
Reformer (of the European regional order, of the international order)
Nonaligned State
Revisionist State
Third World Champion/Champion of Third World Causes

(continues)

Table 3.1.—*Continued*

Level 3

Active Multilateralist
Advocate of Peaceful Coexistence and International Cooperation
Defender (of the faith, of democratic principles and human rights, of international law, of universal human values)
Democracy Promoter
Developer (regional)
Diplomat
Facilitator
Global Trader
Honest Broker
Intermediary
International Collaborator
Mediator-Integrator
Middle Power (emerging)
Moral Crusader
Practitioner of Openness to the Outside World
Promoter (of international cooperation, of global peace and prosperity, /supporter of arms control and disarmament)
Regional Custodian
Regional Subsystem Collaborator
Sub-imperialist-imperialist
Supporter of International Organizations

Level 2

Ally (faithful, independent, regional)
Collaborator/Partner
Good Neighbor
Guardian
Independent
Member of a Democratic Community of States
Military Power
Nuclear Weapon Power
Rival
Superpower in Waiting

Level 1

Bridge (builder, cultural, and civilizational)
Example (liberal, setter)
Junior Partner
Model of National Liberation and Independence
Moral Force
Potential Nuclear Weapon Power
Privileged Partner
Semi-peripheral State

Table 3.1.—*Continued*

Level 0 (Most Passive)
Excluded (from the international system, from restrictive Western institutions)
Instrument for Changing Russia
Internal Developer
International Pariah
Isolate
Leading Civilian Nuclear Power
Liberalizing Autocracy
New Member of the International Community
Protectee
State (African, democratic, developing, developmental, new, sovereign)
Victim

iors; latent roles, in contrast, may be traditional for a country but not salient in a given situation. The active roles in role set can be thought of as a snapshot of identity in a particular time, while the full role set gives a larger sense of historical identity. The active roles give some sense of how policymakers view their country's position in the international system and their responsibilities and duties at a particular point in time. These active roles also are a window into the kind of behavior that might be expected of the country in a particular situation in which they are invoked.

Our method largely observes the active roles operating on behalf of the state at any given point in time. We assume that some of the active roles will become latent, while others will eventually drop out of the role set. This method is not particularly able to distinguish between these phases in a role's duration. For example, we are unlikely to know the difference between a latent role and one that has dropped from the role set until it reappears as an active role. This does not seem to pose a particular problem for this analysis, however, since we are primarily concerned with the active roles in the role set and whether they differ markedly as a result of material competition or more evolutionary foreign policy processes that are also shaped by socialization efforts.

Our method also does not readily distinguish between roles that may be under contention at a given time in a state and those that are settled as the official NRC. As Cantir and Kaarbo (2012, 2016) remind us, NRCs are always subject to a domestic contestation process—particularly in democratic systems, but likely in autocratic systems as well. Thus, we will observe occasions where many roles are suggested for the states (e.g., after the transition from the USSR to Russia). While the Russian leadership actively adopted some of those roles, others became latent roles. Typically, roles that are not officially enacted by the state are still credible, as they draw on the same underlying set of cultural materials (even if the roles contradict one another). Both active and latent roles debated during domestic contestation will appear in the role sets we document. The narratives describing the roles will help clarify which roles are more active than others.

As will become clearer in the analysis of role sets, a fair amount of variance exists across the BRICS. Some have relatively small role sets, with only a few roles seemingly active in any given decade, while others have large role sets that even seem schizophrenic in their contradictions. Some states have role sets that are relatively stable in that they contain the same roles from decade to decade, while others show a fair amount of innovation in roles. The role sets provide a general overview of state identity for the BRICS and offer insights into the dynamics of identity and underlying patterns of behavior as these states have begun their rising process.

Observing Structural Breaks in Militarized and Economic Conflict Behaviors

We complement our qualitative analysis with a quantitative approach utilizing a series of endogenous Bayesian Markov chain Monte Carlo (MCMC) change-point regressions (Chib 1996, 1998; Park 2010, 2011b). If structural theories of international relations are correct, we should observe economic growth and increases in relative material power that are associated with increases in conflict behavior. If our foreign policy approach is on target, we would expect little in the way of structural breaks in militarized or economic conflict behavior outside of dramatic domestic reorganization (e.g., a revolution or coup). We estimate endogenous Bayesian change-point models for both militarized and economic conflict series for each BRICS state to evaluate whether changes take place in the effect of key independent variables such as economic growth and relative power.

Bayesian statistics utilize Bayes's Law to make inferences about parameter estimates based on a specified model, given observed data and prior knowledge.[3] One feature of employing a Bayesian framework is that all parameter estimates are treated as probabilistic. One benefit of this is that it greatly simplifies interpretation of the quantitative analysis. For example,

Bayesian probability intervals describe the degree of confidence that the parameter estimate is within some range. Frequentists' confidence intervals, conversely, have a probability of either 0 or 1 that the specified range contains the true value, since the observed data are treated as an outcome of a random sample of the underlying fixed parameter (Gill 1999, 2009: 62–66). Another benefit is that we can compare models to determine which is best able to explain the observed data, including models that allow the parameters to change in effect size and direction reflecting reorientations in foreign policy making (Park 2010). Finally, by treating all parameters in the model as probabilistic, we can explore whether change-points occur in a gradual, evolutionary manner or in a sudden, abrupt way (Nieman 2016a).

Change-point models work by identifying structural breaks in the effect of a set of covariates. In other words, the effects of the explanatory variables are allowed to be time-dependent and to change between different periods.[4] By allowing for changing effects, change-point models provide a valuable tool for rigorous analysis of social theory propositions (Park 2011a; Nieman 2016a). The timing of change-points is treated probabilistically, allowing for measures of uncertainty regarding when structural breaks occur. These measures of uncertainty can then be used to demonstrate a degree of confidence in the timing of a change-point and can even themselves be analyzed (Park 2010, 2011b; Nieman 2016a).

In substantive terms, the estimator seeks the optimal way to divide the data into subsamples. It does this by examining several models with different possible change-points until it identifies the model with the best fit to the data. The estimator effectively splits the data into subsamples so that the effects of the covariates in the model change in significance or direction from one subsample to the next. The model, in other words, identifies unique subsamples within the larger dataset because it is sensitive to changes in the effect of the explanatory variables. Consequently, change-point models offer a sharp contrast to the traditional large-n assumption that our explanatory variables exert a fixed effect for all units across time and space. To prevent overfitting, several models are estimated and compared using the Bayes Factor, which penalizes models for imposing too much structure.[5]

An endogenous change-point model is a type of Markov model with hidden states and restricted transition properties (Chib 1998).[6] The outcome variable y_t is treated as a function of a set of explanatory variables x_t and temporal regime-specific parameters βs_t, where subscript t represents the temporal observation and s indicates the temporal regime. s_t follows a discrete-time, discrete-state Markov process. This nonergodic Markov process is represented as a one-step transition matrix

$$P = \begin{pmatrix} p_{11} & p_{12} & 0 & \cdots & 0 \\ 0 & p_{22} & p_{23} & \cdots & 0 \\ \vdots & \vdots & \vdots & \vdots & \vdots \\ \vdots & \vdots & 0 & p_{mm} & p_{m,m+1} \\ 0 & 0 & \cdots & 0 & 1 \end{pmatrix}$$

Where $p_{i,j} = \Pr(s_t = j \mid s_{t-1} = 1)$ is the probability of moving to temporal regime j at time t, given that the temporal regime at time $t-1$ is i and m is the number of change-points.[7] While m is selected by the researcher, the placement of the change-points is not (Chib and Greenberg 1996). Instead, MCMCs are used to probabilistically identify the placement of each change-point given the observed data.[8] The use of a sufficiently long MCMC chain ensures that the entire state space is explored.

We identify the probability of the timing of a change-point in two steps (Park 2010: 771): (1) we obtain the probability of each temporal regime at t by taking random draws from each regime's posterior sampling distribution; (2) we obtain the probability of the change-point occurring by taking the first difference of these probabilities. This permits us to identify the probability of a change-point for each t, allowing us to calculate both a point estimate (the median conditional probability) and a confidence range (from adding up the conditional probabilities to the desired degree, e.g., 90%, 95%, etc.). Several models with different numbers of change-points are simulated, and the model with the best fit is selected using the Bayes Factor.

To summarize, temporal regimes are considered latent variables and treated probabilistically when estimating parameters of the explanatory variables. The model is fitted so that the probability of a change-point is endogenous depending on the current time regime (Chib 1998: 223; see also Gill 2009: 345–46). The probabilities of transitioning from one temporal regime to another are used to identify the timing of the change-point. Finally, parameter estimates are obtained from sampling the full state space of the posterior distribution, which accounts for the precision (or imprecision) of the estimated change-point.

The Bayesian change-point model offers several advantages over other approaches in accounting for varying temporal effects of explanatory variables, such as using dummy variables or frequentist change-point models. First, the most common approach for modeling time, imposing temporal dummy variables—that is, temporal fixed effects (Green, Kim, and Yoon 2001)—is often imprecise and does not capture changing effects in explanatory variables.[9] As Park notes (2010: n. 1), temporal dummy variables are poor statistical tools because they provide no guidance regarding the placement, number, or length of temporal regimes. Even when scholars expect that behavior differs between particular time periods, specifying eras is often difficult and starting points are usually selected somewhat arbitrarily (e.g., while the 19th and 20th centuries may mark distinct eras, does the change take place in precisely 1900? Perhaps after World War I?). Moreover, temporal dummy variables capture changes in the baseline probability of an outcome but not changes in the effect of individual explanatory variables. If such changes are present, however, utilizing temporal dummies results in a misspecified model, producing biased estimates and possibly incorrect inferences. Without knowing *ex ante* which temporal regime a state is in and precisely when it started, temporal dummy variables are a poor fit for identifying changes in observed behavior, such as conflict behavior among BRICS states.

Second, frequentist change-point models fail to convey the level of confidence in the placement of a change-point, while the Bayesian model recovers the conditional probabilities of a structural break occurring for each year. This is because, in contrast to the frequentist approach, Bayesian models treat the observed data as given and the parameter estimates, including the change-point, as random variables. The conditional probabilities convey a clearly stated level of confidence that the change-point occurred in year *t* or within a range of years while simultaneously indicating whether a structural break occurred suddenly (high concentration around year *t*) or gradually (low concentration spread over many *t*). These identified breaks can then be compared to the historical record to examine possible causes of the change-point itself.

Model Selection and the Number of Change-Points

To identify the appropriate number of temporal regimes, we estimate a series of change-point models to calculate the marginal likelihood for models including (1) all observations belonging to *n* distinct temporal regimes and (2) observations belonging to *n* + 1 distinct temporal regimes. We then use

Bayes Factor to calculate fit statistics to identify the model with the best fit to the observed data.

We estimate ten endogenous change-point models for the militarized conflict equations and six endogenous change-point models for the economic conflict equations.[10] We then compare the models to one another. We employ diffuse, weakly informed prior distributions for each parameter $\beta_k \sim N(0,10)$ and noninformative, uniformly distributed priors for the probability of the change points.[11] To ensure that each model explores the full state space, we run twenty thousand MCMC chains after discarding a ten-thousand-draw burn-in. All estimates were conducted using MCMCpack in R (Martin, Quinn, and Park 2008; R Development Core Team 2010).

The Bayes Factor is used to compare estimated models, with one model operating as the baseline model and the other as the alternative model. If $BF_{ij} = (m[y/M_i]/ \ m[y/M_j])$ where BF_{ij} is the Bayes Factor, then the baseline model M_i is compared to the alternative model M_j, $m(y|M_i)$ is the marginal likelihood under model M_i, and $m(y|M_j)$ is the marginal likelihood under model M_j. Taking the log of the Bayes Factor, negative values are interpreted as evidence against the baseline model, and positive values are evidence in favor of the baseline (Gill 2009: 209). If we apply Jeffrey's (1961) scale, then values between 3 and 20 offer positive support for the baseline model, and values above this provide strong support for the baseline model (Kass and Raftery 1995).

Data and Research Design

We investigate our hypotheses quantitatively for each BRICS state over the time period 1870–2007 unless otherwise noted. We analyze two types of conflict for each country: militarized and economic.

Militarized conflict is coded as the number of militarized interstate disputes (MIDs) and wars that a rising power has initiated or joined in a given year.[12] The number of MIDs and wars initiated or joined accounts for only those disputes in which the rising power chose to engage, thus reflecting its underlying foreign policy agenda. MID and war data are obtained from the Correlates of War project (Palmer et al. 2015). Given the latent nature of these count data (King 1989), we employ a Poisson change-point model (Park 2010) to analyze militarized conflict behavior.[13]

Economic conflict data are conceptualized as illiberal actions that challenge the Western-led liberal international economic order (LIEO). We operationalize illiberal actions as one of three complementary activities: (1) expropriating assets of U.S. firms, (2) defaulting on sovereign debt (owed to U.S.-based international banks), and (3) increasing financial regulations.[14] Each of these observable actions represents facets of the same underlying challenge to the liberal, free-market normative economic vision of the United States and its Western allies. We treat economic conflict as a dichotomous variable, where the presence of any illiberal action is coded as 1, and 0 otherwise. We employ a probit change-point model (Park 2011b) to analyze economic conflict behavior.[15]

Expropriation and default data are obtained from Tomz and Wright (2010). They treat these two variables as two types of sovereign theft, as each involves the seizure of a foreign firm's assets. Tomz and Wright define expropriation as any case where the government intervenes and takes control over operations of foreign direct investment. They define default as a failure to pay interest or principal within the grace period or making an exchange offer at less favorable terms than the original issue. These data are available for the period 1929–2004. We use financial openness data from Chinn and Ito (2008) to measure financial openness. They construct a continuous measure of financial openness based on the IMF's *Annual Report on Exchange Arrangements and Exchange Restrictions*, where greater values indicate more open policies. One advantage of these data is that they measure the intensity of capital controls rather than just their presence. We treat any policy shifts toward increased government control of the financial market as an illiberal action.[16] These data are available from 1970 to 2007. Taken together, the economic conflict data are available from 1929 to 2007.

We include several explanatory variables that predict a state's likelihood to engage in militarized or economic conflict. Our primary variable of interest is a rising power's *Power Ratio* compared to the sum of all other states within the state's home region using the Correlates of War project's composite index of national capabilities (CINC) variable. CINC measures a country's relative material power based on economic and military capabilities and population size (Singer, Bremer, and Stuckey 1972). We use the Correlates of War state system membership list to identify regional memberships. *Power Ratio* is calculated as the CINC score of the BRICS state divided by the sum of its score and the scores all states within the same region. This variable is bound between 0 and 1, where 1 represents perfect preponderance and 0.5 indicates equal strength between the rising power and the combined strength of the other states within its region. We compare each rising power to its home region because rising powers are likely to be regional powers, and all of the BRICS are land powers against which structural theorists would expect their neighbors to balance (e.g., Levy and Thompson 2010). As a rising power becomes more powerful, structural theories predict that it becomes more assertive in regional and global affairs and initiates and joins an increasing number of conflicts to pursue its interests. To account for the possibility that other states may become more likely to acquiesce to a rising power as it becomes increasingly preponderant, we include a *Power Ratio Squared* term to allow for potential nonlinear effects. We include *Power Ratio* as an explanatory variable for both militarized and economic conflict.[17]

The number of contiguous neighbors that are involved in interstate wars is also expected to influence how active a rising power is militarily. Neighboring conflict provides opportunities for military intervention, either to advance a state's own goals or to resolve a conflict that may be destabilizing to the region. *Neighbor Conflict* data are obtained from Wimmer and Min (2006) and extended by the authors using the Correlates of War militarized conflict data (Palmer et al. 2015). These data are used in the militarized conflict models only.

We include a measure for the *Proportion of Democracies* in each rising power's region. Previous research demonstrates that as the level of democracy initially increases within a system, it is associated with an increase in militarized conflict (Mitchell, Gates, and Hegre 1999; Kadera, Crescrenzi, and Shannon 2003; Rasler and Thompson 2005). This may result from the known tendency of mixed dyads to have conflictual relationships (Raknerud and Hegre 1997; Beck and Jackman 1998). This is especially relevant in the case of the rising BRICS, as all except India are autocratic regimes for most or all of the time period under study. We treat a state as democratic if it has a Polity2 score equal to or greater than 7 (Marshall and Jaggers 2008) and identify regional systems in the same way as discussed previously. *Proportion of Democracies* is included in both the militarized and economic conflict models.

We also account for a state's integration into the world economy. Polachek (1980) argues that the opportunity costs of war are too great for countries that are highly engaged in trade, as war interferes with trading lines (see also Peterson and Thies 2012). In addition, military conquest is an expensive method of gaining access to resources in terms of both blood and

treasure (Rosecrance 1986; Lee and Mitchell 2012). Finally, economic integration reinforces contractual norms and legalistic principles that produce
liberal preferences (Mousseau 2003, 2009). Building on these arguments,
Gartzke (2007) and Gartzke and Hewitt (2010) suggest that a capitalist
peace exists for developed countries as intellectual and financial capital
make territorial possession less important for economic growth, developed
countries increasingly have similar foreign policy objectives, and capital
markets provide new outlets for state competition. We measure *Trade* as a
rising state's total trade flows as a percent of gross domestic product (GDP).
Trade data are obtained from the Correlates of War international trade dataset (Barbieri, Keshk, and Pollins 2008, 2009). *Trade* is included in both
militarized and economic conflict equations.

We include an indicator variable for each country's entry into *World
War I* and *World War II*, where appropriate. These indicator variables capture the instantaneous effect of the world wars on conflict initiation. Any
long-term effects, however, would be captured by a structural break in the
conflict determinants (Mitchell, Gates, and Hegre 1999; Park 2010: 773).
These variables are included in the militarized conflict equation.

We include *GDP Growth* in the economic conflict equation to account
for short-term economic conditions that may cause economic challenges.
Poor economic conditions may make expropriation of foreign assets and
debt default more appealing, while accompanying domestic unrest may increase the attractiveness of populist economic policies.[18] *GDP Growth* is the
logged first difference of GDP in year *t* minus the previous year. GDP data
are obtained from Maddison (2003) and updated with World Bank figures.

Finally, because we run the conflict series separately for each BRICS
state, the constant in each model is effectively absorbing any country-
specific effects not captured by the other variables. This is especially important when thinking about the economic conflict series, as data are unavail-
able for many variables that may be expected to influence the probability of
expropriation or default, such as reliable figures on inflation or foreign aid
as a percent of GDP, especially for early years in the series.[19] Our change-
point approach, however, captures changes in the sign and significance of
any explanatory variable, including the constant. Moreover, in the event
that a change-point exists, our approach allows us to identify the likely time
period and cross-validate our results with significant events in the historical
record that may not be in an existing dataset.

Combining Qualitative and Quantitative Observation and Evidence

If our approach to observing NRCs as identities that are indicative of patterns of behavior and specific economic and militarized incidents of conflict behavior succeeds, then we have provided two parallel streams of data. The qualitative data on NRCs should demonstrate how role sets have changed over time. We can assess whether they have changed dramatically, as one would expect if role transitions were induced by rapid changes in material factors, or whether the change has been more gradual. We can observe what types of NRCs comprise the role set. We can assess whether these NRCs are more reflective of conflict or cooperation. More generally, to assess our hypotheses, do the changes match perceived breaks in foreign policy as a consequence of internal domestic processes or of externally induced changes resulting from competition alone.

The quantitative data are in some ways even more helpful in helping to identify sharp distinctions between time periods in foreign policy for the BRICS. The Bayesian change-point modeling identifies structural breaks in the data without having to rely on any of our theoretical presuppositions about when change might occur. The data-generating process itself helps to identify those changes. We can then assess when these changes match internal domestic changes in foreign policy as well as externally induced changes as a consequence of competition in the material sphere.

Both types of evidence can be usefully combined to assess the presence or types of changes that occur in identity and behavior over time for each of the BRICS. We can consider the time regimes identified by the quantitative analysis in comparison with the role sets identified in the qualitative analysis. We should expect that a switch in the time regime would match dramatic transitions in the role set. We can also assess whether such changes match our general sense of the rise associated with these rising powers. We are engaged in a form of adduction whereby we piece together a plausible account of the structures and agents that theoretically drive changes in identities and behavior. Such an approach has a long history with previous structural realist approaches to the rise and decline of great powers (e.g., Goldstein 1988: 2).

Our approach to mixed methods in this book thus allows both qualitative and quantitative evidence to speak for themselves and to speak to each other. We think this is especially important given the development of the literature on rising powers, which has incorporated both material and ideational aspects of global politics into its study. Of course, some approaches emphasize the material aspects more than others, and all have some grounding in the notion that the rise is a result of economic development and growth. It is also important since most of the current literature on emerging power is largely qualitative in nature, thus ignoring previous quantitative contributions associated with the literature on great power rise and decline (e.g., Organski and Kugler 1980; Goldstein 1988; Doran 1991). We believe our mixed-methods approach thus provides a way to think rather holistically about identity and behavior as well as provides evidence that will be compelling across the spectrum of methodological commitments.

CHAPTER 4

Brazil: A Regional Leader in Need of Followers

The rise of Brazil has caught the attention of decision makers, pundits, academics, and the global media. Brazil's rapid economic growth and development have led many observers to note a more assertive foreign policy orientation in recent years as well as greater interest in the provision and management of regional security. Brazil has campaigned for a seat on the U.N. Security Council and defied traditional alignment with the United States to engage Iran. Are these types of behaviors just the beginning of an assertive and more militarized foreign policy, or will Brazil simply be satisfied with recognition of its status as a regional leader and a member of the exclusive BRICS and IBSA clubs? As we know, structural materialist theories of international relations tend to see a deterministic relationship between rising powers and revisionist foreign policy and conflict behavior designed to bring about system change. Our approach suggests that structural forces may be indeterminate, as competition and socialization work against each other. This leaves plenty of room for more deliberate foreign policy action within Brazil and cautions analysts to recognize the domestic and international constraints on such revisionism. We contribute to this debate by examining Brazil's beliefs about its identity through time as well as its militarized and economic conflict behavior.

We examine both qualitative and quantitative evidence regarding Brazilian identity and behavior. We begin with a qualitative analysis of Brazil's state identity as expressed through national role conceptions (NRCs). The role set of NRCs at any point in time helps us to understand how Brazil conceives of itself. Such self-conceptions provide an internal guide for foreign policy action and provide expectations to the rest of the world about Brazil's international behavior. We look for significant changes in the role set that may lead to major foreign policy reorientation. Such reorientations may also be reflected in changes in Brazil's conflict behavior. Our quantitative analysis uses Bayesian Markov chain Monte Carlo (MCMC) change-point models to investigate whether there have been any dramatic changes in Brazilian militarized or economic conflict behavior over time. By comparing Brazil's words and deeds through NRCs and conflict behavior, we can assess whether claims about potential threats emanating from Brazil's rise are accurate.

Our qualitative and quantitative analyses find little change in Brazil's identity and remarkable continuity in conflict behavior across time. While individual NRCs may come and go, the balance of the role set reflecting Brazil's identity has continuously stressed a role as a regional leader. Our statistical analysis of Brazil's conflict behavior indicates that there were no structural breaks in Brazil's militarized conflict behavior as would be expected from structural materialist theories. We find two potential breaks in Brazil's economic behavior in the 1980s, but these are largely driven by internal weaknesses made clear by the sovereign debt crisis in the region. Overall, we find little evidence in words or deeds, identity, or militarized and economic conflict to lend credence to the notion of an overly assertive or aggressive Brazil as it emerges into potential great power status.

National Role Conceptions and Brazilian Foreign Policy Analysis

A small but growing literature on Brazilian foreign policy refers to roles and status changes. While this literature is not grounded in role theory per se, we use the insights it provides as a coding source for our NRCs. We review the qualitative evidence on NRCs identified by scholars for Brazil as comprising its role set and look for changes in that role set over time. If structural materialist IR theories are correct, then we should see dramatic changes not only in Brazilian NRCs but also in the way they are received by others (especially the United States) as Brazil's power grows. Our consideration of structural forces suggests that both competition and socialization mechanisms may be working at cross-purposes. This leaves room for foreign policy approaches to change that expect major internal and external shocks to bring about foreign policy restructuring, though Harnisch (2001) suggests that those shocks are mediated by the existing role set. Rather than wholesale change, a role-theoretic approach suggests modification of roles based on structural imperatives.

A survey of the foreign policy literature on Brazil finds debates along several fronts related to autonomy (Giacalone 2012). The first axis of this debate concerned whether to practice "confrontational autonomy" or "national autonomy." Confrontational autonomy would involve active confrontation of the hegemon through revolution and would lead to breaking old economic and political ties. Conversely, national autonomy was a strategy for maintaining good relations with the hegemon while supporting Brazil's own development projects. Most of the late military governments pursued a national autonomy strategy through development. The second aspect of the debate concerned "autonomy through distance" versus "autonomy through participation," shifting from the nonautomatic acceptance of international regimes to actively trying to shape those regimes. Democratic governments largely continued national autonomy and became much more active in their participation in international regimes. Giacalone (2012: 338–39) notes a revival of the "confrontational autonomy" approach in the 2000s coincident with the dominant view of Brazil's rise.

In general, the concern with autonomy or the type of autonomy seemed to wax and wane in Latin America based on changes in the environment (Russell and Tokatlian 2003; Seabra 2012; Giacolone 2013). Lima and Hirst (2006: 22–23) argue that changes in Brazil's foreign policy are linked to critical junctures in the prevailing development model. They identify two critical junctures in the 20th century: the 1930s crisis, when the agro-exporting model was replaced by the import-substitution model, and the 1990s exhaustion of protected industrialization and its replacement by integration into the global economy. The former is related to "autonomy through distance," while the latter is associated with "autonomy through participation" and later in the Lula administration with "autonomy through diversification" (Vigevani and Cepaluni 2007: 1313).[1] This focus on methods of attaining autonomy provides some initial confirmation of Holsti's (1982: 198) argument that countries that engage in foreign policy restructuring are mainly attempting to reassert autonomy.

Landry (1974) provides a good overview of Brazilian roles in the 1960s and 1970s, showing that they revolve around themes of autonomy/independence and development. The adoption of the *internal developer role* in the early 1960s, while normally devoid of international reference (see Holsti 1970: 269), was seen as a way to avoid "Chinese or Japanese encroachment into the almost virgin Amazon" (Landry 1974: 24). Indeed, Landry (1974: 27) suggests that the four military administrations that ruled Brazil between 1964 and 1974 advocated authoritarianism and development. Internal security needs were also met by the internal developer role, since economic growth and prosperity could co-opt the growing middle class and the working class. Landry also argues that independence is the other dominant theme of Brazilian foreign policy since the early 1960s (28).[2] The *active independent role* predominated between 1961 and 1964, since there are some trade-offs between internationally financed development and independence. João Goulart especially pushed a *Third World champion* role as part of his approach to independence. While the Branco government saw itself as a privileged partner of the United States after the 1964 military coup (Carranza 2016), over time relations with the United States began to move away from Brazil as a U.S. "viceroy" or *regional-subsystem collaborator role* and toward a "mature partnership" in which Brazil occupied more of a *regional leader role*. The 1971 Médici-Nixon meeting in Washington confirmed that the United States would secure North America and Brazil would take care of South America in this changing conception of the relationship between the two states. Brazil is also viewed as enacting an *anticommunist agent role* in its foreign policy, perhaps even more so than the United States (Landry 1974: 30). Brazil also pursued a *developer role* in the region to provide aid to "under countries" such as Uruguay, Paraguay, and Bolivia.

Landry further notes that by the mid-1970s, the strict bipolarity of the Cold War was beginning to loosen, meaning that neither the United States nor the Soviets could expect to exert complete control over allies. This would apply in particular to Brazil and other countries that occupy a *middle power role*. After reviewing the elements of Brazil's strength, Landry suggests that it could be considered a middle power and even an *emerging power* that contends for great power status in the future. The *rival role* relationship between Argentina and Brazil was not thought to impede this emergence, since Argentina was internally weak at the time and Brazil was strengthening.[3] Selcher (1985) notes that the rival role relationship had been converted to simple competition by the mid-1980s.

Carranza (2016) notes that in the 1970s, Brazil considered itself a "superpower in waiting." By the early 1980s, Brooke (1981: 167) declares that Brazil is emerging as the "superpower of the South." Referencing a 1980 report by the Commission on U.S.-Brazilian Relations, he notes, "Brazil has a different vision of the world, a different role and different responsibilities than we" (168). The vision relates to its emergence as a *Third World power* based on developing the kinds of resources often found in the developing world, such as agriculture and mining. The *internal developer role* is complemented by a *global trader role* and *regional integrator* through its search for new markets and trading opportunities in the region and around the world. Brooke further notes that "Brazil is also bidding for military power" (1981: 174). The *military power role* is supported by the fact that by the 1980s, Brazil had become the sixth-largest arms exporter in the world as a consequence of its homegrown weapons industry. Brooke also describes an unconvincing enactment of the *ally role* with the United States from the U.S. point of view as well as a failure to enact an *anticommunist agent role* internationally, as Brazil increasingly sought out its own national interests rather than those of the hegemon. Finally, Brooke describes a *liberalizing autocracy role* adopted by the Figueiredo regime through its policy of *abertura* (178–80). While this policy is largely aimed at a domestic audience, it does have international ramifications through relations with the United States (especially as President Carter repeatedly condemned Brazil's human rights record) and as Brazil requires stable domestic employment to support its international trading goals.

In a discussion of U.S. national strategy, Chase, Hill, and Kennedy (1996) argue that the United States should consider the role played by major players, including Brazil, as that of a *pivotal state*. In their view, a pivotal state is a "hot spot that could not only determine the fate of its region but also affect international stability" (33). Conceptually, focusing on pivotal states would help integrate new security issues into policymakers' old state-centered mind-set and help to direct U.S. assistance to stabilize key regions around the world. The authors contend that by the mid-1990s, Algeria, Brazil, Egypt, India, Indonesia, Mexico, Pakistan, South Africa, and Turkey had become pivotal states. Brazil was viewed as a pivotal state because it held so much promise in terms of economic development yet still faced many internal challenges, such as "extreme economic inequality, poor educational standards, and extensive malnutrition . . . a burgeoning current account deficit and post-peso crisis skittishness" (44). Brazil's foundering would have severe economic, political, social, and environmental consequences for the entire South American region.

Barbarosa (2001) argues that since the 1991 formation of Mercosur, Brazil has played the role of *regional integrator* or *regional leader* in the economic sphere. The goal is to strengthen the domestic economies of Latin American states through integration so that they can be better competitors on the international market. Part of this project also involved the role of *developer*, as Brazil was key in developing the physical infrastructure to encourage integration, especially along its northern border with Guyana and Venezuela. By 1999, this included welcoming hemispheric integration through the Free Trade Agreement of the Americas (FTAA). Burges (2006) agrees that Brazil pursued a *regional leader role* in South America that aimed toward consensus rather than coercion in leading neighboring states during the Cardoso era (1992–2003).

Alden and Vieira (2005) reinforce Brazil's *middle power role* and *regional leader role*, arguing that since 2003 it has also occupied a *trilateral leadership role* with South Africa and India that is distinctive of the multilateralism associated with middle powers. The authors note that in the 20th century, Brazil pursued a policy of maintaining friendly and constructive relations with its neighbors in the region, including pursuing a *mediator-integrator role* to settle territorial disputes diplomatically as well as push for increasing open economic regionalism through Mercosur and other regional trade agreements.[4] Brazil has also pursued an "unwritten alliance" or *allied role* with the United States alongside multilateral approaches to problems. The pursuit of trilateralism for Brazil began with Lula's 2003 election, and the resulting IBSA Forum was formalized in the Declaration of Brasilia signed that same year by the foreign ministers of the three states. The trilateral role relationship envisions "formalized cooperation between regional hegemons who pool together their material and principled assets to achieve clear national interests in multilateral fora of negotiation" (Alden and Vieira 2005: 1086). Alden and Vieira (2005: 1086) also note that domestic support for this trilateral role relationship is limited, suggesting that its enactment may be inconsistent when international and domestic political priorities conflict. Brands (2011) similarly sees Brazilian grand strategy under Lula moving to hasten the end of unipolarity and move toward multipolarity with more multilateral cooperation that will favor Brazil's interests.

While Brands (2011) does not particularly frame his discussion around trilateralism, he notes the continuing evolution of the *military power role*, the *middle power role*, and the *regional leader role*. The regional leader role is much the same conceptualization as employed under trilateralism. In fact, Brands agrees with Burges's (2008) assertion of Lula's intent to enact a *consensual hegemon role* in the region through continued regional integration that brings political and economic benefits while tying Latin America closer to Brazil (cf. Giacalone 2012: 338–39). Carranza (2016) concurs, suggesting that during the Lula period (2003–10), Brazil pursued foreign policy goals of autonomy, universalism, and "destiny of grandeur." Similar to Alden and Vieira, Brands finds somewhat inconsistent domestic support for this type of active international role, especially when it imposes domestic costs.

Internationally, support for this role may also fall prey to competing national interests, as the BRIC and IBSA groups often express solidarity for each other until they disagree on some issue, such as Brazil's bid for a UN Security Council seat (Brands 2011: 39). The international support also varies by country. For example, Wehner (2015) notes that such secondary powers as Argentina, Chile, and Venezuela accept Brazil's regional leadership to varying degrees and in different contexts. Argentina aims to be a soft balance to Brazilian leadership, often drawing Mexico into "regional" discussions when Brazil has explicitly redefined its leadership role to South America and away from the larger Latin American sphere (Malamud 2011). Argentina views Brazil in the *mediator* role, as an *ally*, and in a *regional power* role that does not extend to the global level. Chile similarly views Brazil as a regional leader but often draws Mexico in as a way of balancing, especially in the economic arena, where Chile and Mexico have more in common. Chile recognizes Brazil's roles as *mediator, facilitator*, and *crisis manager* in the region. Venezuela also supports Brazil as a regional power and leader while maintaining that Venezuela, too, could enact such roles. Venezuela expresses more limited support for the *mediator* role. Flemes and Wojczewski (2010) suggest that more broadly, Brazil's claims to regional leadership are "contested" by states that support some aspects of the role and not others. Brands (2011: 40) suggests that the U.S. partnership may be approaching a *rival role* relationship, especially when Lula engaged Iran or opposed the FTAA (cf. Hakim 2002: 154; Lima and Hirst 2006: 33).

The increasingly assertive foreign policy under Lula has been matched with a general acceptance of Brazil as a rising power in academic and policy circles (Hurrell 2010: 60; Sotero 2010; Engstrom 2012: 835; Seabra 2012: 194). Engstrom (2012) argues that a great deal of continuity would persist from Lula to Dilma, especially as Dilma continued to press for global institutional reforms, pursued South-South dialogues, increased the formalization of the IBSA forum, and preferred soft over hard power, although the focus on the region versus the global led him to call Brazil an "ambivalent regional leader." Flemes and Wehner (2012: 12) similarly indicate ambivalence in regional leadership, as Brazil is currently not ready to pay the costs of economic integration but is willing to provide regional security.[5] The low levels of multilateral leadership and selective distributional leadership open the door to regional contestation of Brazil's leadership role.[6] For example, since 2003, this has resulted in a competitive partnership role emanating from a balance of power strategy from the perspective of Argentina—more cooperative at the regional level and more competitive at the global level.

Malamud (2011) takes the argument one step further to suggest that Brazil has not succeeded at achieving recognition with the region for its *regional leader role* but has had much more success in attaining an *intermediate global power* or *middle power role* on the global scene. Malamud suggests that there have been only erratic attempts at region building, a lack of regional support for Brazil's global goals, and rival contenders in Argentina and Mexico (and even Venezuela under Chávez for regional leadership). Perhaps more charitably, Soares de Lima and Hirst (2006: 32) note that "assuming the role of a regional power has generated unprecedented demands on Brazil and seems to require capabilities that go beyond Itamaraty's unquestioned diplomatic skills." While we remain primarily interested in how Brazil sees itself, many of these issues raise questions about what exactly constitutes a regional power (Flemes 2010; Nolte 2010; Prys 2010).

Speculating on the future of nonpolarity, Haas (2008) identifies six *major powers*: China, the European Union, India, Japan, Russia, and the United States. In addition, there are numerous *regional powers*—Brazil, Argentina, Chile, Mexico, Venezuela, Nigeria, South Africa, Egypt, Iran, Israel, Saudi Arabia, Pakistan, Australia, Indonesia, and South Korea. Haas notes the difficulties that come with diplomacy in a nonpolar world but suggests that the United States should help encourage a form of cooperative multilateralism or "concerted nonpolarity." Thus, even if Brazil has not achieved recognition for the regional power or regional leader role within South America, it may be increasingly recognized that way in the United States. Stephen (2012: 293) argues against considering Brazil or any of the other rising powers in this group as middle powers. Instead, he sees Brazil, like India, as aspiring to a global power role given its capabilities. Such rising powers may at times engage in spoiling or balancing or may be co-opted into international institutions.

The analysis of Brazilian foreign policy suggests several key shocks related to the economic development models that *could* induce major foreign policy change: the 1930s crisis when the agro-exporting model was replaced by the import-substitution model, and the 1990s exhaustion of protected industrialization and its replacement by integration into the global economy. Conversely, there is also some discussion of an agent-moderated shock of a global/domestic realization of increased Brazilian power resulting in potentially more aggressive foreign policy under Lula beginning in 2003 (though whether he pursued a form of confrontational autonomy or consensual hegemony is disputed).

The narrative history of Brazilian NRCs briefly summarized in table 4.1 demonstrates a slowly evolving and relatively consistent Brazilian identity. While the decade-by-decade portrait of NRCs masks some variation in NRCs according to traditional breaks in Brazilian foreign policy, it does paint a picture of a generally stable and evolving Brazilian identity. NRCs related to regional leadership emerge in the 1970s, prior to the 1990s shift in development models. It is true that the language of regional leadership becomes more grandiose in the 1980s "superpower of the South" or "Third World power," and by the 2000s the NRCs are focused on Brazil's emergence on the global scene. This could be evidence of the 1990s structural break that was moderated during the Cardoso administration but ultimately led to a more aggressive foreign policy stance under Lula. The NRCs in the 2000s do reflect the entire gamut of regional leadership and global aspirations, from "military power" to "consensual hegemon." It is therefore possible to interpret the changes in NRCs to a more evolutionary growth in Brazilian power with a possible structural change in the 2000s. Yet one also

Table 4.1. Brazil's Role Sets

1930s	*internal developer*
1940s	*regional-subsystem collaborator, U.S. ally, Argentine rival*
1950s	*regional-subsystem collaborator, U.S. ally, Argentine rival*
1960s	*internal developer, active independent, Third World champion, Argentine rival, U.S. ally/ privileged partner*
1970s	*regional leader, U.S. ally, anti-communist agent, developer, middle power, emerging power, internal developer, Argentine rival, superpower in waiting*
1980s	*superpower of the South, Third World power, internal developer, global trader, regional integrator, military power, liberalizing autocracy*
1990s	*regional integrator, regional leader, developer, pivotal state*
2000s	*intermediate global power, middle power, regional leader, trilateral leader, military power, consensual hegemon, U.S. ally?, U.S. rival?, Argentine ally, mediator, regional power, rising power, facilitator, regional crisis manager*

might easily argue that agents in the form of Cardoso and Lula significantly affected the way Brazil represented itself on the regional and global scene despite relatively constant Brazilian power in relation to its neighbors in the 1990s and 2000s.

The data in table 4.2 provide some additional information regarding our theoretical model of the operation of socialization and competition mechanisms on emerging powers. As in the earlier discussion, the number of roles occupied by Brazil increases dramatically by the 1970s, as does the overall level of activity associated with those roles. While the number of roles declines a bit in the 1980s and 1990s, the average level of activity (on the active-passive scale) still remains high—in fact, it is the highest in the 1990s. In the first decade of the 21st century, we find the highest number of roles occupied by Brazil, the highest overall activity, and a generally high average activity level associated with the role set. In general we see a steady increase in the number of roles and their activity level over time, with some potential structural changes in the 1970s and 1990s/2000s. What do these changes in foreign policy roles suggest for Brazil's conflict behavior? Will militarized and economic conflict behavior match purported dramatic changes in material power or be consistent with our review of NRCs that suggests more evolutionary changes?

A separate literature on zones of peace also intersects with our project at this point. It is possible that the regional culture of South America has been evolving in a more peaceful direction over time. Kacowicz (1998) argues that South America went through a period of negative peace (1883–1980s), then stable peace in the Southern Cone (early 1980s–1991), then perhaps a pluralistic security community (1991–?). He argues that satisfaction with the territorial status quo largely ensured a negative peace alongside evolv-

Table 4.2. Active-Passive Dimensions of Brazil's Role Sets

Decade	Number of Roles	Overall Activity	Low	High	Mean
1930s	1	0	0	0	0
1940s	3	7	2	3	2.3
1950s	3	7	2	3	2.3
1960s	5	12	0	4	2.4
1970s	9	28	0	5	3.1
1980s	7	19	0	5	2.7
1990s	4	18	3	5	4.5
2000s	14	50	2	5	3.6

ing norms of peaceful conflict resolution, as well as the presence of Brazil as a regional hegemon, among other factors. The stable peace in the Southern Cone resulted from the return to democracy among the states in the region as well as increased economic integration in the 1980s. According to this analysis, these and the other factors mentioned earlier may well have resulted in the formation of a pluralistic security community by the early 1990s. Thies's (2008) quantitative assessment of this argument produced mixed findings. We should remain open to the possibility that the regional culture of international relations may exercise a pacifying effect on Brazil's conflict behavior—something we may not encounter in other regions with emerging powers. The structural breaks we observe may occur in the early 1980s and again in the early 1990s, but they would contradict H1 in the sense that despite rising Brazilian power, Brazil may be more peaceful at each break.

Militarized Interstate Disputes and Brazilian Conflict Behavior

We move from our qualitative analysis of Brazil's NRCs to a quantitative test of its militarized and economic conflict behavior using change-point models. We test militarized conflict in two steps: after a brief overview of Brazil's militarized conflict behavior over the period 1870–2007, we estimate ten endogenous Poisson change-point regressions, varying the number of change-points, and use Bayes Factor to select the model with the best fit to the observed data. We then report and interpret the summary statistics of the posterior distribution of the best-fitting model. If structural theories of international relations are correct, we should observe that economic growth and increases in Brazil's relative material power are associated with increases in conflict behavior. If our foreign policy approach is accurate, we would expect little in the way of structural breaks in militarized or economic conflict behavior outside of dramatic domestic reorganization (such as military coups).

Figure 4.1 reports the number of MIDs initiated or joined by Brazil between 1870 and 2007. It is clear that military engagement by Brazil is relatively sparse, with only a brief spike in 1944. Yet this simple examination of the data does not tell us whether any changes have occurred in the determinants of conflict, such as whether power dynamics matter in the later years as Brazil rises. A change-point model, however, lends itself well to this type of analysis.

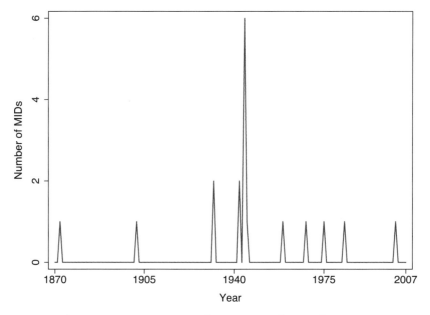

Fig. 4.1. Military Dispute Initiations and Interventions by Brazil, 1870–2007

We estimate the full militarized conflict model outlined in chapter 3.[7] We identify South America as Brazil's region for calculating the *Power Ratio* measure.[8] In addition, we include the United States in the *Power Ratio* measure, as the United States has long-standing involvement in the South American region (Kacowicz 1998; Mares 2001; Thies 2008).[9] We also analyze models without the United States included in calculating *Power Ratio*.

To select the most appropriate model representing Brazil's militarized conflict behavior, we estimate ten endogenous Poisson change-point models and employ a Bayes Factor comparison of each model's marginal likelihood. Each model is titled M and given a subscript indicating the number of change-points in the model. The parameter estimates of the explanatory variables from the model with the best fit are then analyzed.

Table 4.3 reports the logged Bayes Factor comparison of the marginal likelihood for each model, where the numerator in the Bayes Factor ratio is the column (baseline model) and the denominator is the row (alternative model). As chapter 3 demonstrates, because the ratios are logged, negative values are evidence against the baseline, while positive values are evidence in favor of the baseline. Applying Jeffrey's (1961) scale to the values in table

4.3, model M_0 has "decisive" support as the best model fit. This suggests that the data best fits a model with zero change-points, indicating that the determinants associated with Brazil's military conflict behavior have not changed in the period under review.

We now turn to exploring the effect of the explanatory variables on militarized conflict behavior. In particular, we are interested in the effect of *Power Ratio*, as structural theories would expect it to be positively related to militarized conflict behavior. We report summaries of the posterior parameter estimates of each endogenous variable in table 4.4.

Table 4.4 presents the results of two models: one including the United States as a regional member and one without the United States. Model 1

Table 4.3. Comparison of Poisson Change-Point Models of Brazil's Militarized Conflict Behavior

	M_0	M_1	M_2	M_3	M_4	M_5	M_6	M_7	M_8	M_9
M_0	0	9.49	3.96	8.28	16.69	21.40	24.93	35.15	40.36	38.43
M_1	−9.49	0	−5.53	−1.21	7.19	11.91	15.44	25.66	30.87	28.94
M_2	−3.96	5.53	0	4.32	12.73	17.44	20.97	31.19	36.4	34.47
M_3	−8.28	1.21	−4.32	0	8.40	13.12	16.65	26.87	32.08	30.15
M_4	−16.69	−7.19	−12.73	−8.40	0	4.71	8.24	18.47	23.68	21.75
M_5	−21.40	−11.91	−17.44	−13.12	−4.71	0	3.53	13.75	18.96	17.03
M_6	−24.93	−15.44	−20.97	−16.65	−8.24	−3.53	0	10.23	15.44	13.5
M_7	−35.15	−25.66	−31.19	−26.87	−18.47	−13.75	−10.23	0	5.21	3.28
M_8	−40.36	−30.87	−36.4	−32.08	−23.68	−18.96	−15.44	−5.21	0	−1.93
M_9	−38.43	−28.94	−34.47	−30.15	−21.75	−17.03	−13.5	−3.28	1.93	0

Note: $\ln(BF_{ij} = m[y|M_i]/m[y|M_j])$ where BF_{ij} is the Bayes Factor comparing model M_i to a baseline model M_j, $m(y|M_i)$ is the marginal likelihood under model M_i, $m(y|M_j)$ is the marginal likelihood under model M_j. Columns are M_i and rows are M_j. MCMC chains are run 20,000 times after discarding 10,000 burn-in draws.

Table 4.4. Poisson Estimation of Brazil's Militarized Conflict Initiation with Zero Change-Points

	With U.S.		Without U.S.	
	Mean	S.D.	Mean	S.D.
Power Ratio	−1.112	0.450	−0.006	0.155
Power Ratio Squared	0.671	0.313	−0.078	0.219
Neighbor Conflict	0.310	0.439	0.125	0.421
Democratic Proportion	0.006	0.036	0.011	0.023
Trade	−0.339	0.224	−0.178	0.175
World War I	−1.824	2.308	−1.398	2.251
World War II	1.452	0.841	1.988	0.833
Constant	2.082	1.498	−0.185	3.126

Note: Mean and standard deviation drawn from the posterior distribution. MCMC chains are run 20,000 times after discarding 10,000 burn-in draws.

identifies *Power Ratio, Power Ratio Squared, Trade*, and *World War II* as significant predictors of militarized conflict. The two *Power Ratio* estimates are significant with greater than 95 percent confidence, *Trade* is significant with 85 percent confidence, and *World War II* is significant with greater than 90 percent confidence. In contrast to structural theories, *Power Ratio* is associated with a *decrease* in expected militarized conflict. *Power Ratio Squared* has a positive coefficient, indicating that the rate of decline slows as Brazil's degree of relative material power increases.[10] These results support the stable foreign policy account of Brazil's militarized conflict behavior and offer some support for the "zones of peace" argument that South America has a culture of peace that constrains even rising powers. Model 1 of table 4.4 also shows that increases in *Trade* are associated with a pacifying effect on Brazil's foreign policy. The *World War II* indicator variable captures the instantaneous positive effect of Brazil's entry into that war on its militarized conflict behavior. We find little evidence that *Neighbor Conflict, Proportion of Democracies*, or entry into *World War I* are significant determinants of Brazil's militarized conflict behavior, as each parameter estimate is within one standard deviation of 0.

Model 2, which does not include the United States as a member of Brazil's region, finds only *Trade* (roughly 68% confidence) and *World War II* (more than 95% confidence) to be significant predictors of militarized conflict. None of the other explanatory variables, including the *Power Ratio* variables, appear to exert a significant impact on militarized conflict in this model, as 0 is well within one standard deviation of the mean parameter estimate.

The quantitative results offer support for foreign policy accounts and argue against structural theories in the case of militarized conflict. There are no change-points in the underlying data-generative process of Brazilian militarized conflict behavior. *Power Ratio* is significant in the model including the United States in the region but has a pacifying effect, running directly against the expectations posited by structural theories. The quantitative results are consistent with our qualitative analyses, finding much stability in Brazil's militarized foreign policy.

Brazilian Economic Conflict

We now turn to analyzing Brazil's economic conflict behavior for 1929–2007, the period for which data are available. Brazil's early NRCs as *Third*

World Champion and *Superpower of the South* raise the prospect for potential economic conflict with the liberal international economic order (LIEO). Brazil engaged in six economic challenges during this period. Brazil twice defaulted on its sovereign debt in the 1930s—in 1931 and 1937. Brazil engaged in a series of foreign asset expropriations in 1959, 1962, and 1965, a period when the global risk of expropriation was highest (Korbin 1984; Hajzler 2012) and domestic hyperinflation, which encourages expropriation as compensation in real terms is reduced (Rosenn 1974–75), was prevalent. Finally, Brazil again defaulted on its sovereign debt in 1983, at the end of a period of military rule and during South America's "lost decade" of economic stagnation. To analyze Brazil's economic conflict behavior, we estimate six probit change-point regression models, varying the number of change-points between models. We use the Bayes Factor to select the model with the best fit to the observed data using the economic conflict model outlined in chapter 3.[11]

Table 4.5 reports the results of the Bayes Factor comparisons of the logged marginal likelihood of each model. The results indicate that model M_2, a model with two change-points, is the best-fitting model. That is, three distinct temporal regimes, each with its own data-generating process, explain Brazil's economic conflict behavior. Figure 4.2 displays the posterior probability of each temporal regime and the probability of the change-point for each year between 1929 and 2007. The top of figure 4.2 shows the posterior density for each temporal regime. The bottom two graphs in figure 4.2 show the posterior probability density for a change-point in each year.

Figure 4.2 shows that there are two relatively stable temporal regimes separated by a sharp, temporary regime and that the change-points happen

Table 4.5. Comparison of Probit Change-Point Models of Brazil's Economic Conflict Behavior

	M_0	M_1	M_2	M_3	M_4	M_5
M_0	0	3.36	−12.5	−2.48	39.79	36.73
M_1	−3.36	0	−15.9	−5.83	36.44	33.38
M_2	12.52	15.87	0	10.04	52.31	49.25
M_3	2.48	5.83	−10.04	0	42.27	39.21
M_4	−39.79	−36.44	−52.31	−42.27	0	−3.06
M_5	−36.73	−33.38	−49.25	−39.21	3.06	0

Note: $\ln(BF_{ij} = m[y|M_i]/m[y|M_j])$ where BF_{ij} is the Bayes Factor comparing model M_i to a baseline model M_j, $m(y|M_i)$ is the marginal likelihood under model M_i, $(y|M_j)$ is the marginal likelihood under model M_j. Columns are M_i and rows are M_j. MCMC chains are run 20,000 times after discarding 10,000 burn-in draws.

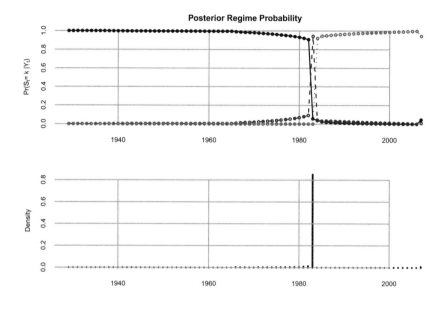

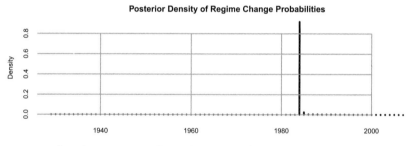

Fig. 4.2. Identifying Structural Breaks in Brazil's Economic Conflict Behavior, 1929–2007. (*Note:* Expected modal change-points: 1983, 1984. Local means for each time regime: 0.093, 1, and 0 economic challenges.)

very quickly and in rapid succession in 1983 and 1984. From 1929 until 1982, defaults and expropriations follow a similar process during the period that Brazil adhered to import-substitution and interventionist economic policies. In 1983, however, Brazil's default on its sovereign debt does not follow this process. After Brazil's economy begins to improve in 1984 after three years of stasis, the determinants that account for the 1983 default no longer seem to apply. Following the transition from military rule and the return to democracy in 1985, Brazil appears to follow the U.S.-led LIEO.

Table 4.6 displays summaries of the posterior parameter estimates for the endogenous predictors of economic conflict for each of the three identified temporal regimes. During the first temporal regime, *Trade* is the only significant predictor of economic conflict and is associated with a negative effect with greater than 90 percent confidence. This suggests that as Brazil engages more with the global economy, it is less likely to challenge the economic order. None of the other predictors have a mean more than one standard deviation away from 0.

In the second temporal regime, *Trade* is no longer a significant predictor, as 0 is within one standard deviation of its mean. *Proportion of Democracies* is positive and significant, with approximately 70 percent confidence. This means that as the number of South American democracies increases, Brazil is more likely to initiate an economic challenge. None of the other variables are significant.

In the third temporal regime, *Proportion of Democracies* is again significant, again with approximately 70 percent confidence. The coefficient, however, is now negative, indicating that as the number of South American democracies increases, Brazil is less likely to initiate an economic challenge. The changes in the effect of *Proportion of Democracies*—from null to positive to negative—highlight the utility of using a change-point model, and the shift in effect from positive to negative coincides with Brazil's transition from military dictatorship to democracy.

The quantitative results find little evidence to suggest that Brazil's rise has made it more conflictual economically. *Power Ratio* was not a significant predictor in any of the temporal regimes. The economic conflict results contrast with structural theoretic accounts of conflict behavior. The quanti-

Table 4.6. Probit Estimation of Brazil Economic Conflict Initiation with Two Change-Points

	Pre-1982		1983		Post-1984	
	Mean	S.D.	Mean	S.D.	Mean	S.D.
Power Ratio	−0.211	0.307	0.054	3.218	−0.841	2.932
Democratic Proportion	0.069	0.223	1.708	1.610	−1.138	1.070
Trade	−1.620	0.918	0.125	3.110	1.064	2.106
Constant	1.580	1.928	−0.056	3.182	−0.018	3.147

Note: Mean and standard deviation drawn from the posterior distribution. MCMC chains are run 20,000 times after discarding 10,000 burn-in draws. The median posterior probability for the two breaks in the model were 1983 and 1984. Estimates of the posterior average over the full state space, accounting for the precision (or imprecision) of the estimated change-points.

tative results suggest that while Brazil calls for changes to the global economic system, such reforms to agricultural trade and subsides, in practice it largely adheres to the legitimacy of the existing LIEO.

Conclusion

Our analysis finds that changes in Brazil's identity and conflict behavior are more consistent with foreign policy approaches than structural theories. Brazil's role sets have varied over time, but the core has evolved to a form of regional leadership based on consensus. While Brazil has continued to invest in its military power, this particular regional power may have evolved in a region that has become increasingly pacified over time. Scholars and policy analysts have never been as suspicious of Brazil's intentions as they are of other emerging powers, such as China, but structural theories do suggest that at some point, growth in power should lead to increasingly aggressive foreign policy and conflict behavior. However, no structural breaks in Brazil's militarized conflict behavior have occurred. There is little evidence to suggest that power disparities in the Latin American subsystem, with or without the United States, has any effect on Brazilian conflict behavior. If anything, Brazil views itself as a partner in a mature relationship with the United States—an example of successful long-term socialization by the United States. Brazil also sees itself as contributing to a group of emerging powers that balance hegemony through multilateralism. Structural materialist theories tend to ignore the relations of authority present in the hierarchical international order, whether designed by the United States or by emerging powers themselves.

There is more action on the economic conflict aspect of Brazil's behavior, with two closely grouped structural breaks occurring in 1983 and 1984. This was a turbulent economic time for all Latin American states, as it represents the immediate aftermath of the debt crisis that began in 1982. The International Monetary Fund (IMF) worked closely with the Brazilian government in 1983 to manage its mounting deficit and debt problems, though the IMF recommendations were at odds with traditional Brazilian economic policy (see Boughton 2001, 372–84). Late in 1983, the Paris Club was satisfied with the negotiations and agreed to reschedule nearly three billion dollars of Brazil's debt. Brazil implemented more realistic interest rates, engaged in tighter controls over the monetary base, and began restraining wage demands as a result of these negotiations—all reforms designed to cut inflation to more manageable levels. Yet as the first election of a civilian president in nearly two decades loomed, the IMF became strongly concerned that these difficult adjustments would be hard to maintain. In January 1985, Tancredo Neves was elected president. Brazil's commitment to the austerity program had already begun to weaken during the preceding year, and by 1985 the country had stopped paying interest on bilateral debts and requested another rescheduling agreement through the Paris Club. Thus, while this turbulent period marked structural breaks in Brazil's economic behavior, they clearly represent weakness on the international stage rather than strength. The NRCs during this period also do not change dramatically.

What does our analysis suggest for the future? Brazil's identity, comprised of an evolving role set, is largely one of a regional leader that prefers to work in concert with its neighbors and with other emerging powers on the global scene. This does not preclude conflict in the future if Brazil does attain great power status, as great powers engage in a significant percentage of all conflict (Bremer 1992; Chiba, Martinez Machain, and Reed 2014). It would be unusual for a great power not to manage the affairs of its home region, including through the use of periodic militarized conflict. Latin America is somewhat peculiar in that it may be moving toward zones of negative and stable peace in the Southern Cone alongside some persistent zones of conflict in the northern tier of South America and in Central America. In general, our analysis suggests that Brazil will continue to view its identity as a regional leader that engages in infrequent militarized disputes in its home region, but a dramatic shift in foreign policy orientation or conflict behavior is unlikely. The same is true in terms of Brazil's economic conflict. The concerns for Brazil are largely related to internal weaknesses, such as the sovereign debt crisis of the 1980s and more recent charges of mismanagement and corruption leading to a slowdown in economic activity under the Rousseff administration and her eventual impeachment. While Brazil may band together with the other BRICS to launch projects such as the development bank, it seems unlikely that the country will take an active role in challenging the U.S.-led LIEO.

CHAPTER 5

Russia: A Once and Future Great Power?

The reemergence of Russia as an actor with an active foreign policy, global military capabilities, and autocratic tendencies has caught the attention of decision makers, pundits, academics, and the global media. Russia's natural-resource-fueled economic growth plus its aspirations for control of the near abroad have led many observers to note a more assertive foreign policy orientation in recent years. Russia's 2008 intervention in Georgia, invasion of Crimea and support of separatists in Ukraine, and intervention in Syria are viewed as evidence of a renewed Russian threat. Some observers have even suggested the dawn of a new Cold War as the United States and other Western allies attempt to contain an aggressive Russia that hearkens back to the days of traditional great power politics. Are these types of behaviors just the beginning of an assertive and more militarized foreign policy, or will Russia simply be satisfied with recognition of its complementary status as a great power as a (suspended) member of the G8 and continued membership in the UN Security Council? We continue our examination of rising powers by reviewing Russia's beliefs about its identity through time as well as its military and economic conflict behavior.

We examine both qualitative and quantitative evidence regarding Russian identity and behavior to look for significant changes in the role set that may lead to major foreign policy reorientation. We also explore whether foreign policy reorientations have resulted in changes in Russian militarized or economic conflict behavior over time using change-point models. By comparing Russia's words and deeds through NRCs and conflict behavior, we can assess whether claims about potential threats emanating from rising powers such as Russia are accurate.

Our qualitative and quantitative analyses find some changes in Russian identity that match the traditional narrative of the country's foreign policy, which is accompanied by relative continuity in conflict behavior over the past seventy years. We find a small but consistent role set from the 1930s through the 1970s, followed by changes associated with Gorbachev in the 1980s that carry through to the post-Soviet period. Our statistical analysis reveals one structural break in militarized conflict behavior around 1938, but the timing and supporting evidence suggests this was likely affected by domestic events that produced changes in foreign policy orientation—the great purges that consolidated Joseph Stalin's hold on power—rather than changes to the structural environment itself. We also find one structural change in economic conflict behavior that coincides with the end of the Soviet Union in 1991. The post-Soviet period is certainly one of a search for an appropriate identity (of the many NRCs present in the role set), and it represents a transition from one of the poles of power in the system to a smaller but still substantial successor state. However, it does not seem to indicate a move toward a more revisionist foreign policy orientation based on rising power status. Overall, while we find some evidence of changes in words, we find little evidence of changes in deeds in Russia's militarized or economic conflict behavior; instead, the determinants of Russian foreign policy have remained relatively constant from Stalin and Khrushchev to Medvedev and Putin.

National Role Conceptions and Russian Foreign Policy Analysis

We review the qualitative evidence on NRCs identified by scholars for Russia as comprising its role set and look for changes in that role set over time. The obvious candidates for internal shocks that would change the identity and self-conceived roles of Russia include the formation of the USSR in the aftermath of the Russian Revolution in October 1917 and the breakup of the Soviet Union in December 1991. As Kassianova (2001: 821) notes about the latter, "Russia offers a very striking example of an international actor whose self-perception over the first decade of its independent existence has suffered numerous adverse and challenging impacts originating from both within and without." Gorbachev's arrival in 1985 and the introduction of his "New Thinking," including the policies of glasnost and perestroika, may also have ideational impacts on Soviet identity. Ivanov (2001: 12) adds the loss of a generation of Soviet diplomats during Stalin's repression of the

1930s as a setback to communicating the Soviet role to the world. Thus, we have four potential internal shocks: 1917, 1930s, 1985, and 1991.

In their well-known analysis of Soviet roles, Thibault and Lévesque (1997) suggest that at the close of World War II, the Soviet Union adopted a number of roles that guided foreign policy into the 1980s. These roles (drawing on Holsti 1970) included *anti-imperialist agent, defender of the faith, regional liberator, guardian,* and *example.* The role of *U.S. rival* is also implicit in their discussion. The United States largely accepted this adversarial role, though it avoided open conflict with the USSR and was less likely to intervene in conflicts involving states within the Soviet sphere (Nieman 2016b). Holsti (1970) identified eight roles during the 1960s in descending order of importance: *anti-imperialist agent, regional-subsystem collaborator, regional protector, example, liberation supporter, developer, defender of the peace,* and *defender of the faith.*

These roles remained relatively constant despite occasional disagreements within the upper echelons of Soviet elites. For example, despite Khrushchev's "Secret Speech," in which he exposed Stalin's brutality and raised the prospect of greater equality between Moscow and its satellites in Eastern Europe, Russia maintained its leadership role in the communist world and sought to expunge challenges that it perceived as weakening this role and by extension communism more broadly (Valdez 1993). This view of itself as an *example, leader,* and *defender of the faith* helps explain Soviet interventions and support of local governments in Poland, Hungary, and Czechoslovakia, as domestic changes in its satellites that produce shifts away from Soviet dominance would imply a weakening of international communism (Valdez 1993).

Chafetz (1996: 667) suggests that Gorbachev resolved the tension between the Soviet role as a *status quo power* and the (Bolshevik) *revolutionary power* role in favor of the former (see also Valdez 1993). Gorbachev also pushed for the role of *integrator of Russia with the West.* By 1989, foreign minister Shevardnadze had classified the USSR as a *member of a democratic community of states.*

After the breakup of the Soviet Union, there was significant domestic contestation over what roles best represented the new Russia.[1] Andrei Kozyrev, Boris Yeltsin, and the radical liberals subsequently pushed for roles aligned with three major priorities: integration into Europe, establishment of friendly relations with the United States, and normalization of relations with Japan (Thibault and Lévesque 1997: 20). Ukrainian independence, among other factors, brought criticism of this pro-Western position. The Eurasians within the Russian political elite responded with the idea of a more "enlightened" continuity with the Soviet past, including foreign policy priority to the Commonwealth of Independent States (CIS), the near abroad, and Eastern Europe. This group proposed a role of *guarantor of political and military stability throughout the entire territory of the former USSR* (Thibault and Lévesque 1997: 21). The fear was that a pro-Western orientation simply cast Russia in the role of *junior partner to the United States*.[2] Instead, Russia is a *Eurasian power* at the crossroads of East and West, North and South, and can serve as an *intermediary* (Thibault and Lévesque 1997: 22). Neocommunists and extreme right-wing movements argued that Russia should take the role of *leader of pan-Slavic movement* (Thibault and Lévesque 1997: 22).[3]

Between 1989 and 1991, Thibault and Lévesque (1997: 23) identify six main roles expressed by the Soviet leadership. These include, in descending order of importance, *promoter of arms control and disarmament, international collaborator, reformer of the international order, reformer of the regional European order, defender of universal human values*, and *supporter of international organizations*. The first three roles comprised nearly two-thirds of all official statements about Soviet roles. Thibault and Lévesque also identify references to status in Soviet official discourse (31). These statuses can also be considered roles, including in descending order of importance, *new member of the international community, collaborator/partner, independent and influential player, great power*, and *excluded from the international system*.[4] While *great power* is listed fourth, the authors note that it "permeates the discourse of the leadership" (32).

After the dismantling of the USSR and its replacement by the successor state of Russia in 1992, the officially expressed roles experienced some changes. The four most important roles, in descending order of importance, were *promoter of a regional geopolitical order, integrator of Russia into the Western world, promoter of international cooperation, protector of the Russian state, and independent player* (Thibault and Lévesque 1997: 26). Additional roles included *instrument for changing Russia, defender of democratic principles and human rights, supporter of international organizations, supporter of arms control and disarmament*, and *normal, nonaggressive great power* (as opposed to the great power status in the previous Soviet regime) (Thibault and Lévesque 1997: 34). Thibault and Lévesque (1997: 28) note the tension between the promoter of a regional geopolitical order role, which was motivated by the desire to reassert Russian control over the post-Soviet space, and the integrator of Russia into the Western world role, which produced an ambivalent and ambiguous foreign policy orientation.

Former Russian ambassador to the United States Vladimir Lukin (1992: 67) argues that the international role of Russia is as *stabilizer of the Eurasian geopolitical environment*. Kassianova (2001: 830) also identified *collaborator/partner, integrator of Russia into the Western world, promoter of international cooperation, great/leading power, democratic state*, and even *U.S. ally* as roles identified in the "Foreign Policy Concept of 1993." Chafetz, Abramson, and Grillot (1996: 734) identified *global system leader* and *regional protector* as Russian roles with specific attention focused on post–Cold War nuclear nonproliferation. Kassianova (2001: 831) notes changes in the "National Security Concept of 1997," such as the reduced references to Russia as a *great power* or a *democratic state*; instead, Russia describes itself as an *influential European and Asian power*. Petersson (1998) interviewed Russian legislators for their view of Russia's role in the world, which included *international problem solver, protector of Slavic peoples, influential power, example* (e.g., spiritual example, example of successful transition), *promoter of international peace, bridge* between Europe and Asia, and *integrator of Russia into Europe*. Legislators also agreed that Russia was a *great power*, even if it failed in some aspects of that role, such as economic power.

The roles emanating from the "Foreign Policy Concept of 2000" include *Eurasian power, excluded from restrictive Western institutions*, and *collaborator/partner* (Kassianova 2001). The "National Security Concept of 2000" includes roles such as *leading power* and *supporter of international organization*.[5] Cummings (2001) analyzes the emerging relationships between Russia and the Central Asian countries in Putin's first year in office.[6] She suggests that the West had previously given Russia the role of *regional peacekeeper* for Central Asia. Under Putin, the role of *collaborator/partner* has assumed prominence, as has some acceptance in the region of Russia as a *leader* as opposed to a *hegemon* or *bloc leader*. Foreign minister Ivanov (2001) notes the vigorous debate over Russian identity in the first ten years after the demise of the Soviet Union, noting that Russia still occupies the role of a *new state*. Russia also draws on its historical foreign policy traditions of being a *reformer* and reinforces roles developed during the Soviet era as a *defender of democratic principles and human rights, supporter of international organization*, and *supporter of arms control and disarmament*.

Ivanov also evokes the *Eurasian power* role and rejects any kind of *neoimperial* role associated with prerevolutionary Russia and the Soviet era. Ivanov also contends that the long span of Russian history has always shown Russia to be a *defender of international law*.

Foreign minister Lavrov (2006) stresses that Asia and Europe are equally important to Russia, reinforcing a *Eurasian power* role. Further, Russia's role of a *cultural and civilizational bridge*—or more accurately an *intermediary* and *problem solver* between the East and West—is needed more than ever (71). Lavrov refers to Russia as one of an orchestra of *leading powers* that should collectively govern the world (76). Russia views itself as a *regional integrator* and *cooperator/partner* in Asia. Lo (2004) documents that Russia views itself simultaneously as a principal *partner* with China and as a *civilizational barrier* against the barbarian East.

Aksenyonok (2008: 75) describes the West's attempts to altercast Russia into the roles of *aggressor* and *violator of the norms of international law* in the aftermath of the 2008 intervention in Georgia, whereas Russia viewed itself as a defender and Georgia as the warmonger. Allison (2008: 1146) describes the Georgian intervention as an attempt to assert a *regional superpower* role in the CIS states befitting Russia's rising status in the international system as an *aspirant global power*. He also notes the *defender of the peace* or even *defender of human rights* role advocated by President Medvedev. This replaced the *peacekeeper* role adopted in 1992 after the cease-fire between Georgia and South Ossetia.

Others suggest that Russia still has not found a new role for itself nearly two decades after the breakup of the USSR (Trenin 2009). It sits on the periphery of both Asia and Europe, it attempted and failed to integrate into the West in the 1990s, and then abandoned such aims by the second term of Putin's presidency. Putin thus advocated a role of *independent great power* as a default position. After 2008, this involved creating a "zone of privileged interests" in the CIS for Russia—what Rahr (2007) refers to Russia's self-conception in the post-Soviet space as a *neoimperial role*. Unfortunately, Russia's role partners in the post-Soviet space are not all equally eager for such a return to Russian dominance. Further, Trenin (2009: 70–71) notes that Russia will not accept a *junior partner* role with the European Union or United States even as they refuse to treat it as an equal. MacFarlane (2006) attempts to assess whether Russia is an *emerging power*, which he defines to include regional preponderance, aspiration to a global role, and the contestation of U.S. hegemony. In contrast to Russian self-conceptions, MacFarlane argues that Russia is not an emerging power in the usual sense of the expectations associated with the role. Instead, Russia's foreign policy is dedicated to reversing the decline of the 1980s and 1990s and laying the foundation for a return to real great power status. This includes the attempt at reasserting *regional hegemony* over the former Soviet space.

The debate within Russia and Europe may be about whether Russia is a *European power* (Baranovsky and Utkin 2012). The preservation or resurrection of *great power* status is often described as one of the unifying elements of Russian foreign policy (e.g., Smith 2005: 47). Russia historically views itself as a *balancer and guardian of global stability* (e.g., Lo 2002: 19–20; Tsygankov 1997: 251). As Chafetz (1996: 679) notes, all of the various Russian factions agree that Russia must achieve the *great power* role, but what constitutes the role is under contention. Makarychev (2008: 202) asserts that Russia is attempting to adopt the *normal great power role*, with practices that resemble those of the West, but is not viewed by Europe as a normative power. Light (1996: 36–38) and Mendras (1997) examine the transition of Russia from an *imperial state* to a *normal state* after 1991. President Putin described Russia as a *sovereignty democracy* to emphasize its view of the role of democratic state as not subject to outside interference (Tocci 2008: 309). Rahr (2007) and Mankoff (2007) suggest that the United States is again considered a Russian rival by 2006.

As Nau and Welt (2013: 1) presciently point out, "What happens in places like George, Central Asia or Ukraine will tend to reflect more what Russia does than what the United States does." Russia may approach the various issues confronting the world from a globalist, nationalist, or great power orientation. From a nationalist view, Russia believes that the international role of the United States is shrinking and that emerging powers like itself are becoming more important. Conversely, the great power view is that the world is unpredictable and Russia should not rely on alliances. Globalists think that Russia's resurgence is accidental and that it should reintegrate into the West if it wants to maintain its power. Thus, a variety of outcomes are possible depending on which view wins out in Russia.

Table 5.1 summarizes this narrative history of Soviet/Russian NRCs. The Soviet role set exhibited a fair amount of consistency from the close of World War II through the 1970s. The 1980s, particularly with the arrival of Gorbachev, produced a fairly dramatic change in the Soviet role set. Many of the roles originating in this time period are revisited in the aftermath of the dissolution of the USSR, and the post-1991 period is marked by the search for Russian identity. As a result, the NRCs advocated by the Russian government and debated within domestic society and by international actors have proliferated. On the one hand, there is a fair amount of stability in the Soviet/Russian role set from the 1980s onward, with constant reference to promoter/supporter of arms control and disarmament, supporter of international organization, collaborator/partner, and others. Integration or exclusion from Western institutions changes from the 1990s to 2000s, as does the view of what it means to be a great power; a Eurasian power role has been added, the United States has been abandoned as an ally and a return to traditional rivalry has occurred, and so on. It is difficult to discern a real structural break from the 1980s on as a result of the overlap of NRCs, yet a break between the 1970s and 1980s or perhaps coinciding with the arrival of Gorbachev is a possibility.

Table 5.1. Soviet Union/Russia's Role Sets

1940s	*anti-imperialist agent, defender of the faith, regional liberator, guardian, example, U.S. rival*
1950s	*anti-imperialist agent, defender of the faith, regional liberator, guardian, example, U.S. rival*
1960s	*anti-imperialist agent, regional-subsystem collaborator, regional protector, regional liberator, example, liberation supporter, developer, defender of the peace, defender of the faith, guardian, example, U.S. rival, revolutionary power*
1970s	*anti-imperialist agent, regional-subsystem collaborator, regional protector, regional liberator, example, liberation supporter, developer, defender of the peace, defender of the faith, guardian, example, U.S. rival, revolutionary power*
1980s	*status quo power, integrator of Russia with the West, member of a democratic community of states, promoter of arms control and disarmament, international collaborator, reformer of the international order, reformer of the regional European order, defender of universal human values, supporter of international organizations, new member of the international community, collaborator/partner, independent and influential player, great power, excluded from the international system*
1990s	*promoter of a regional geopolitical order, integrator of Russia into the Western world, promoter of international cooperation, protector of the Russian state and independent player, instrument for changing Russia, defender of democratic principles and human rights, supporter of international organizations, supporter of arms control and disarmament, (normal nonaggressive) great power, stabilizer of the Eurasian geopolitical environment, democratic state, U.S. ally, new state*
2000s	*Eurasian power, excluded from restrictive Western institutions, collaborator/partner, leading power, (normal) great power, supporter of international organizations, regional peacekeeper/defender of the peace, reformer, defender of democratic principles and human rights, supporter of international organizations, supporter of arms control and disarmament, defender of international law, cultural and civilizational bridge, intermediary, regional integrator, balancer and guardian of global stability, U.S. rival, major power*

Table 5.2. Active-Passive Dimensions of the Soviet Union/
Russia's Role Sets

Decade	Number of Roles	Overall Activity	Low	High	Mean
1940s	6	17	1	5	2.8
1950s	6	17	1	5	2.8
1960s	13	43	1	5	3.3
1970s	13	43	0	5	3.1
1980s	14	44	0	5	2.7
1990s	13	38	0	5	2.9
2000s	17	57	0	5	3.4

Holsti's (1970: 286) scale of activity-passivity in NRCs is not helpful in these latter three decades either. Table 5.2 shows an increase in the number of roles performed between the 1950s and 1960s and again between the 1990s and 2000s. The overall level of activity remains quite high in the entire post-1960 period, with a notable increase between the 1990s and 2000s. The average activity level of NRCs in the role sets is fairly constant at around 3 until the 2000s, when it inches up to 3.4.

The narrative history of the Soviet Union/Russia demonstrates a slowly evolving and relatively consistent Russian search for identity. While the decade-by-decade portrait of NRCs masks some variation according to traditional breaks in Russian foreign policy, it does paint a picture of a generally stable and evolving Russian identity at least since the 1980s.

Militarized Interstate Disputes and Russian Conflict Behavior

We move from our qualitative analysis of Russia's NRCs to a quantitative test of its militarized and economic conflict behavior using change-point models. We begin by examining Russia's militarized conflict behavior over the period 1870–2007 using an endogenous Poisson change-point regression. If structural theories of international relations are correct, we should observe that increases in Russia's relative material power are associated with increases in conflict behavior. If our foreign policy approach is on target, we would expect little in the way of structural breaks in militarized or economic conflict behavior outside of dramatic domestic reorganization (such as revolution, coup, or regime consolidation).

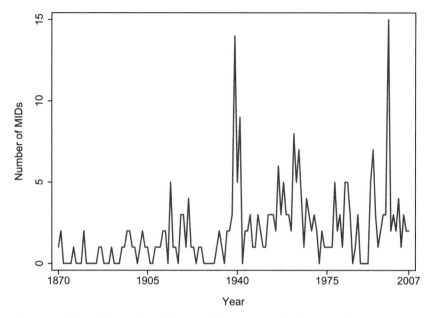

Fig. 5.1. Military Dispute Initiations and Interventions by Russia, 1870–2007

Figure 5.1 displays the number of MIDs initiated or ongoing MIDs joined by Russia between 1870 and 2007. It is clear that the number of disputes in which Russia willingly engages increases in the second half of the twentieth century. This simple examination of the data does not, however, inform us whether this increase results in changes in the determinants of militarized conflict or whether this is simply a reflection of an increase in power capabilities or some other factor. It is also unclear how many structural breaks occur and where they take place. Thus, a change-point model is exceptionally useful for this type of analysis.

We estimate the full militarized conflict model outlined in chapter 3. In contrast to the other rising powers, we identify Russia's region as global when calculating its *Power Ratio* variables.[7] Given its previous *great power* status and unique geopolitical location spanning the Eurasian land mass, Russia has consistently held far-reaching and global interests.

We estimate ten endogenous Poisson change-point models and use the Bayes Factor to select the best model. Table 5.3 reports the logged Bayes Factor comparisons of the marginal likelihood for each model. Applying Jeffrey's (1961) scale to the values in table 5.3, model M_1 has "decisive" support as the best model fit. This suggests that the data best fits a model with one change-point with two temporal regimes. Hereafter, we focus on the results from this model.

We now turn to figure 5.2 to examine the timing of the change-point. Figure 5.2 displays the posterior probabilities for each temporal regime and the probability of a change-point during each year from 1870–2007. The top of figure 5.2 concerns the posterior density for the two temporal regimes. The bar graph at the bottom of figure 5.2 reports the probability densities of the change-point for each year.

Figure 5.2 indicates that the change-point occurred during the 1930s, prior to the outbreak of World War II, with the modal probability in 1936 and the median probability in 1938. While the USSR invaded Poland in 1939 and fought Finland in 1939–40, not until Nazi Germany invaded in 1941 did the USSR began to face severe wartime costs. The probability that the change-point occurred in 1939–41, however, is less than 20 percent, compared to 57 percent that it occurred before the start of the war. This suggests that some factor other than war led to the change in Russian militarized behavior.[8]

The relatively short time period identified in figure 5.2 indicates that the structural break occurred rather quickly. This result fits well with our knowledge of Soviet history. The identified time period overlaps with the Great Purge, a period of intense internal conflict within the USSR when Stalin removed political rivals and consolidated his power (Pristland 2009). In fact, the expected break (modal) of 1936 coincides with the First Mos-

Table 5.3. Comparison of Poisson Change-Point Models of the Soviet Union/ Russia's Militarized Conflict Behavior

	M_0	M_1	M_2	M_3	M_4	M_5	M_6	M_7	M_8	M_9
M_0	0	−6.41	2.28	6.83	14.80	20.20	22.68	26.36	35.09	35.59
M_1	6.41	0	8.69	13.23	21.20	26.61	29.09	32.77	41.50	41.99
M_2	−2.28	−8.69	0	4.54	12.51	17.92	20.40	24.08	32.81	33.30
M_3	−6.83	−13.23	−4.54	0	7.97	13.38	15.85	19.54	28.26	28.76
M_4	−14.80	−21.20	−12.51	−7.97	0	5.41	7.88	11.57	20.30	20.79
M_5	−20.20	−26.61	−17.92	−13.38	−5.41	0	2.48	6.16	14.89	15.38
M_6	−22.68	−29.09	−20.40	−15.85	−7.88	−2.48	0	3.68	12.41	12.91
M_7	−26.36	−32.77	−24.08	−19.54	−11.57	−6.16	−3.68	0	8.72	9.22
M_8	−35.09	−41.50	−32.81	−28.26	−20.29	−14.89	−12.41	−8.73	0	0.50
M_9	−35.59	−41.99	−33.30	−28.76	−20.79	−15.38	−12.91	−9.22	−0.50	0

Note: $\ln(BF_{ij} = m[y|M_i]/m[y|M_j])$ where BF_{ij} is the Bayes Factor comparing model M_i to a baseline model M_j, $m(y|M_i)$ is the marginal likelihood under model M_i, $(y|M_j)$ is the marginal likelihood under model M_j. Columns are M_i and rows are M_j. MCMC chains are run 20,000 times after discarding 10,000 burn-in draws.

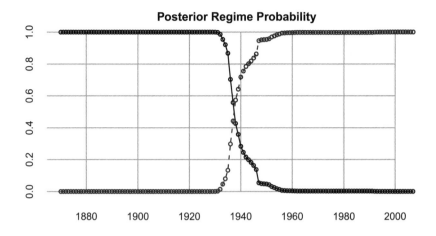

Fig. 5.2. Identifying Structural Breaks in Russia's Militarized Conflict Behavior, 1870–2007. (*Note:* Expected modal change-point: 1938. Local means for each time regime: 0.868 and 3.014 militarized disputes.)

cow Trial, where senior communist officials were charged with conspiring to kill Stalin and promptly executed. This was in the midst of Yezhovsh-china, a period of especially intense repression.[9]

An alternative account may be that the 1930s were a period of rapid industrialization and economic growth—with growth rates over 7 percent annually from 1934 to 1937 and a peak at 14 percent in 1936—and that this led to the change in Russian militarized conflict behavior. The lack of evidence for a subsequent break, however, suggests that the Soviet Union largely maintained the same foreign policy practices that Stalin implemented once he had secured power, at least in observable determinants of military conflict. This runs in contrast to the industrialization argument, as economic growth after World War II continued at even higher rates.

Taken together, these results suggest that the Great Purge was an important moment for Russian foreign policy, as Stalin's domestic power consolidation had a significant and lasting impact that continued in the policy even after the demise of the USSR and the end of the Cold War. The increase in the local means of conflict involvement between the two temporal regimes—0.867 in the first period, 3.014 in the second period—indicate a more robust foreign policy after the change-point.

Beyond knowing how many structural breaks occurred and when they took place, we are interested in examining the effect of key explanatory variables on militarized conflict involvement, especially *Power Ratio*. We report summaries of the posterior parameter estimates for each endogenous variable in table 5.4.

Table 5.4 presents the two simultaneously and probabilistically estimated models: a pre-1938 and post-1938 model. During the pre-1938 era, both *Trade* and *World War I* are significant predictors of militarized conflict, with 94 percent probability. *Trade* has a negative coefficient, indicating that as the level of trade as a percent of GDP increased, Russia was less likely to initiate or intervene in a militarized conflict. *World War I* is positively correlated with military conflict, suggesting that the start of World War I

Table 5.4. Poisson Estimation of the Soviet Union/Russia's Militarized Conflict Initiation with One Change-Point

	Pre-1938		Post-1938	
	Mean	S.D.	Mean	S.D.
Power Ratio	0.413	0.984	−1.677	2.217
Power Ratio Squared	0.190	3.150	0.031	3.097
Neighbor Conflict	0.035	0.076	0.068	0.260
Democratic Proportion	0.003	0.027	0.036	0.020
Trade	−1.225	0.646	−0.035	0.015
World War I	1.774	0.556	0.017	3.148
World War II	0.582	2.697	0.928	2.068
Constant	0.495	0.984	0.324	0.841

Note: Mean and standard deviation drawn from the posterior distribution. MCMC chains are run 20,000 times after discarding 10,000 burn-in draws. The median posterior probability of a break in the model was 1938. Estimates of the posterior for the pre-1938 and post-1938 average over the full state space, accounting for the precision (or imprecision) of the estimated change-point; hence, a parameter for World War II is included in each time period, as there is a small probability that the change-point occurred after 1945 (see figure 5.2).

increased the likelihood that Russia initiated militarized conflict. The coefficients for *Power Ratio Squared, Neighbor Conflict, Proportion of Democracies*, and *World War II* are all within one standard deviation of 0, suggesting that they exert little impact on militarized conflict involvement.[10]

Following Stalin's consolidation of power and continuing with subsequent Soviet premiers and Russian presidents, several explanatory variables change in their effect on conflict behavior in the post-1938 period. The effect of *Trade*, while still a significant predictor, declines, though the amount of trade as a percentage of GDP increases dramatically over time. Conversely, the *Proportion of Democracies* is associated with an increase in conflict involvement in the post-1938 period. The result indicates that Russia engages in increasingly conflictual militarized behavior as the proportion of democracies in the world increases around it. The association between increases in democratization and Russian military involvement offers an explanation for Russia's interventions in Georgia in 2008 and Ukraine in 2014–15, though the data are only suggestive, as both crises are out of sample. None of the other variables—*Power Ratio, Power Ratio Squared, Neighbor Conflict, World War I and II*—are significant predictors, as 0 is included within one standard deviation from their mean values.

The quantitative results offer evidence against structural theories and in support of foreign policy accounts for militarized conflicts. Few changepoints are present, and the one in 1938 appears to be associated with changes in domestic politics rather than international geopolitical factors. *Power Ratio* does not appear to be a significant predictor of militarized conflict in either temporal regime, running in contrast to the expectation of structural theories. These quantitative results are consistent with our qualitative analyses of Russian NCRs, that Russian conflict behavior is best explained by foreign policy accounts rather than structural theories.

Russian Economic Conflict Behavior

We now quantitatively analyze Russia's economic conflict behavior. For much of the 1929–2007 period, Russia did not interact with the global capitalist marketplace and operated outside of the world economy. Prior to the late 1970s, for example, Russia did not accept U.S. investment and was financially closed off from the West. This lack of global involvement and ideological opposition to capitalism did not, however, mean that the Soviet Union was completely isolated. The Soviet Union, for example, subsidized trade to validate the superiority of the communist economic model and gain support from subordinated governments (Marrese and Vanous 1983). Moreover, terms of trade between Soviet satellite states and Russia actually became *negative* following the end of the Cold War, indicating that the USSR subsidized bilateral trade with its Eastern bloc allies (Oblath and Tarr 1991; Rodrik 1992). Evidence also indicates that the USSR offered incentives to encourage trade among other Warsaw pact members (Rodrik 1994; D. K. Rosati 1994).

After the end of the Cold War and the collapse of the communist system, Russia defaulted on its sovereign debt in 1991 and 1992. After the shock therapy of economic liberalization in the 1990s, Russia began to close its financial sector off from the world, increasing the degree of capital controls in 1998, 1999, and 2001, possibly in response to the 1997–98 Asian financial crisis, its aftershocks, and the Russian public's subsequent disillusionment with liberalism and the beginning of a return to economic nationalism. An extension of this economic nationalism was the introduction of the Eurasian Economic Union (EEU) in 2015: union membership requires standardization of products and shared trade and monetary policy with Russia but increases tariffs outside the group. The EEU represents, to some degree, a return to Soviet-style economic foreign policy in that Russia subsidizes trade among its members in an effort to promote the economic union.[11] To more systematically examine economic conflict behavior, we estimate a series of probit change-point regression models using the economic conflict model from chapter 3.

The results of the logged marginal likelihood comparisons are displayed in table 5.5. The results suggest that model M_1, with a single change-point,

Table 5.5. Comparison of Probit Change-Point Models of the Soviet Union/Russia's Economic Conflict Behavior

	M_0	M_1	M_2	M_3	M_4	M_5
M_0	0	−6.76	−3.35	−1.06	42.87	45.66
M_1	6.76	0	3.41	5.70	49.63	52.42
M_2	3.35	−3.41	0	2.29	46.22	49.01
M_3	1.06	−5.70	−2.29	0	43.93	46.72
M_4	−42.87	−49.63	−46.22	−43.93	0	2.79
M_5	−45.66	−52.42	−49.01	−46.72	−2.79	0

Note: $\ln(BF_{ij} = m[y|M_i]/m[y|M_j])$ where BF_{ij} is the Bayes Factor comparing model M_i to a baseline model M_j, $m(y|M_i)$ is the marginal likelihood under model M_i, $(y|M_j)$ is the marginal likelihood under model M_j. Columns are M_i and rows are M_j. MCMC chains are run 20,000 times after discarding 10,000 burn-in draws.

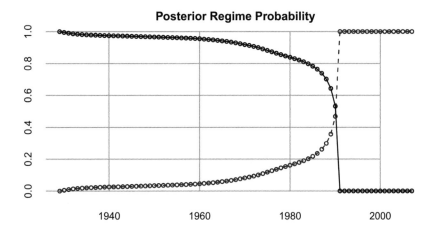

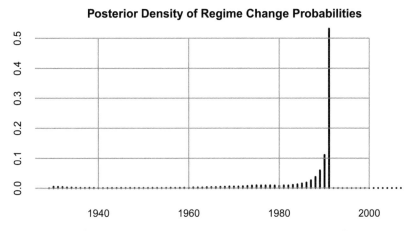

Fig. 5.3. Identifying Structural Breaks in Russia's Economic Conflict Behavior, 1929–2007. (*Note:* Expected modal change-point: 1991. Local means for each time regime: 0 and 0.294 economic challenges.)

has the best fit to the observed data. Figure 5.3 displays the posterior probability for each temporal regime (top) and the posterior probability of the change-point (bottom) for each year between 1929 and 2007.

The probability of the change-point increases rapidly in the mid-1980s, coinciding with the perestroika and glasnost reforms instituted by Gorbachev, before spiking in 1991 with the collapse of the Soviet Union. The expected change-point in 1991 indicates that following this dramatic political event, the effect of the predictors of economic challenges changed. The underlying rate of observable economic challenges increased from 0 when Russia failed to engage with the capitalist global economy prior to 1991 to a rate of 0.294 economic conflicts afterward.

Summaries of the posterior parameter estimates for each endogenous variable are reported in table 5.6. *Proportion of Democracies* is a significant predictor of economic conflicts in the first temporal period, exerting a negative impact with a probability of 99 percent, while none of the other explanatory variables have a meaningful effect. In the post-1991 period, however, *Trade* is the only significant indicator and has a negative effect. That is, increases in international trade reduce the likelihood of economic conflict in the second temporal period. Neither *Power Ratio* nor *GDP Growth* are significant indicators in either temporal period, as evidenced by their means being within one standard deviation of 0. That *Power Ratio* is insignificant suggests that changes in relative material power have no effect on economic challenges. Moreover, the lack of significance associated with *GDP Growth* suggests that domestic economic changes are not responsible for Russia's economic foreign policy.

The quantitative results support foreign policy rather than structural materialist theoretic accounts of its behavior as a rising power. The one identified change-point coincides with dramatic domestic change and, while the collapse of the Soviet Union had profound international effects, there is no evidence that changes in Russia's relative material power impacts its economic foreign policy. These quantitative results are consistent with the qualitative analyses of Russian NRCs, which demonstrate the lack of economic–based roles after the end of the Cold War.

Table 5.6. Probit Estimation of the Soviet Union/Russia's Economic Conflict Initiation with One Change-Point

	Pre-1991		Post-1991	
	Mean	S.D.	Mean	S.D.
Power Ratio	−0.003	3.150	−0.612	3.277
GDP Growth	−0.384	0.967	0.027	0.069
Democratic Proportion	−1.294	0.478	0.067	0.095
Trade	−1.334	2.333	−0.217	0.128
Constant	−0.061	3.148	0.024	3.550

Note: Mean and standard deviation drawn from the posterior distribution. MCMC chains are run 20,000 times after discarding 10,000 burn-in draws. The median posterior probability of a break in the model was 1991. Estimates of the posterior for the pre-1991 and post-1991 average over the full state space, accounting for the precision (or imprecision) of the estimated change-point.

Conclusion

We find that Russian identities and conflict behavior are more consistent with our foreign policy approach than with structural materialist theories. While Russia's role sets have varied over time, the core evolved slowly, even during times of significant structural upheaval. Russia did not experience changes to factors influencing conflict involvement, even following the end of the Cold War. In the early to mid-1990s, when Russia's words suggested a more collaborative relationship with United States and European powers, Russia's actions remained largely unchanged since the purges of the mid-1930s. Russia has remained interested in playing a leading role in managing disputes within the near abroad and its sphere of influence. Russia's economic conflict behavior only demonstrated one significant structural change that coincided with the end of the Soviet Union in 1991. In many ways, this is perhaps unsurprising, given that the size of the economic actor reduced rather dramatically due to internal decisions about what constituted the state. This is by no means a story of rising power producing economic conflict. In fact, the story of Russia might more accurately reflect changes in declining power. Regardless, the economic and militarized conflict regimes have remained stable in the post-Soviet era.

What does our analysis suggest for the future? Russia's identity is comprised of a fairly stable role set since the 1980s. Russia continues to see itself as a leading power and as a balancing force against the United States and EU. Russia has maintained a very active and industrious military, frequently involving itself as a manager of global disputes and conflicts, and this is unlikely to change in the immediate future. In general, our analysis suggests that Russia will continue to see itself as a great power that balances the interests of the United States and EU, frequently involving itself in militarized disputes, especially in its home region, but a dramatic shift in foreign policy orientation or conflict behavior is unlikely.

CHAPTER 6

India: From Nonalignment to Nuclear Power

India is the world's largest democracy and the world's second-most-populous state. Its economic growth and potential for future development have led those within and outside of India to consider it an emerging or rising power. But will gains on the economic front translate into political revisionism? Structural materialist theories of international relations tend to see a deterministic relationship between rising powers and revisionist foreign policy and conflict behavior designed to bring about system change, while our approaches to foreign policy analysis recognize the domestic and international constraints on such revisionism. We continue our analyses of these contending approaches to rising power by examining India's beliefs about its identity through time as well as its conflict behavior.

We accomplish this by examining both qualitative and quantitative evidence regarding Indian identity and behavior. Our qualitative analysis focuses on India's state identity as expressed through national role conceptions (NRCs). Our quantitative analysis uses change-point models to investigate whether any dramatic changes have occurred in Indian militarized or economic conflict behavior over time. These approaches allow us to compare India's words and deeds to assess claims about the foreign policies of rising powers.

Our qualitative and quantitative analyses find some changes in Indian identity that match the traditional narrative of the country's foreign policy; these changes are accompanied by relative continuity in conflict behavior across time over the past sixty years. We find a small but consistent role set from the 1940s through the late 1960s, followed by changes associated with the breakup of Pakistan in 1971 that seem to carry through to the present. Our statistical analysis reveals no structural breaks in Indian militarized or economic conflict behavior. Thus, while we find some evidence of changes in words, we find little evidence of changes in India's conflict behavior deeds; instead, the determinants of Indian foreign policy have remained relatively constant since Nehru.

National Role Conceptions and Indian Foreign Policy Analysis

We review the qualitative evidence on NRCs identified by scholars for India as comprising its role set and look for changes in that role set over time. If structural materialist IR theories are correct, then we should see dramatic changes in Indian NRCs as well as the way they are received by others as India's power grows. Foreign policy approaches to change would also expect that major internal and external shocks could bring about foreign policy restructuring, though these shocks should be mediated by the existing role set. Rather than wholesale change, a role-theoretic approach suggests modification of roles based on structural imperatives considering the countervailing effects of both competition and socialization.

There are several obvious candidates for internal shocks that would change the identity and self-conceived roles of India. The first is between partition and Indian independence in 1947 and the 1948 war with Pakistan. A second shock may be the 1962 war with China, which for practical purposes ended Nehru's policy of nonalignment. Many analysts divide Indian foreign policy as pre- and post-1962. A third shock could be Bangladesh's 1971 independence, which dismembered Pakistan and assured Indian dominance of the subcontinent. A fourth shock might have occurred sometime between 1975, when Prime Minister Indira Gandhi declared emergency rule, and 1977, when the Janata Party replaced the Congress Party in power. A fifth shock might have occurred after the end of the Cold War in 1989 and the collapse of the USSR in December 1991, which ended the de facto alliance with the Soviets.

Early work on Indian foreign policy identifies a number of postindependence roles for India under Nehru, including *nonaligned state, regional leader, anti-imperialist agent*, and *developer*, with the regional leader and developer roles focused specifically on Asia (Barton 1950). Hussain (1962: 242) remarks that neither the Soviets nor the Chinese believed the initial Indian pronouncement of a *nonaligned* role. Both expected that India would join the "imperialist powers," though India's subsequent behavior convinced both that the commitment to nonalignment was real. The Chinese believed that a *nonaligned* role was anathema to an independent state, even though this role was adopted by a number of other new states entering the system closely thereafter. Zinkin (1955) reinforces the importance of the *anti-imperialist agent* role for India in the first years of its independence.

Pan-Asianism has a long tradition in Indian political thought (Keenleyside 1982). This line of thinking predated independent India, with many political leaders espousing the idea of a Greater India that would encompass most of South Asia and even creep into Southeast Asia. By 1947, Nehru reiterated the idea that India was a natural *regional leader* for Asia through some type of federation. India's support for liberation movements and its anti-imperial and anticolonial stances were also wrapped up in causes that linked such movements to larger underlying cultural or civilizational unities (e.g., Pan-Islamism). Politicians and academics would repeat the call for Pan-Asianism through federation with Indian leadership again in the 1950s and 1960s, though the 1962 war with China briefly dampened enthusiasm for the idea.

Srivastava (1960) argues that India's foreign policy from 1927 through 1960 had essentially been Nehru's policy, an assessment with which most scholars agree.[1] The two most important roles identified for India by Nehru were that of *nonaligned state* and *anti-imperialist agent* (see also Fontera 1960). While Srivastava believes that Nehru frequently violated the behavioral expectations associated with these roles in his governmental dealings, there is no doubt that these roles remained enshrined in India's identity. Kripalani (1959) similarly argues that even before independence, the Congress Party enunciated what would become India's foreign policy roles— *nonaligned state* and *anti-imperialist agent*. Kripalani at times equates the *nonaligned* role with a *neutral* role, but he notes that such a neutral role is not passive but active (48), which squares more with the traditional use of nonalignment.[2] Appadorai (1960) identifies the key roles he believes have been a part of India's foreign policy, though they may have been misunderstood until the mid-1950s. These include *nonaligned state, anti-imperialist agent, internal developer,* and *mediator/integrator*. Mack and Mack (1957) identify a constellation of roles for postindependence India, including *honest broker for peace, neutral,* and *independent*. On closer inspection, the meaning behind the term *honest broker* fits with the *mediator/integrator* role in the pursuit of peace, and the *neutral* role is again a much more active conception that fits with the *nonaligned* role identified by others. Power

(1964) also uses the *independent, neutral,* and *nonaligned state* roles somewhat interchangeably.

During the 1960s, some degree of internal contestation over India's foreign policy roles occurred between the opposition and governing Congress Party (Erdman 1966). The Swatantra (Freedom) Party viewed India as a *rival* to China and to Pakistan, though China was seen as the true threat. Swatantra also argued against the *nonaligned* role and favored adopting an *allied* role across an expansive region of all noncommunist countries from Israel to Australia to Japan. The party's view of this *allied* role would require it to be a regional protector if the domino theory held true and regimes fell one after another to the communists across Southeast Asia. Ultimately, Swatantra advocated an *allied* role with the United States and the Western democracies. The Bharatiya Jan Sangh (Indian People's Party) saw both China and Pakistan as *rivals* but viewed *allied* roles with the United States or Western democracies as against its *anti-imperialist agent* role. Instead, India must be an active *independent state* and pursue nuclear weapons to guarantee its security.

A survey of Indian intellectuals found that 83 percent supported the *nonaligned* role because it permits freedom of action, allows India to receive economic assistance from all sides, promotes general peace, and is timely given the international environment (Singh 1965). Baljit Singh's intellectuals also identify India's choice of *nonalignment* as having auxiliary roles of *balancer* for the region and a *bridge* role between East and West. The minority respondents in his group said that the *mediator* role was no longer necessary, and a few advocated *ally* roles with the United Kingdom, United States, or USSR.

The classic work by Holsti (1970) identifies six roles cited by foreign policy decision makers in India during the 1966–68 period, including *regional leader, active independent, liberator-supporter, mediator/integrator, independent,* and *internal developer.* Holsti notes that India occupies the *nonaligned* role in most assessments (280), but his analysis most often invokes the *mediator* role.

Kapur (1971) describes a world of three great powers (United States, USSR, and China) and India as a *major power.* Narayanan (1972) describes three *Asian great powers* (China, Japan, and India). Kapur also believes that the 1962 conflict with China dealt a setback to the *nonaligned* role, so that India became a *revisionist state.* Further, India would serve as the *balancer* in the South Asian region to prevent both Soviet hegemony and a militarily strong Pakistan with a Muslim majority. Kapur also reinforces that non-alignment did not mean the traditional passive form of neutrality but a wish to eschew any inhibitions on India's freedom of action. Again, this *nonaligned* role generated the auxiliary role of *balancer* to prevent any great power from achieving dominance or any power from achieving a sphere of influence in Asia. Kapur explicitly states that Indian foreign policy "has two distinct eras": prior to and after 1962. After 1962, and particularly after the 1965–68 debate on Nuclear Nonproliferation Treaty (which India did not sign), Indian foreign policy began to emphasize security more than peace. India's role shifted from *leading civilian nuclear power* to *potential nuclear weapon power* after its atomic test in 1974. Wood and Vaagenes (1984: 723) also argue that the *nonaligned* role was abandoned after the 1962 war with China. The Indo-Soviet treaty of 1971 created a *Soviet ally* role despite the fact that the government argued that the treaty did not exclude the *nonaligned* role. Wood and Vaagenes (1984: 723) suggest that since 1971, Indian foreign policy has been built on a *regional power* role that minimizes superpower influence in South Asia.

Some observers have noted that the 1977 transition from the Congress Party to the Janata Party was not expected to produce a dramatic change in foreign policy (Karunakaran 1979). If anything, the new prime minister promised a return to a true *nonaligned* role, even as Indian leaders promised to continue warm relations with the Soviets (see also Thomas 1981: 706). However, the change was quite pronounced. Thomas (1980: 223) suggests changes in three roles: a reinterpretation of the *nonaligned* role, transition from the *civilian nuclear power* role to *potential nuclear weapon power*, and a general reorientation toward a *military power* role and away from its traditional *civilian power* role. Karunakaran (1979) suggests that anti-imperialism no longer resonated in India in the late 1970s. India had become recognized as an *emerging power* or at least a *regional power* in South Asia, making its traditional Pakistani *enemy* nervous. Though after the India-supported breakaway of Bangladesh from Pakistan in 1971, the importance of Pakistan in India's foreign policy is argued to have declined. Nonalignment is argued to have been a smokescreen during India's search for power, and now that it is acquiring military power, that role is obsolete. Narayanan (1972) describes India as the principal military power in South Asia in the aftermath of the birth of Bangladesh. Thomas (1981) notes how U.S. and Indian interests repeatedly clash in South Asia because the United States is explicitly pursuing a regional balance of power, while India often attempts to serve as *balancer* for the region while pretending to occupy the *nonaligned* role and pursue a policy of peaceful coexistence. Thomas (1981: 696) notes that as late as 1979, Indian officials still claimed to occupy the *nonaligned, anti-imperialist, liberator-supporter* roles.

The 1979 Soviet invasion of Afghanistan again challenged the Janata government's profession of a true *nonaligned* role, and in 1980 Prime Minister Indira Gandhi reiterated a *Soviet ally* role in her support of the invasion (Ghosh and Panda 1983). Despite the widespread global condemnation of the invasion, India stood firm in its support of the USSR. In some measure, this was in response to the U.S. arming of Pakistan, which continued to push India in the direction of the Soviets.

Kapur (1985) argues that the continuity that has been observed by others in foreign policy since 1962 continued up through 1985. Prior to 1962, Nehru's vision of India as a *nonaligned* state as a model for the globe held true, while after that time the *military power* role and *regional power* role for South Asia became ascendant. The 1971 Bangladesh crisis marked another turning point that reinforced these trends. Kapur (1988) reinforces his earlier analysis to suggest that the post-1971 period was marked by Indian efforts to achieve regional power and dominance in South Asia (an "Indocentric" power structure). Ayoob (1987) emphasizes India's view of itself as the preeminent South Asian power and suggests a strong desire for this to extend to all of Southeast Asia by working with anti-imperialist (and anti-China) regimes in Vietnam and Indonesia.

The dissolution of the USSR in December 1991 was a shock to India, since it meant the end of the de facto *allied* role with the Soviets (Chiriyankandath 2004). The defeat of the Congress Party not long after the end of the Cold War in 1989, combined with the end of the USSR, meant that much of what formed the foundation of Indian foreign policy (*Soviet ally* and *nonaligned* roles) evaporated. It left India thinking about whether and how to align with the United States.

Indian policymakers had a difficult time as they began to revise their view of the United States during the Gulf War (Malik 1991). Initially, India's main concern was the safety of a huge number of Indians working in the Gulf, including Kuwait, as well as the fact that almost a majority of India's oil was imported from either Iraq or Kuwait. India was alarmed at the possibility of unilateral U.S. intervention in the conflict and was thus initially soft in its condemnation of Iraq—despite the long-standing stance of anti-imperialism and anticolonialism. This policy was shifted by the Singh government to support of U.N. Resolution 678 authorizing the use of force in Iraq and the possibility of alignment with the United States. Jayaramu (1991: 187) interprets this as India accepting the emerging Pax Americana while still suggesting that nonalignment is a fundamental feature of Indian foreign policy. India ultimately accepted more neoliberal/Washington Consensus principles in the management of the economy after briefly reviving the *internal developer* role in the early 1990s through *swadeshi*, a form of economic nationalism that emphasized India's need to develop on its own (Alden and Vieira 2005: 1088).

Indian elites viewed China as a serious rival from 1962 to 1989, when things improved slightly upon Rajiv Gandhi's visit to Beijing; another downturn followed India's 1998 nuclear tests (Ollapally 2014: 350). Egreteau (2012: 8) also agrees that despite the series of disputes that led up to the 1962 war, that was the beginning of the enduring rivalry between China and India. Despite escalatory and deescalatory dynamics over time, the peak occurred in 1987 with some particularly bloody border skirmishes. Again, the bilateral visits that started with Gandhi seemed to smooth relations momentarily until India's nuclear test in 1998, which India intended as a means to an end of achieving nuclear parity with China (not Pakistan). Relations continued with ups and downs, but the rivalry between the two generally seems to have solidified.

Malik (1994) views an evolving *rivalry* between India and China over Southeast Asia (focused on Myanmar) and a contest for *regional hegemony* as characterizing the 1990s despite apparent rapprochement in the late 1980s (Garver 1996). The end of the Cold War and the breakup of the Soviet Union meant that the U.S.-USSR rivalry no longer overlaid the regional dynamics of South Asia. Once this was removed, the Sino-Indian rivalry came into sharper focus as a central feature of post–Cold War Asia. Anderson (2001: 768) explains that Southeast Asia is the focal point of the rivalry since India's orientation is primarily toward the Indian Ocean and China's is to the east—Southeast Asia lies in between. Tanham (1992) describes the debate between those in India who prefer it become a great power versus those who wish it would remain a moral power. All are agreed about *regional hegemony* on the subcontinent, but some are more committed to the idea of India as *regional peacekeeper* and a *Pax India*. Tanham (1992: 134) suggests that as of the 1990s, India's self-conceived identity was not quite yet matched by the strategic thinking needed to underpin its activity in this regard. Somewhat relatedly, Sridharan (1996: 19) points out that in the

1990s, parliamentary debates on foreign policy clung to the Cold War era, with emphases on themes related to the *nonaligned, anti-imperial agent,* and *antihegemonism* roles.

In a discussion of U.S. national strategy, Chase, Hill, and Kennedy (1996) argue that the United States should consider the role of major players, including South Africa, to be that of a *pivotal state.* In the authors' view, a pivotal state is a "hot spot that could not only determine the fate of its region but also affect international stability" (33). Conceptually, focusing on pivotal states would help integrate new security issues into policymakers' old state-centered mind-set and help to direct U.S. assistance to stabilizing key regions around the world. They argue that Algeria, Brazil, Egypt, India, Indonesia, Mexico, Pakistan, South Africa, and Turkey are pivotal states by the mid-1990s. India and its neighbor, Pakistan, are pivotal to the South Asian region as a consequence of their forecasted population growth and composition, which produces a huge youth bulge, the obvious issues of religious tension, nuclear ambitions, and the political rivalry between the two.

Anderson (2001) and other scholars argue that the 2000s mark a reorientation of Indian foreign policy away from simply being a *regional power* in South Asia to a *major Asian power* on the world stage. In the context of Sino-Indian relations, Garver (2002) notes that both China and India view each other as *major powers* (see also Yuan 2007) and that both engage in the role of *balancer* in South Asia and East Asia, respectively, in the attempt to neutralize each other's influence in their home regions. Garver's (2002: 33) ultimate judgment is that India is acting as a revisionist power in the larger South Asia–Indian Ocean Region, especially with regard to Pakistan and Myanmar by 2002. Scott (2006: 120) notes that by the mid-2000s, India began developing grand strategy and doctrine for control of the Indian Ocean, conceived of as "their nation's rightful and exclusive sphere of influence." But, as Pant (2009) notes, by the late 2000s, a large mismatch persists between India's ambitions and capabilities in this regard.

Formed in 2003, the India–Brazil–South Africa Dialogue Forum (IBSA) was meant to serve as a forum for cooperation on a wide array of economic, political, environmental, and defense-related issues. IBSA also established each of the three founders as *regional leaders* in furthering cooperation across regions in the developing world (Alden and Vieira 2005).

Some argue that India is on the verge of becoming a *great power,* reflecting the sense for some time that India has occupied the *emerging power* role (Mohan 2006: 17). Mohan (2006) suggests that India occupies a *swing state*

role in the global balance of power. India's grand strategy is argued to encompass three concentric circles: dominance over the immediate neighborhood, balance of power over the extended neighborhood in Asia and
the Indian Ocean, and great power aspiration in the global arena. Thus,
regional power, balancer, and emerging power are by the 2000s a consistent
feature of Indian foreign policy. Further, the signing of the nuclear pact in
2005 between the United States and India under President George W.
Bush acknowledged India as a nuclear weapon power despite the Nonproliferation Treaty. India (and Pakistan) had previously formally declared
themselves nuclear weapons powers in 1998 (Singh 1998). By the 2000s,
great power rivalry over South Asia had largely receded with greater co-
incidence of U.S. and Indian interests in the region, renewed attempts to
settle border issues with China, and some movement with Pakistan on
Kashmir. While India floated the idea of an ally role with the United States
in the late 1990s, President Bill Clinton preferred to improve relations
rather than pursue a formal alliance. The tables were turned by the early
2000s, when the Bush administration began to seek formal alliance with
India and such efforts were mildly rebuked in India due to some lingering
sense of India as a nonaligned state.

Mohan (2006) documents a number of other roles, including regional
leader for regional economic and political cooperation in forums such as
ASEAN, the East Asian Summit, the Gulf Cooperation Council, the Shanghai Cooperation Organization, and the African Union. India has also
emerged as a developer in becoming a major aid donor after decades as a
recipient of foreign aid. The vision of India as a rising power is also articulated more forcefully in the late 2000s, as is the Sino-Indian relationship in
light of their mutual rising (Guihong 2005). Clearly, by the mid-2000s, India is a military power that is consciously developing strategic doctrine for
both the South Asian landmass and Indian Ocean (Zaman 2006: 231),
where it confronts its rival China (Brewster 2010).

India seems to desire achieving "global recognition of India's importance" through the goal of attaining a permanent seat on the UN Security
Council (Abraham 2007: 4209). It did not achieve that goal in the mid-
2000s, nor had it made much progress in its regional leader role in groups
such as the South Asian Association for Regional Cooperation. Abraham
(2007) is also skeptical of India's influence in the World Trade Organization
and in the efficacy of the IBSA. Further, the moral power India once had as
a nonaligned state committed to global peace has dissipated now that it

routinely acts like any other state seeking its interests. The trade-off for becoming a military power is this loss of moral power. Abraham suggests that India's attempts to mimic the great powers have failed and urges it return to its moral power.

The biggest challenge for India in the coming years, according to Pant (2008: 226), is to maintain its economic rise. To achieve its aspirations as an *emerging power*, it needs to maintain the momentum of economic growth and development. Mukherjee and Malone (2011: 103) similarly point out that "economic prosperity . . . is now seen as the key to India's attainment of Great Power status," but they highlight a number of concerns shared by Pant (2008). These concerns are related to a standstill in the reform process by the end of the 2000s plus the onset of global recession. Without continued economic growth, India's ability to maintain and expand its military will fall short. Issues with internal security arising from terrorist attacks are also a potential drag on economic growth. Pant notes that some Indian policymakers are still clinging to Cold War mentalities and the *nonaligned* and *anti-imperialist* roles that may be getting in the way of further cooperation with the United States (234). Finally, Pant suggests that while "the rise of India might be an idea whose time has come . . . the challenges confronting Indian foreign and security policy today are varied and not amenable to easy solutions" (237). Ollapally and Rajagopalan (2010) document that the *rising power* role is a continuous part of Indian identity into the 21st century.

In his analysis of the IBSA states, Stephen (2012: 293) suggests that India has dual roles as a *regional power* and a *rising power*. He argues against considering India or any of the other rising powers in this group as middle powers. He argues that India, like Brazil, can aspire to a global power role given its capabilities. Such rising powers may at times engage in spoiling and balancing or may be co-opted in international institutions. India has fulfilled many roles typical of middle powers, especially in light of its activity in the area of human rights. Hansel and Möller (2015) identify *internal developer, regional integrator, advocate of developing nations, active independent, moral force, great power, liberal example,* and *democracy promoter* as frequently invoked roles during the 2001–12 period in their analysis of Indian policymakers' speeches on responsibility to protect and international criminal law. This analysis is consistent with Vasudevan (2010) and others who describe Indian foreign policy as a "moralistic running commentary."

Stewart-Ingersoll and Frazier (2010) suggest that India is in fact in a unipolar or *hegemonic* situation vis-à-vis the South Asian regional security complex, even with Pakistan's nuclear weapons. Yet as a consequence of the lack of others' support, this is more like a power-restraining power system. The authors do not believe that India performs the role of *regional leader* as a consequence of the rivalries with China and Pakistan despite India's self-conceptions in that regard. Even so, Stewart-Ingersoll and Frazier note that India has devoted more effort to promoting a global role for itself than a regional role. India has been more active as a *regional custodian* in maintaining the existing security order. India conceives of itself as a *regional protector* as part of its goal of being viewed as a *major power*.

The ambivalence often found in studying Indian foreign policy is reflected in what Ollapally (2011: 202) calls India's role as a *bridging power*, which he defines as "a power that comfortably straddles different global power structures, engages multiple regions and audiences and promotes seemingly inconsistent normative values and practices, and importantly, offers itself as a successful negotiator between these worlds and ideas." Prior to 1991, India was an *autonomous power* with no formal alliance structure and no use of force to settle disputes. This is consistent with many analyses focused on Indian autonomy and independence. Nau and Fontaine (2012: 3) suggest the existence of a neonationalist version of autonomy that focuses on nonalignment, disarmament and anticolonialism and a hypernationalist version that rejects India's historical military self-restraint. According to Ollapally (2011), the bridging power role is a function of various long-running aspects of Indian state identity, including notions of civilizational exceptionalism, postcolonial nationalism, partition trauma, pluralism and tolerance, secular democracy, inheritor of the British Raj, developing country, and major power.

Table 6.1 summarizes the narrative history of Indian NRCs. The Indian role set exhibited a fair amount of consistency from independence through the 1960s. A number of new roles appear after the 1971 dismembering of Pakistan. The transition to these new roles, mostly reflecting movement away from the *nonaligned* role in pursuit of global peace toward roles representing *military power* and *regional power* appeared to be fairly smooth. It is difficult to discern any major reorientations after 1971, since the role set contains mostly related roles from that point on. If anything, 1971 seems to be the crucible for change in India's identity as expressed through NRCs. While the decade-by-decade portrait of NRCs masks some variation in NRCs according to traditional breaks in Indian foreign policy, it does paint a picture of a generally stable and evolving Indian identity at least since the 1970s.

Table 6.2 shows an increase in the number of roles and overall activity by the 1960s and 1970s, followed by declines through the 1990s and another surge in the 2000s. The average activity level associated with the role sets is fairly constant at just above 3 for most of the postindependence era, with peaks in the 1970s and 2000s. What do these changes in foreign policy roles suggest for India's conflict behavior? Will conflict behavior match purported dramatic changes in material power or be consistent with our review of NRCs that suggests more evolutionary changes?

Table 6.1. India's Role Sets

1940s	*nonaligned state, anti-imperialist agent, internal developer, mediator/integrator, regional leader, developer, independent, Pakistani enemy, autonomous power*
1950s	*nonaligned state, anti-imperialist agent, internal developer, mediator/integrator, regional leader, developer, independent, Pakistani enemy, autonomous power*
1960s	*nonaligned state, anti-imperialist agent, internal developer, mediator/integrator, regional leader, developer, independent, Pakistani enemy, active independent, liberator-supporter, balancer, bridge, autonomous power, Chinese rival*
1970s	*nonaligned state, anti-imperialist, liberator-supporter, Soviet ally, regional power, emerging power, balancer, major power, military power, revisionist state, leading civilian nuclear power, potential nuclear weapon power, Pakistani enemy, Chinese rival, Asian great power, autonomous power*
1980s	*nonaligned state, Soviet ally, regional power, emerging power, military power, potential nuclear weapon power, autonomous power, Chinese rival*
1990s	*nonaligned state, internal developer, regional power, nuclear weapon power, rival (with China), regional hegemon, regional peacekeeper, pivotal state, Chinese rival*
2000s	*regional leader, developer, internal developer, regional power, emerging power, balancer, major power, swing state, nuclear weapon power, Chinese rival, rising power, major Asian power, military power, major power, great power, regional integrator, advocate of developing nations, active independent, liberal example, democracy promoter, moral force, regional protector, regional custodian, bridging power*

Table 6.2. Active-Passive Dimensions of India's Role Sets

Decade	Number of Roles	Overall Activity	Low	High	Mean
1940s	9	30	0	5	3.3
1950s	9	30	0	5	3.3
1960s	14	45	0	5	3.2
1970s	16	54	0	5	3.4
1980s	8	25	2	5	3.1
1990s	9	30	0	5	3.3
2000s	24	84	0	5	3.5

Militarized Interstate Disputes and Indian Conflict Behavior

We next quantitatively analyze India's militarized and economic conflict behavior using change-point models. We estimate and report the results of a Poisson change-point model for the period 1947–2007. According to structural theories of international relations, we should observe that economic growth and increases in India's relative material power are associated with increases in conflict behavior. Our foreign policy approach, however, leads us to expect little in the way of structural breaks in militarized or economic conflict behavior, outside of dramatic domestic reorganization.

Figure 6.1 displays the number of MIDs initiated or ongoing MIDs joined by India between 1947 and 2007. The frequency of military involvement initiated by India appears to change little over the period.

To more systematically analyze the data, we estimate the full militarized conflict model outlined in chapter 3. We treat Asia as India's relevant region of analysis.[3] Neither world war is included in the model because although India contributed to both war efforts, it did not formally enter the state system as an independent state until 1947.[4]

Table 6.3 reports the logged Bayes Factor comparisons of the marginal likelihood for each model. Using Jeffrey's (1961) scale, model M_0 has "decisive" support as the best model fit. This suggests that the data best fits a model with no change-points.

Table 6.4 reports the summary of the posterior estimates for each endogenous variable. To assess the structural theories, we pay special attention paid to *Power Ratio*. *None* of the explanatory variables included in the model have a significant impact on militarized conflict. In other words, none of the variables have a mean posterior estimate more than one standard deviation away from 0. This suggests that none of the variables included in the model are systematically associated with conflict initiation.

Taken together, the results are solidly against the structural theory explanation and much more supportive of foreign policy accounts. That no change-point is present provides evidence against the structural expectation that several structural breaks should occur congruent with increases in changes in India's status as a rising power. In addition, *Power Ratio* appears to have no significant impact on India's conflict behavior. Instead, India's foreign policy agenda, at least as it pertains to militarized conflict, appears to have experienced no major changes over the period, and structural vari-

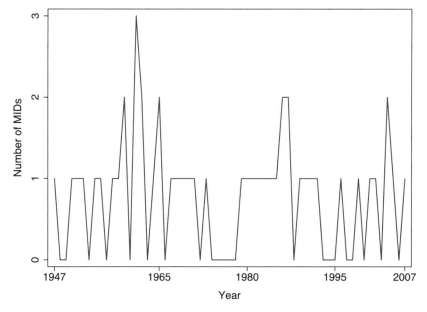

Fig. 6.1. Military Dispute Initiations and Interventions by India, 1947–2007

ables are unable to account for India's behavior. Instead, India's militarized conflict behavior appears idiosyncratic rather than systematic. Combined with the qualitative analysis of India's NRCs, the results suggest that the role transitions that did occur in the 1970s did not lead India to be more conflictual, at least in a militarized sense.

Indian Economic Conflict Behavior

We now analyze India's economic conflict behavior between 1947 and 2007. India's early NRCs as *anti-imperial agent, liberator-supporter,* and *revisionist state* raise the prospect for potential economic conflict with the liberal international economic order (LIEO). India undertook seven economic challenges during this period, all expropriations of foreign assets. The first occurred in 1956, relatively soon after independence. The event is not altogether surprising, as expropriation is commonly linked with newly independent states' efforts to control their economies, particularly with regard to industries or firms associated with colonialism (Korbin 1984: 339–40). The next five expropriations were clustered, occurring every two years between 1967

Table 6.3. Comparison of Poisson Change-Point Models of India's Militarized Conflict Behavior

	M_0	M_1	M_2	M_3	M_4	M_5
M_0	0	9.25	12.78	12.96	23.80	33.13
M_1	−9.25	0	3.52	3.706	14.55	23.88
M_2	−12.77	−3.52	0	0.185	11.03	20.36
M_3	−12.96	−3.71	−0.19	0	10.84	20.17
M_4	−23.80	−14.55	−11.03	−10.842	0	9.33
M_5	−33.13	−23.88	−20.36	−20.17	−9.33	0

Note: $\ln(BF_{ij} = m[y|M_i]/m[y|M_j])$ where BF_{ij} is the Bayes Factor comparing model M_i to a baseline model M_j, $m(y|M_i)$ is the marginal likelihood under model M_i, $(y|M_j)$ is the marginal likelihood under model M_j. Columns are M_i and rows are M_j. MCMC chains are run 20,000 times after discarding 10,000 burn-in draws.

Table 6.4. Poisson Estimation of India's Militarized Conflict Initiation with Zero Change-Points

	Mean	S.D.
Power Ratio	−0.038	0.071
Power Ratio Squared	−0.015	3.154
Neighbor Conflict	0.090	0.438
Democratic Proportion	0.023	0.030
Trade	−0.071	0.080
Constant	0.052	1.468

Note: Mean and standard deviation drawn from the posterior distribution. MCMC chains are run 20,000 times after discarding 10,000 burn-in draws.

and 1975. Though the global risk of expropriation was greatest during this period, the number of expropriations by the Indian government is still rather high (Korbin 1984; Hajzler 2012). The final expropriation took place in 2001. To analyze the determinants of India's economic conflict behavior, we estimate a series of probit change-point regression models.

Table 6.5 reports the Bayes Factor comparisons of the logged marginal likelihood of several models. The results indicate that model M_0, with zero change-points, has the best fit to the data. This result indicates that there are no structural breaks in India's economic conflict behavior.

Table 6.6 presents the summary statistics for posterior parameter estimates for each endogenous explanatory variable of economic conflict. All but one of the variables is shown to exert a significant influence on economic conflict. *Power Ratio* is negative and significant, with greater than 80 percent confidence. This suggests that in contrast to structural theories, increases in relative material power are associated with a *declining* likelihood of engaging in economic conflict. *GDP Growth* has a positive effect, with approximately 88 percent confidence. That is, India is more likely to engage in economic conflict, such as expropriation of foreign assets, during periods of economic growth. This result parallels the finding by Aguir and Gopinath (2006) that loan default is countercyclical to growth and the current account. The finding also lends support to an assumption in the formal theoretic literature that expropriation is somewhat driven by opportunism: as the value of foreign assets increase, the propensity to seize them increases as well (Eaton and Gersovitz 1984; Tomz and Wright 2010). Finally, *Trade* is associated with a decrease in the likelihood of an economic challenge, with greater than 95 percent confidence. As India engages more with the international economy, it is less likely to initiate an economic challenge. *Propensity of Democracy* is insignificant in the model, as the standard deviation around the mean includes 0.

The quantitative results of economic conflict provide support for a stable foreign policy and run counter to the expectations of structural theo-

Table 6.5. Comparison of Probit Change-Point Models of India's Economic Conflict Behavior

	M_0	M_1	M_2	M_3	M_4
M_0	0	3.38	15.32	12.98	4.83
M_1	−3.38	0	11.94	9.60	1.45
M_2	−15.32	−11.94	0	−2.34	−10.49
M_3	−12.98	−9.60	2.34	0	−8.15
M_4	−4.83	−1.45	10.49	8.15	0

Note: $\ln(BF_{ij} = m[y|M_i]/m[y|M_j])$ where BF_{ij} is the Bayes Factor comparing model M_i to a baseline model M_j, $m(y|M_i)$ is the marginal likelihood under model M_i, $(y|M_j)$ is the marginal likelihood under model M_j. Columns are M_i and rows are M_j. MCMC chains are run 20,000 times after discarding 10,000 burn-in draws.

Table 6.6. Probit Estimation of India's Economic Conflict Initiation with Zero Change-Points

	Mean	S.D.
Power Ratio	−0.177	0.132
GDP Growth	0.142	0.091
Democratic Proportion	0.014	0.049
Trade	−0.391	0.170
Constant	1.842	2.487

Note: Mean and standard deviation drawn from the posterior distribution. MCMC chains are run 20,000 times after discarding 10,000 burn-in draws.

ries. *Power Ratio*, for example, is associated with decreases in economic conflict. The process underlying India's economic foreign policy has remained largely unchanged during the period under review, at least in terms of conflictual behavior. On balance, decisions about challenging the economic order depend on whether the positive effects of opportunism (growth) are matched by the constraining effects of integration (trade). As trade has become more central to India's economy over time, these constraining effects appear to have overwhelmed the positive effects. The quantitative results suggest that while India has been a vocal critic of the LIEO, calling for reforms to the terms of trade for developing states, among other criticisms, it has increasingly adhered to those same standards as it integrated into the international economy.

Conclusion

Our analysis finds that changes in Indian identity and conflict behavior are more consistent with our foreign policy approach than with structural materialist theories. While India's role sets have varied over time, the core evolved slowly up through the late 1960s and perhaps exhibited a reorientation only following the dismemberment of Pakistan. Most of the candidates for foreign policy reorientation identified in the literature did not manifest themselves in dramatic changes to India's role set. Perhaps even more important, India did not experience changes to factors influencing militarized or economic conflict involvement during the entire postindependence period.

What does our analysis suggest for the future? India's identity is comprised of a fairly stable role set prior to 1971 and then again after the late 1970s. Since that time, India has seen itself as regional power and an emerging global power. While these roles have entailed an increasing emphasis on military power and the emulation of previous great powers, India has not been inclined to engage in militarized conflict in a different way in its recent history. In contrast to structural materialist theories, we do not foresee any dramatic shift in foreign policy orientation or conflict behavior for India. Consistent with a role-theory approach to foreign policy, we expect that India's current roles emphasizing regional power and emerging global power are likely to prevail, shaping and molding foreign policy discourse and behavior in the near future.

CHAPTER 7

China: Responsible Stakeholder or Revisionist Great Power?

The rise of China weighs heavily on the minds of decision makers and pundits. Many worry that China's rapid economic growth and development may lead to a more assertive foreign policy orientation and militarized conflict behavior. China's handling of the 2001 U.S. spy plane incident and the ongoing militarization of the Spratly Islands seem to fit such an aggressive vision for a rising power. Academics tend to have mixed views on whether China's growing economic clout will result in attempts to transform the international order through conflict (e.g., Ross and Feng 2008). We examine the case of China through the same analytical lenses used in the previous chapters to understand its beliefs about its identity through time as well as its militarized and economic conflict behavior.

We begin with a qualitative analysis of Chinese state identity as expressed through its role sets to understand how China conceives of itself. Such self-conceptions provide an internal guide for foreign policy action and provide expectations to the rest of the world about China's international behavior. Sudden changes in role sets may lead to major foreign policy reorientation and changes in conflict behavior. We employ quantitative methods to investigate changes in militarized and economic conflict behavior. Our mixed-method approach allows us to investigate both China's words and deeds to assess whether claims about the growing China threat are accurate.

Our qualitative and quantitative analyses find decreasing radicalization in China's identity and remarkable continuity in conflict behavior across time. While individual national role conceptions (NRCs) may come and go, the balance of the role set reflecting Chinese identity has become more peaceful and less revisionist. Our statistical analysis of Chinese militarized and economic conflict behavior shows no structural breaks, indicating little change in the factors that produce conflict behavior over modern Chinese history. Overall, we find little evidence in words or deeds, identity or conflict behavior that lends credence to the notion of a China threat.

National Role Conceptions and Chinese Foreign Policy Analysis

A small but growing literature on Chinese foreign policy uses roles and role theory to analyze China's foreign policy orientation.[1] We review the qualitative evidence on NRCs identified by scholars for China as comprising its role set and look for changes in that role set over time. If structural IR theories are correct, then we should see dramatic changes in Chinese NRCs as well as the way they are received by others (especially the United States) as China's power grows. Foreign policy approaches to change would also expect that major internal and external shocks could bring about foreign policy restructuring, though Harnisch (2001) suggests that those shocks are mediated by the existing role set. Rather than wholesale change, a role-theoretic approach suggests modification of roles based on structural imperatives.

One of the early contributions to role theory analyzing Chinese foreign policy comes from Beylerian and Canivet (1997), who provide a useful historical overview of Chinese NRCs in the modern era.[2] The narrative provided by these scholars also indicates how they believe internal and external shocks, including changes in power, affected Chinese selection of NRCs. They argue that in the immediate aftermath of the founding of the People's Republic, the only real role available to China was that of *junior partner and faithful ally* of the Soviet Union. A number of secondary roles emerged soon thereafter, as China developed relations with India and Indonesia: *supporter of national liberation, regional collaborator, anti-imperialist agent,* and *model of national liberation and independence* (see also Holsti 1970; Shih 1993). In the late 1950s and early 1960s, China moved to distance itself from the USSR and develop the *independent ally* role. Mao Zedong clearly wanted to put the Sino-Soviet relationship on a more equal footing rather than have China in a subordinate role to the USSR. China was also domestically absorbed with the Great Leap Forward (1958–61). China's early role set was fairly receptive to the Soviet system status quo, and auxiliary radical roles were primarily directed against the U.S. bloc.

As relations with the Soviets deteriorated, China paid more attention to its *supporter of national liberation* and *anti-imperialist agent* roles to develop support among newly independent states as well as the *anti-revisionist* role to maintain good relations with the international communist movement. The Cultural Revolution (1966–76) led to the suspension of normal foreign relations, and the main role conception occupied by China during this time was *bastion of world revolution and of socialism*. After the Soviets invaded Czechoslovakia in 1968, China added the role of *opponent of Soviet social imperialism* to its role set. Through the 1960s, China's roles became increasingly radical and completely antisystem with the break from the Soviets.

By the end of the 1960s, Beylerian and Canivet (1997: 189–90) note, China had a limited number of roles couched in very moralistic language. Mao Zedong and Zhou Enlai worked to end China's isolation by reaching out to the United States. Through this rapprochement with the United States, China adopted the role of *opponent of Soviet expansionism*, now framed in geopolitical rather than ideological terms. The United States altercast China in the role of *great power*.[3] China began to downgrade roles such as *bastion of world revolution and of socialism* and switched to *champion of Third World causes* as a result of Mao Zedong's theory of the three worlds articulated in 1974. This role was also accompanied by *active promoter of a united front against the hegemony of the two superpowers* (Shih 1993). Beylerian and Canivet (1997: 190) note that these roles did not displace *anti-imperialist agent* and *anti-revisionist* agent in the role set. Near the end of the 1970s when U.S. declinism was reaching its peak, China revised its role to one of *anti-Soviet hegemony*, thinking that the United States no longer posed a hegemonic threat. Thus, by the beginning of the 1970s, China's radicalism was on the wane as it became more of a stakeholder in the international system—even to the extent that the United States began to consider China a great power to balance the Soviet Union.

During the Mao years (1949–76), China developed a reputation for settling many territorial disputes militarily. Blanchard and Lin (2013) note that for decades after the 1911 revolution, China's foreign policy was primarily directed at protecting the borders (after defining them) and reestablishing sovereignty and independence. Li (2013) develops an argument that Mao had a Hobbesian worldview (Wendt 1999) in which a militarized approach to foreign policy made sense to a revolutionary challenger to the international system. After Mao's death and the introduction of reforms, China has increasingly been integrated into the international system and its general

Lockean culture. Militarized foreign policy makes less sense in a live-and-let-live Lockean world where threats are not existential (Wendt 1999). Li (2013) creates a more fine-grained demarcation as well, based on statements from leaders and officials about Chinese perceptions of the likelihood of war. China has considered war inevitable from 1949 to 1953 and 1960 to 1974, postponable (20–40% chance) from 1954 to 1959 and 1974 to 1984, and avoidable from 1985 to the present. He then conducts an empirical investigation of whether China engaged in militarized interstate disputes (MIDs) with other states based on this variation in threat perception and finds confirming evidence that greater threat perception led to more MIDs.

China has engaged in more territorial disputes than any other country since the end of World War II, but according to Fravel (2010: 507), it has settled the majority of those disputes through bilateral agreements. Curiously, given those who argue about the weight of history on the present, this has often come at the expense of sovereignty. While Li (2013) highlights the idea that greater threat perceptions produced more MIDs, it is important to note that a MID can involve the threat, display, or use of force. As Fravel (2010: 507) notes, while China has used force in some disputes, it has typically not seized land that it did not already control prior to hostilities. There are a number of outstanding territorial disputes involving India, Bhutan, and the Paracel, Spratley, and Senkaku Islands, among other places. After a review of the costs, pressures for and against, benefits, and means of territorial expansion, Fravel concludes that China will not pursue territorial expansion.

Deng Xiaoping's economic and social reforms introduced at the end of 1978 meant the adoption of the role of *practicing openness to the outside world*, which would enable China to modernize and develop economically with great speed. China continued to pursue the *anti-Soviet hegemonic role*, although the U.S. support of Taiwan under Reagan moved China closer to the USSR. By 1982, China's role set began to revolve around the role of *independent actor*. According to Beylerian and Canivet (1997: 191), the *independent actor* role meant opposition to hegemony, developing relations with all states based on the five principles of peaceful coexistence, and solidarity and cooperation with the Third World.

The external shock of the end of the Cold War and the dissolution of the USSR caused China's leadership to rethink its role set, according to Beylerian and Canivet (1997: 192). China maintained the roles of *independent actor* and *anti-hegemony* but modified their meaning. The role of *openness to the outside world* was also maintained. In addition, China began to focus on its regional security environment, though the *regional collaborator* role was not resuscitated; instead, the *regional reconciler* role was adopted.[4] China also worked to develop the role of *promoter of global peace and prosperity* through its position on the UN Security Council. Finally, there is some evidence that China may be pursuing the role of *promoter of a new international order*, which leads some to classify China as a *dissatisfied power*.

Beylerian and Canivet (1997) also conduct a content analysis of foreign policy speeches and interviews for the immediate post–Cold War era (1989–1993). They identify nine major roles in China's role set for this time period: *reformer of the international order, reconciler of regional conflicts, advocate of peaceful coexistence and international cooperation, practitioner of openness to the outside world, good neighbor, opponent of hegemonism, consolidator of the United Nations and defender of world peace, independent actor,* and *unifier of the Sinic world.* The *advocate of peaceful coexistence and international cooperation* role is most frequently mentioned in Beylerian and Canivet's analysis, followed by *reconciler of regional conflicts* and *reformer of the international order.* Ultimately, the authors argue that China's leaders "modified, but did not fundamentally alter the structure of China's international roles after 1989" (221). The new addition to the role set is the advocacy for peaceful coexistence and international cooperation, coupled with supporting roles such as *reconciler of regional conflict* and *good neighbor.* The *reformer of the international order* role suggests that they are not fully satisfied, but China's foreign policy role set seems to contradict what structural theories would tell us about the direction of change in foreign policy doctrine.

Brittingham (2007) focuses on the post–Cold War role of *great power* era, which he and Rozman (1999) claim has long been a central feature of Chinese foreign policy. Given that all roles imply counterroles to form a role relationship, Brittingham examines how the great power NRC has been received by its significant other, the United States. He argues that the United States has tried to altercast China into the *troubled modernizer* role with its attempts at modernization and economic reforms that should ultimately lead to the end of the communist system and the embracing of Western political and economic ideals (Madsen 1995). Yet the 1989 events in Tiananmen Square shattered this view of China as a liberalizing state; hence, China is now cast in the role of *failed modernizer* and potential *rogue.* This role requires that outsiders "save" China from itself and results in policies such as sanctions, the attempt to link MFN status to human rights issues, and the emergence of the discourse of the "China threat" in the aftermath of the 1995–96 Taiwan Straits Crisis. Thies (2015a) suggests that the United States also attempted to altercast China as a *protectee* during the crisis by enacting the traditional regional protector role.[5] China contested these counterroles offered by the United States, leading to a resurgence of Chinese nationalism and anti-Americanism. Brittingham (2007: 161–62) suggests that this may open the door to conflict between the United States and China, yet a variety of factors, including overwhelming U.S. capabilities, Chinese restraint, and other "webs of restraint," may limit outright conflict.

In his analysis of the Taiwan Straits Crisis, Thies (2015a), drawing on an expert survey by Moore (2016) of Chinese watchers of America and American watchers of China identified a number of salient roles. One of the central findings from the Moore survey is that "sacred commitments" were at stake for China. These include fostering a sense of dignity among the Chinese people as they seek to end the foreign oppression and domination experienced during the "Century of Humiliation," in part by regaining Taiwan. While China may have been a *victim* in the past and draws on that historical role in the present to justify the Communist Party's continued rule, it is also an *anti-imperialist agent* and *opponent of hegemonism* in its efforts to restore Taiwan to China against U.S. wishes. Another sacred commitment is the belief that China must be unified to be great. Thus, Taiwan is part of the stumbling block preventing China as a *rising power* from being a truly *great power*, even as the aspirations for great power status have preoccupied post–Cold War China. A third sacred commitment is to complete the revolution started in 1911 and continued in 1949: Taiwan remains unfinished business, and China conceives itself in the role of *bastion of world revolution and socialism*. The final sacred commitment is to Chinese identity, which accords Taiwan an important place in the national discourse on unity, sovereignty, and territorial integrity. This commitment affirms support for China as a *sovereign state* and the *unifier of the Sinic world*. As Thies notes, all of these roles are primarily achieved rather than ascribed (as expected of a major member/rising power). Thies also notes that most accounts considered China and the United States as rivals from 1949 to 1972, and the crisis reignited the *rival* role, which continues to this day.

Drawing on the resurgence of Chinese nationalism in recent years, Breslin (2010) argues that the *great power* role is increasingly attractive in China, especially given the country's historical strength and subsequent subjugation during the Century of Humiliation beginning with the First

Opium War (1839–42) and concluding with the foundation of the People's Republic.[6] While the United States may have granted China the role of *great power* by when formal diplomatic relations were reestablished, China now has the capacity to act as a great power. However, China is a great power in an international political order designed by the United States with an array of institutional features and power structures that serves its interests and those of its allies. China is therefore a dissatisfied great power that has not yet acted in a revisionist or revolutionary way on the world stage. Instead, Breslin (2009: 822; 2010: 53) argues that China has adopted the role of a *responsible great power* that promotes global peace, stability, and growth. Contrary to power transition theory expectations or those who promulgate the "China threat," China has thus far indicated a willingness to follow rather than challenge the existing order. For example, China has promoted the idea of a responsible power through its work on UN peacekeeping (Richardson 2011). Buzan and Cox (2013: 113) date China's peaceful rise to the 1978 reforms but say that the term *peaceful rise* was in vogue in China only from 2003 to 2004.[7] The logic remains in place, and China maintains a cold peace with the United States, Japan, India, Russia, and indeed most of Southeast Asia.

Atanassova-Cornelis (2012) identifies two major strands of post–Cold War identity beyond that of the *great power* role, including *victim* and *developing country*.[8] She argues that the Chinese leadership drew on the Century of Humiliation in the aftermath of the Tiananmen Square incident to garner public support for the regime. The Chinese Communist Party was portrayed as saving the nation from hostile foreign powers such as Japan and the United States. Taiwan often forms a focal point in this identity, since it was a Japanese colony from 1895 to 1945 and is the source of constant irritation with U.S. military support to maintain its independence today. The *developing country* aspect of Chinese identity began with Deng Xiaoping's economic reforms. Domestic policy is geared toward development and forms the basis for China's diplomacy as it seeks a peaceful environment. Neither Japan nor the United States freely accepts the *developing country* role for China, which is often seen as instrumentally used in trade or environmental negotiations. Finally, the *great power* identity is useful domestically to garner support in pursuit of rightful international respect and status. As we know, the *great power* role also engenders fear of China as a rising power in Japan and the United States, especially with regard to the development of its military might. Thies (2015a) also argues that China occupies a *rising power* master status by the mid-1990s, which is why the Taiwan Straits Crisis was so contentious. China has pursued the *responsible great power* role or *responsible stakeholder* role and language of the peaceful rise/harmonious world/peaceful world to try to assuage its key role partners (Breslin 2009: 822; Atanassova-Cornelis 2012).

Haas (2008) identifies China as a major power that occupies a status above the rank of the numerous regional powers. Yet Shambaugh (2013) somewhat curiously describes China as a "middle power" that has joined the ranks of other middle powers—Australia, Brazil, Canada, Germany, India, Indonesia, Iran, Japan, Russia, South Africa, South Korea, and Turkey. This use of the middle power designation does not fit with the usual understanding of middle powers as primarily democratic, pro-Western, and system supportive.

China is engaged in rivalries with a number of key states in the international system. Park (2013), Calder (2006), and Dreyer (2006) all identify a "simmering" but ongoing rivalry with Japan. Given that both are regional powers with regional leadership aspirations, this is not surprising. But, as Park (2013: 93) reminds us, both have difficulties finding followers in East Asia. Ollapally (2014: 350) notes that Indian elites viewed China as a serious rival from 1962 to 1989, when relations improved slightly with Rajiv Gandhi's visit to Beijing before taking another downturn after India's nuclear tests in 1998. Egreteau (2012: 8) agrees that despite the series of disputes that led up to the 1962 war, that was the beginning of the enduring rivalry between China and India. Despite escalatory and deescalatory dynamics over time, the peak occurred in 1987, with some particularly bloody border skirmishes. Again, the bilateral visits started with Gandhi seemed to smooth relations until India's 1998 nuclear test, which India intended as a means to an end of achieving nuclear parity with China (not Pakistan). Relations continued with ups and downs, but the rivalry between the two generally seems solidified.

The literature is filled with speculation about the future Sino-American relationship and the likelihood of conflict between the two (e.g., Ross and Feng 2008). Friedberg's (2005) review of liberal, realist, and constructivist international relations theory as well as the optimistic and pessimistic versions of each supports almost all kinds of future relationships between the United States and China. Foot's (2006) review of Chinese scholarship suggests that a majority of the elite hope for accommodation with the United

States, though they doubt that this will occur. One minority view is much more optimistic about Sino-U.S. accommodation even though it will be tough. Finally, another minority opinion expects U.S. and Chinese conflict since the United States will never tolerate China as a true great power or even a regional Asia-Pacific power. Sutter (2014) notes that the relationship has been strained since at least the Taiwan Straits Crisis but remained manageable until the 2012 U.S. presidential and congressional campaigns, when even President Obama referred to China as an "adversary." The academic discussion also shifted to a great divergence framework that acknowledges positive economic ties between the two states but a precarious security situation. Sutter suggests that the two states are practicing a kind of constructive engagement, recognizing the economic interdependence that characterizes the relationship along with more pressing domestic problems in both countries and common goals in many international forums.

Buzan and Cox (2013) compare the U.S. and Chinese rises and find a number of similarities and differences. They conclude, however, that a peaceful rise for China is possible despite the weight of international relations theory that expects conflict and war. A Chinese rise that could avoid direct confrontation with the United States while bullying regional neighbors would look much like the U.S. case of peaceful rise. China is also emerging at a time when neither empire building nor great power war is no longer acceptable. The normative constraints on China's rise essentially help to channel it toward more peaceful avenues. Of course, China can attempt to challenge and redefine the rules without risking economic or military conflict with the United States (Odgaard 2013). Xiaoyu (2012) refers to this as "two-way socialization." China faces a world of industrialized powerful states that were not so numerous when the United States rose, and its home region is more troubled. Acharya (2014) offers a number of possible directions that an Asian security order could take with Chinese participation and ultimately advocates a consociational security order rather than one dominated by China. Buzan and Cox (2013) also note that China cannot take advantage of global wars to grow, as the United States did, nor will it likely emerge as a singular hegemon to replace the United States, in part because China lacks both the desire for this position on a global level and a vision for a Chinese-led global order. Wolf's (2014) concern that China, like Imperial Germany, is too wrapped up in status and may make the same mistakes that lead to conflict is appropriate in this context as well.

Finally, Buzan and Cox (2013: 131) argue that China risks avoiding great power managerial responsibility too long during its peaceful rise, much like the United States did, an approach that is detrimental to the global order.[9]

The analysis of Chinese foreign policy suggests several key shocks that *could* induce major foreign policy change: the 1949 foundation of the People's Republic of China, the 1954 enunciation of the five principles of peaceful coexistence when establishing relations with India, the start of the Cultural Revolution in 1966, the economic and social reforms initiated in 1978 by Deng Xiaoping, the 1989 Tiananmen Square incident, and the 1995–96 Taiwan Straits Crisis, which is conventionally cited as the origin of the China threat, especially as China's material power had grown dramatically by this point in time.

Conversely, the narrative history of Chinese NRCs briefly summarized in table 7.1 demonstrates a slowly evolving Chinese identity. While the decade-by-decade portrait of NRCs masks some variation according to traditional breaks in Chinese foreign policy, it does paint a picture of a generally stable and evolving Chinese identity. If anything, it is a self-conceived

Table 7.1. China's Role Sets

1950s	*junior partner and faithful ally, supporter of national liberation, regional collaborator, anti-imperialist agent, model of national liberation and independence, independent ally, U.S. rival*
1960s	*supporter of national liberation, anti-imperialist agent, anti-revisionist agent, bastion of world revolution and of socialism, opponent of Soviet social imperialism, U.S. rival, Indian rival*
1970s	*opponent of Soviet expansionism, champion of Third World causes, active promoter of a united front against the hegemony of the two superpowers, anti-imperialist agent, anti-revisionist agent, anti-Soviet hegemony, Indian rival, great power (altercast by United States)*
1980s	*practitioner of openness to the outside world, anti-Soviet hegemony, independent actor, rising power, Indian rival*
1990s	*independent actor, anti-hegemony/opponent of hegemonism, practitioner of openness to the outside world, regional reconciler, promoter of global peace and prosperity, promoter of a new international order, reformer of the international order, advocate of peaceful coexistence and international cooperation, good neighbor, unifier of Sinic world, victim, developing country, anti-imperialist agent, rising power, bastion of world revolution and of socialism, sovereign state, U.S. rival, Indian rival, rising power* Altercast roles (by U.S.): *dissatisfied power, troubled modernizer, failed modernizer, rogue, protectee*
2000s	*great power, responsible great power, responsible stakeholder, major power, U.S. rival, rising power, middle power, Indian rival, Japanese rival*

Table 7.2. Active-Passive Dimensions of China's Role Sets

Decade	Number of Roles	Overall Activity	Low	High	Mean
1950s	7	20	1	5	2.9
1960s	7	25	2	5	3.6
1970s	7	26	2	4	3.7
1980s	5	15	2	4	3.0
1990s	19	55	0	5	2.9
2000s	9	32	2	5	3.6

identity that appears to move toward a more peaceful orientation to the world. While radical, revolutionary, and revisionist NRCs dominated in the 1950s and early 1960s, they began to give way toward system-supportive NRCs by the 1980s and 1990s. Table 7.2 shows a high level of activity associated with the role sets in the 1960s and 1970s that declines in the 1980s and 1990s. Thus, the growth in material power over time that should give rise to revisionist NRCs is contradicted by the evidence: as Chinese power grows, its self-conceived identity becomes more peaceful and system-supportive. What is also unusual about the Chinese case is the amount of altercasting that occurs from the United States as dominant power in the system in the 1990s, although this is not new to the U.S.-Chinese relationship (Thies 2015b). The qualitative evidence about Chinese identity seems to contradict our first hypothesis and support the second. China has not been compelled toward NRCs that demonstrate aggressive self-conceived identities, as structural theories would expect. Table 7.2 does show that despite a small number of roles in the 2000s, the level of average activity associated with them is high, and they relate to relatively peaceful global identities that require a high degree of activity and external involvement.

Militarized Interstate Disputes and Chinese Conflict Behavior

In our quantitative tests, we analyze China's militarized conflict behavior from 1870 to 2007 using a Poisson change-point model. Structural theories of international relations lead to the expectation that increases in China's relative material power are associated with increases in conflict behavior, while our foreign policy leads us to expect little in the way of changes in conflict behavior.

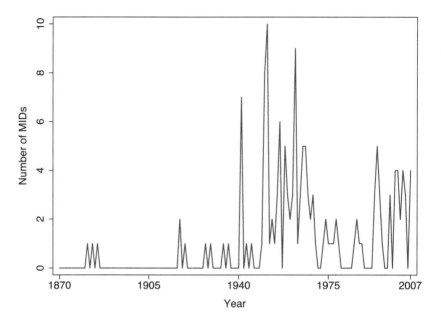

Fig. 7.1. Military Dispute Initiations and Interventions by China, 1870–2007

Figure 7.1 shows the number of MIDs initiated or joined by China between 1870 and 2007. The number of disputes in which China engages increases over the second half of the 20th century and into the 21st. To more systematically assess the possible determinants of China's militarized behavior, we estimate a change-point model using the conflict specification outlined in chapter 3.[10] We identify Asia as China's primary region for the purposes of calculating its *Power Ratio*.[11]

Table 7.3 reports the logged Bayes Factor comparison of the marginal likelihood for several models. Looking at table 7.3 and applying Jeffrey's (1961) scale, we identify model M_0, a model with zero change-points, as having "decisive" support as the best fit. This suggests that the determinants associated with China's military conflict behavior have not changed in the period under review.[12]

We now explore the effect of the explanatory variables on militarized conflict behavior. In particular, we are interested in the effect of *Power Ratio*, as structural theories expect this variable to be positively related to conflict. We report summaries of the posterior parameter estimates of each endogenous variables in table 7.4.

Table 7.4 shows that *Power Ratio Squared* is significant, with approximately 70 percent confidence. That the sign of the coefficient is negative, combined with the insignificant result of *Power Ratio* (0 is within one standard deviation of the mean), indicates that increases in relative material power are associated with *decreases* in militarized conflict. This result directly contradicts structural expectations of increased conflict as the material power of rising states increase. We also find that *Neighbor Conflict* is positive and significant at the 88 percent confidence level. That China is likely to intervene in its neighbors' conflicts suggests that China views itself as having a conflict management role in the East Asia region. *Proportion of Democracy* has a positive and significant impact on China's militarized con-

Table 7.3. Comparison of Poisson Change-Point Models of China's Militarized Conflict Behavior

	M_0	M_1	M_2	M_3	M_4	M_5	M_6	M_7	M_8	M_9
M_0	0	9.42	31.50	26.99	32.31	53.13	66.48	75.74	95.01	90.64
M_1	−9.42	0	22.08	17.58	22.89	43.71	57.06	66.32	85.59	81.22
M_2	−31.50	−22.08	0	−4.51	0.80	21.63	34.98	44.24	63.51	59.14
M_3	−26.99	−17.58	4.51	0	5.31	26.14	39.48	48.74	68.01	63.65
M_4	−32.31	−22.89	−0.80	−5.31	0	20.83	34.17	43.43	62.70	58.33
M_5	−53.13	−43.71	−21.63	−26.14	−20.83	0	13.35	22.61	41.87	37.51
M_6	−66.48	−57.06	−34.98	−39.48	−34.17	−13.35	0	9.26	28.53	24.16
M_7	−75.74	−66.32	−44.24	−48.74	−43.43	−22.61	−9.26	0	19.27	14.90
M_8	−95.01	−85.59	−63.51	−68.01	−62.70	−41.87	−28.53	−19.27	0	−4.37
M_9	−90.64	−81.22	−59.14	−63.65	−58.34	−37.51	−24.16	−14.90	4.37	0

Note: $\ln(BF_{ij} = m[y|M_i]/m[y|M_j])$ where BF_{ij} is the Bayes Factor comparing model M_i to a baseline model M_j, $m(y|M_i)$ is the marginal likelihood under model M_i, $(y|M_j)$ is the marginal likelihood under model M_j. Columns are M_i and rows are M_j. MCMC chains are run 20,000 times after discarding 10,000 burn-in draws.

Table 7.4. Poisson Estimation of China's Militarized Conflict Initiation with Zero Change-Points

	Mean	S.D.
Power Ratio	0.060	0.063
Power Ratio Squared	−0.065	0.061
Neighbor Conflict	0.131	0.086
Democratic Proportion	0.103	0.019
Trade	−0.035	0.017
World War I	2.470	0.879
World War II	−0.411	0.528
Constant	−3.041	1.387

Note: Mean and standard deviation drawn from the posterior distribution. MCMC chains are run 20,000 times after discarding 10,000 burn-in draws.

flict behavior at well over the 95 percent confidence level. This result indicates that China has increasingly conflictual relations as the number of democratic states in its region increases. This suggests that China identifies distinct policy dissimilarities with neighboring states as they democratize. *Trade* is also a significant predictor of conflict, with greater than 95 percent confidence. Increases in *Trade* are associated with a decrease in the likelihood of militarized conflict. This result is especially important given the dramatic increase in trade as a percent of GDP in China since Deng's reforms. While the effect of a one-unit increase in trade has been constant, the volume of trade has increased, contributing a large pacifying effect on conflict behavior. Finally, *World War I* is positive and significant at above the 95 percent confidence level. This indicates that entry in the World War I produced an increase in militarized conflict.

The quantitative results suggest that structural theories are unable to account for China's militarized conflict behavior. Instead, at least in terms of observable behavior, China's foreign policy has remained remarkably stable, as the same indicators matter in the same way across the entire period under review. While the finding that democratization in Asia is associated with conflict is disconcerting, China's integration into the world economy has had the most dramatic change in terms of the effect on foreign policy, and this change is reflected in the evolution of NRCs. The quantitative results are consistent with our qualitative analysis in that China's militarized behavior has not kept pace with its rise in capabilities.

Chinese Economic Conflict Behavior

We now quantitatively analyze China's economic conflict behavior. As was the case with Russia, China's economic conflict behavior is interesting in that for much of the 1929–2007 period, China was largely outside of and did not interact with the world economy. This, of course, reflects the ideology of the communist government that has ruled China since its consolidation in 1949. This implies that from 1949 until Deng's reforms in 1979, China had few foreign assets it could expropriate and essentially had a closed financial sector.

Following the 1979 reforms, however, China became increasingly engaged in the global economy. In fact, in recent years, China has become an alternative lender to Western banks and international institutions, such as the World Bank and International Monetary Fund (IMF). China has, for example, provided many African states with loans featuring favorable, back-loaded payment plans that do not require the structural reforms, such as privatization of state-owned firms, often mandated by the World Bank and IMF. Moreover, China often accepts payment in kind rather than in hard currency and technical support on private and public works in return for input on project planning and access to resources (Carmody and Owusu 2007). Since 1984, China has opened its financial market and dramatically increased its public debt (Gunter 2004).

Despite the significant fluidity in China's interactions with the world economy, it has only two instances of economic challenge. In 1939, China defaulted on its sovereign debt as a consequence of its inability to finance both its international commitments and the war effort against Japan. Following the slight easing of capital controls in 1984, China briefly increased the degree of capital controls in 1987 before easing them again in 1992. To explain economic conflict behavior, we estimate a probit change-point model using the economic conflict model outlined in chapter 3.[13]

Table 7.5 reports the results of the logged marginal likelihood comparisons of several models. The results indicate that model M_0, with no change-points, has the best fit to the data. This result suggests that there are no structural breaks in China's economic conflict behavior, with one underlying process that best explains this behavior.

Table 7.6 reports the summary of the posterior estimates for each endogenous variable, with special attention paid to *Power Ratio*. *None* of the explanatory variables included in the model have a significant impact on

Table 7.5. Comparison of Probit Change-Point Models of China's Economic Conflict Behavior

	M_0	M_1	M_2
M_0	0	3.29	10.01
M_1	−3.29	0	6.72
M_2	−10.01	−6.72	0

Note: $\ln(BF_{ij} = m[y|M_i]/m[y|M_j])$ where BF_{ij} is the Bayes Factor comparing model M_i to a baseline model M_j, $m(y|M_i)$ is the marginal likelihood under model M_i, $(y|M_j)$ is the marginal likelihood under model M_j. Columns are M_i and rows are M_j. MCMC chains are run 20,000 times after discarding 10,000 burn-in draws.

economic conflict. None of the variables have a mean posterior estimate more than one standard deviation away from 0. Given the particularity of the events—the 1939 default tied to war with Japan, the 1987 tightening of capital controls after decades of completely closed financial markets—the lack of systematic behavior is perhaps unsurprising.

The lack of a structural break and absence of *Power Ratio* having a significant effect on China's economic conflict behavior provides evidence against structural explanations. No major changes in economic conflict behavior appear to occur over the 1929–2007 period, suggesting a more gradual and evolutionary change in its economic statecraft.

Conclusion

Our analysis finds change in Chinese identity and conflict behavior more consistent with our foreign policy approach than with structural materialist theories. China's role sets have varied over time, but the core evolved from radical, revisionist identities in the first few decades of the People's Republic of China to system-supportive identities in recent decades. Today, most of China's NRCs relate to the idea of a responsible great power committed to maintaining the international system at peace. While many may be suspicious that such words represent China's true self-image and intention, our analysis of China's conflict behavior largely corroborates this view of China's foreign policy orientation. No structural breaks have occurred in either China's militarized or economic conflict behavior. Some evidence suggests that an increase in the proportion of democracies in the region may lead to militarized conflict. Those advocating a China threat are likely to view this

Table 7.6. Probit Estimation of China's Economic Conflict Initiation with Zero Change-Points

	Mean	S.D.
Power Ratio	−0.026	0.031
GDP Growth	−0.009	0.062
Democratic Proportion	−0.034	0.048
Trade	−0.058	0.114
Constant	−0.199	2.024

Note: Mean and standard deviation drawn from the posterior distribution. MCMC chains are run 20,000 times after discarding 10,000 burn-in draws.

finding as supportive of their claims. Yet as Lake (2009: 181–84) argues, we may just as likely see China integrated into the existing authority structures of the international system. Increased trade between China and its neighbors seems to ameliorate conflict, and such trade tends to be governed by the rules and norms of the U.S.-led LIEO. Structural materialist theories tend to ignore the relations of authority present in the hierarchical international order designed by the United States, with a great deal of legitimacy conferred by the acquiescence of other major powers.

What does our analysis suggest for the future? We contend that China's identity, comprised of an evolving role set, is largely one of a responsible great power. This does not preclude conflict, as great powers engage in a significant percentage of all conflict. It would be unusual for a great power not to manage the affairs of its home region, including through the use of periodic militarized conflict. Asia, of course, is a peculiar region given the presence of Japan as another great power that has adopted the civilian power role for the time being. Chinese relative power seems to have no effect on the likelihood of militarized conflict in the region. A dramatic increase in the proportion of democracies in the region also seems unlikely anytime soon, so that source of potential militarized conflict for China should also not be an issue. In general, our analysis suggests that China will continue to view its identity as a responsible great power that engages in infrequent militarized disputes in its home region, but a dramatic shift in foreign policy orientation or conflict behavior is unlikely. Efforts to involve China in the expansion of trade agreements may also result in less militarized conflict.

CHAPTER 8

South Africa: Punching above
Its Weight as a Middle Power

South Africa is an interesting case of a state that has been accorded rising power status by other conventionally acclaimed rising powers. The BRIC designation that caught on with the media, pundits, and policymakers initially did not include South Africa, yet the other BRIC countries invited South Africa to join them in 2010. South Africa, like the other BRICS, is a G20 member and is recognized as one of the most capable states in Africa. Many view it as a regional hegemon or leader of southern Africa, though these stylized facts have run into the internal difficulties experienced as the country transitioned from apartheid to African National Congress (ANC) rule. Much of the moral authority inherent in the person of Nelson Mandela seems to have evaporated under his successors. South Africa's focus in recent years has largely been internal, and the country has not pursued an active foreign policy. Thus, South Africa may represent the weakest claim to the structural materialist hypothesis that rising power may produce revisionist foreign policy.

We conclude our series of case studies by analyzing South Africa's self-conceived identity and conflict behavior over time. Our qualitative analysis of South African state identity looks for significant changes in the role sets that may lead to major foreign policy reorientation. Role transitions can be difficult even under the best of circumstances. Such reorientations may also be reflected in changes in South Africa's conflict behavior. Our quantitative analysis investigates whether dramatic changes have occurred in South African militarized or economic conflict behavior over time using change-point models. By comparing South Africa's words and deeds through national role conceptions (NRCs) and conflict behavior, we can assess whether claims about potential threats emanating from rising powers like South Africa are accurate.

The qualitative and quantitative analyses provide a plethora of potential foreign policy reorientations. Qualitatively, we see two potential reorientations in South African foreign policy role sets: the creation of the Republic of South Africa in 1961 and the end of apartheid circa 1994. These foreign policy reorientations do not appear to be correlated with major changes in material power for South Africa. We find one change in South African militarized behavior that coincides with the formation of the Republic of South Africa and a truly independent foreign policy. We also find one major break in economic conflict behavior in 1973. The likely impetus for this structural change was the Durban strikes, which were the first action that united the working classes and began the movement for equality for the majority black population. These events drew the attention of the world, leading to a UN resolution condemning the apartheid government. Altogether, these changes do not provide support for structural materialist approaches to understanding South Africa as a rising power. Instead, the changes are more clearly related to internal political and economic decisions—often reflecting international pressure as channeled through domestic political processes.

National Role Conceptions and South African Foreign Policy Analysis

We review the qualitative evidence on NRCs identified by scholars for South Africa as comprising its role set and look for changes in that role set over time. If structural IR theories emphasizing solely material factors are correct, then we should see dramatic changes in South Africa's NRCs as well as the way they are received by others as the country's power changes over time. Foreign policy approaches to change that consider the effect of both material and ideational aspects of structure and their coaction with agents would also expect that major internal and external shocks could bring about foreign policy restructuring, though those shocks are mediated by the existing role set. Rather than wholesale change, our role-theoretic approach suggests modification of roles based on structural and domestic imperatives.

The literature on South African foreign policy suggests a long period of relative stability in the country's overall foreign policy orientation, followed by a dramatic break with the end of apartheid. Even so, there are several candidates for internal shocks that could change the identity and self-conceived roles of South Africa. The first could be its formation as the Union of South Africa in 1910 as a dominion of the British Empire. The second could be the passage of the Statute of Westminster (1931), which established the legislative independence of self-governing dominions of the empire and allowed for an independent South African foreign policy.[1] The third could be the 1961 formation of the Republic of South Africa, which coincided with a change in the ANC's orientation and the massive wave of decolonization that swept across Africa. The fourth is the adoption of the "Total National Strategy" in 1978. The final potential shock is the end of apartheid, which occurred by law in 1991, though it is often dated to the 1994 general elections, when nonwhites were first allowed to vote and the country elected its first nonwhite president. Indeed, most of the scholarly literature focuses on post-apartheid foreign policy as markedly distinct from all of South Africa's preceding foreign policy orientations. This post-apartheid period of foreign policy is often cast as one of incoherence and inconsistency. In many ways, it is similar to Russia's search for identity after the dissolution of the Soviet Union in that many roles are being conceived and played, sometimes in particular contexts and time periods.

The Union of South Africa was formed in 1910, with the ANC following two years later. The ANC began by working within the existing framework of governance by seeking redress of grievances and universal franchise in all provinces of the union, in keeping, the party argued, with the Native Land Act of 1913 and the new South African constitution. As Evans (1996: 250) notes, "They were singularly unsuccessful." The ANC even lobbied at the Versailles Conference, drawing on U.S. President Wilson's Fourteen Points, but the party was for decades hampered by the fact that as a nonstate actor, it had no legal standing to develop a foreign policy (Evans 1996: 250). South Africa, conversely, was an original member of the League of Nations and was even entrusted with being a mandate holder. The foreign policy of the state of South Africa from 1948 to 1994 was "dramatically simple—it was a single-issue affair revolving around strategies to ensure the survival of the white regime" (Evans 1999: 623). As Schraeder (2001: 229–30) notes, the foreign policy cost to South Africa was being branded as an *international pariah* conducting the "diplomacy of isolation."

According to Evans (1996: 251), not until after the 1960 Sharpeville Massacre and its repressive aftermath did the ANC begin to develop a co-herent foreign policy goal: having apartheid declared a "crime against humanity" and obtaining international pariah status for the new Republic of South Africa, formed in 1961. According to Evans, the ANC became progressively more radical, integrating its larger goal into the Cold War struggle and embracing Marxist/Leninist principles as it forged connections with revolutionary movements and anti-apartheid groups around the world. Its efforts paid off as South Africa was increasingly seen as an *international pariah*.

In the 1960s, South Africa sought to directly incorporate Botswana, Lesotho, and Swaziland, which had previously been administered by the British high commissioner through South Africa. This would have reduced these nations to the status of South African Bantustans, or a kind of internal colony with limited independence. Britain did not accede to South Africa's desire to continue as a *colonizer*, so the Verwoerd government proposed a common market/commonwealth for southern Africa with the goal of establishing such strong economic relationships that a regional political institution with South Africa as the "mother country" or *regional leader* would likely emerge (Davies and O'Meara 1985: 186). When this project failed to materialize, and in the face of rapid decolonization in the 1960s and increasing condemnation of apartheid, the Vorster government sought an "outward looking" or "dialogue initiative" approach to foreign policy, which sought *regional ally* role relationships with other states in the Organization of African Unity (OAU). This met with some initial success but was eventually blocked by a 1971 OAU initiative to end South Africa's attempts to divide the continent and end its isolation (Davies and O'Meara 1985: 187).

Holsti's (1970) seminal study on foreign policy roles identified the following roles for South Africa in the 1965–68 period: *regional-subsystem collaborator, defender of the faith, independent,* and *isolate*. His analysis indicated that these roles were rather vaguely defined. South Africa also falls in the middle of the states he analyzed in terms of the number of roles expressed, and its roles tend toward the middle on an active-passive scale, placing it in the second group of states overall in terms of foreign policy role activity. What he terms the *regional-subsystem collaborator* role relates to the facilitation of regional economic and political cooperation, which we see clearly in the proposals for a common market/commonwealth for the region. Holsti does not indicate what the *defender of the faith* role in this context means, though it likely refers to liberal economic values. The *isolate* role indicates some early trouble in terms of South Africa's distinctiveness from the rest of the region in terms of its apartheid policy and white rule.

The expression of an *independent* role is not unusual for states, particularly a newly declared republic seeking to demonstrate that it makes its own foreign policy.

South African policy in the southern African region thereafter consisted of largely propping up colonial governments that were in power in the states around it or destabilizing unfriendly regimes (Davies 1985; Davies and O'Meara 1985). Hirschmann (1979: 177) describes Lesotho as a "hostage" since it is physically surrounded by South Africa, though he more accurately describes it as a client, casting South Africa as its *patron*. The process of supporting the Portuguese colonies of Angola and Mozambique as well as the settler-ruled British colony of Rhodesia and South Africa's own colony of Namibia produced a series of buffer states that isolated South Africa from more distant liberation struggles and provided an itinerant pool of labor for its economy (Davies 1985). The collapse of the Portuguese colonial occupation led to a reformulation of South African foreign policy in 1974. South Africa, acting as a *regional hegemon*, began to consider setting up a bloc of independent states surrounding it. This led to both covert and overt attempts to install regimes sympathetic to South Africa, including the invasion of Angola in 1975.

The 1978 Total National Strategy aimed to construct a regional alliance with South Africa in the *pivotal state* role, including economic development projects that would demonstrate the superiority of South African capitalism over Marxist alternatives. Thus, the *regional ally* role would be complemented by the *regional developer* role. The Botha government thought that by pursuing a regional solution to a regional problem, South Africa would become globally recognized as a *regional power* if not a *regional superpower*. The Total National Strategy was designed to combat what was seen as a "total onslaught" of threats against the country deriving from Marxist movements as well as efforts to undermine apartheid (Geldenhuys 1981). As Metz (1986: 492) notes, the destabilization of its neighbors has become one of the most important concerns of the South African government since 1978.

Zimbabwe's independence under an unfriendly government, followed by the 1980 establishment of the Southern African Development Coordination Conference in opposition to South Africa's economic domination of the region were seen as clear blows to South Africa's designs. South Africa continued its covert and overt activities designed to destabilize unfriendly regimes in the region in the early 1980s. While these activities were seen as softening up neighboring regimes, they also undermined the goals of promoting South African capitalism and external recognition of South Africa as a *regional power*. South Africa and Mozambique signed the Nkomati Accord in 1984, effectively ending the destabilizing activities and offering the possibility for South Africa to break out of its *international pariah* role and into a more normal *regional power* role (Davies 1985: 18). Botha's visit to Western Europe in 1984 (impossible prior to this time) seemed to indicate some success in this regard (Davies 1985: 54–55).

From the mid-1970s to 1980s, South Africa also pursued a *nuclear weapons state* role. Liberman's (2001) research demonstrates that the Vorster government had decided by 1969 or 1970 to acquire a nuclear deterrent and to build nuclear weapons around 1974 or 1977. The exact dates are often difficult to know as many policymakers are now deceased or refuse to talk about these decisions. There is some sense that the 1974 Indian nuclear test galvanized the South African government to move forward with the militarization of nuclear technology. The country's first two nuclear devices were completed in 1978 and 1979, though the first device deliverable by bomber came in 1982, all under the Botha government. South Africa came under increasing sanctions associated with its nuclear program, which was ended in 1989. This seems largely to have been a decision by De Klerk to help rehabilitate South Africa and end its international pariah role.

By the 1980s, U.S. policymakers were actively thinking about how to bring about change in South Africa that could produce a stable partner "without constraint, embarrassment or political damage" (Crocker 1980: 324). It was clear that the United States, as a multiracial democracy, could not endorse apartheid. Further, respect for human rights, democracy, and a strong market economy would depend on how change would occur in South Africa. Finally, some believed evolutionary change, as opposed to revolution, might still be possible. The question was how to engage with South Africa to move it away from white rule to a more pluralist democracy, thus ending its role as an *international pariah*. For the United States, there were obvious security implications given that a more truly democratic South Africa would ideally fit into the Western system of alliances in opposition to the Soviet bloc.

The Botha government formulated the "New Diplomacy" in 1989 as a way to ensure South Africa's position as a *regional hegemon* even if the ANC eventually came to power. The elements of the policy included the ideas that South Africa is part of Africa, African problems must be solved by Africans, southern Africa is characterized by security interdependence, and regional issues should be approached in a neighborly fashion; in addition, a conference should be held to design and implement these principles (Evans 1996: 255–56). The New Diplomacy also recognized that military power lacked utility given the new security issues developing in the region, thus abandoning the principles associated with the Total National Strategy. Evans (1996: 256) notes that the goal of South Africa as a dominant *regional power* was left intact, but the means to pursue it changed from military coercion to diplomacy, trade, and cooperation. Evans (1996: 256) also suggests that this was more a change in style than in substance, since the goal of an unrivaled "regional superpower" was still in place.

Nelson Mandela (1993: 88) made it clear that "human rights will be the light that guides our foreign policy" on the eve of elections that would ultimately bring him and the ANC to power in 1994. According to Alden and le Pere (2004: 284), Mandela's foreign policy was imbued with the spirit of the antiapartheid struggle by promoting human rights, civil liberties, and democratization—in essence, a version of the *defender of the faith* role adopted by the United States during the Cold War period (Thies 2013) or the *moral crusader* role in Alden and le Pere's (2004: 286) terms. The southern African region received special priority, since South Africa had dominated the landscape both economically and politically for the previous century. In fact, government officials believed that South Africa needed to work closely within the region to address many negative externalities that could diminish South Africa's and the region's economic growth and development through both an *internal developer* and *regional developer* roles (see Cooper 1998 on the debate over pursing one or the other; Evans 1996 on the transformation in the ANC economic agenda). Landsberg (2005: 728) sees the internal and regional developer roles fused into a single *developmental state* role as it evolves over time. Mandela's government also sought to pursue greater involvement in multilateral institutions, such as the OAU, the Non-Aligned Movement, and the Southern African Development Community (SADC). Within a year after Mandela took office, South Africa had reestablished diplomatic relations with most states and been readmitted to the United Nations, the Commonwealth, and the SADC, thus ending its *international pariah* role and diplomacy of isolation.

Barber (2005) analyzes the great uncertainty over the appropriate role for South Africa in the post-apartheid period. He notes that Mandela initially proclaimed that South Africa was an *African state*, just like any other. Mbeki later restated this idea when he was inaugurated as president. Of course, although South Africa may be a small or medium-sized state in global terms, it is a giant in the African context. Barber suggests that Western states were eager to see Mandela pursue a more continental leadership role to help Africa develop economically and politically. Mandela's first attempt to take on such a role ended in failure when he sought to have Nigeria suspended from the Commonwealth and its oil boycotted for executing leaders of the Ogoni people who were protesting the destruction of their land by the oil industry. Barber notes that Africans actually saw Nigeria as a continental leader, since it had supported liberation struggles and was a major contributor to the OAU. Mandela later shifted to pursuing a *mediator-integrator* or *honest broker* role in attempting to resolve regional conflict (Cooper 1998: 710).

In a discussion of U.S. national strategy, Chase, Hill, and Kennedy (1996) argue that the United States should consider the role played by major players, including South Africa, as that of a *pivotal state*. In their view, a pivotal state is a "hot spot that could not only determine the fate of its region but also affect international stability" (33). Conceptually, focusing on pivotal states would help integrate new security issues into policymakers' old state-centered mind-set and help to direct U.S. assistance to stabilizing key regions around the world. They argue that by the mid-1990s, Algeria, Brazil, Egypt, India, Indonesia, Mexico, Pakistan, South Africa, and Turkey are pivotal states. Post-apartheid South Africa in its early years was viewed as having navigated its political divisions and as being "blessed with a strong infrastructure, a sound currency, and vast natural resources" (45). The biggest advantage for the state was that it was no longer viewed as an *international pariah*. The concerns, which have surfaced in recent years, are that South Africa could easily succumb to instability, ethnic conflict, and economic stagnation. Despite the internal nature of these threats, failure of the South African state would have calamitous effects for the region and for global commodity prices. Thus, the U.S. discussion of South Africa returned to an idea advocated within South Africa as part of the Total National Strategy.

According to Alden and le Pere (2004), the end of apartheid and the pursuit of policies of human rights and development have moved South Africa from a position of *international pariah* to potential *leader of the African continent* in a short period of time. Yet this ambitious foreign policy agenda is tempered by a lack of resources, need for investment, limited institutional capacity, a failure to comprehend the complexity of the African continent's politics, and ambiguity in how South Africa's identity is viewed from both within and abroad. Even bureaucratic politics seemed to intervene in the promotion of a post-apartheid foreign policy, as the Department of Foreign Affairs routinely clashed with other executive agencies, a situation that might be expected given the literature on domestic role contestation (Cantir and Kaarbo 2012; Brummer and Thies 2015). All of these limitations led others to view South Africa's aspirations to continental leadership rather skeptically.

The Mbeki government understood these problems when it assumed power in 1999. According to Alden and le Pere (2004: 287), Mbeki understood that his plans to lead an "African Renaissance" were being held back by South Africa's status as a *developing country* in a poor region and political and bureaucratic problems at home. Yet Mbeki believed that as a middle-income country, South Africa could champion the cause of other developing countries to lead an African renewal. His vision also included concerns for institutional accountability and democratic governance along with a neoliberal version of economic growth. And, as with Mandela, Mbeki led through multilateral institutions. The moral crusade on behalf of human rights that was central to Mandela's vision of South Africa largely fell to the wayside under Mbeki (see Barber 2005). The call for South Africa's leadership of the African Renaissance also failed to resonate across Africa, though Mbeki was influential in shaping the transition from the OAU to the African Union, including its good-governance policies (Evans 1999; Alden and le Pere 2004: 290).

Nel, Taylor, and Van der Westhuizen (2000; 2001: 16–18) suggest that under Mbeki, South Africa had aspired to or perhaps achieved a *middle power* role, like that occupied by Canada and Sweden. Barber (2005: 1091) notes that Mbeki began to pursue a *peacekeeper* role by providing troops to both UN and African Union peace missions, which is often a hallmark of middle powers. The *peacekeeper* and *peacemaker* roles have been found to vary in practice compared to the rhetoric with which they are advocated (Williams 2000a). Others suggested that South Africa was still largely a *semiperipheral state* whose influence was limited to being a benevolent *regional hegemon* or having at most some sway in continental affairs (McGowan and Ahwireng-Obeng 1998: 165–95; Klotz 2000). This scholarly ambiguity rests to a large degree on the expectations-capability gap that frequently plagues post-apartheid South Africa. As Alden and le Pere (2004: 289–90) note, South Africa has had difficulty managing conflicts in its own region, including the postwar reconstruction of Angola and the ongoing problems in Congo, Burundi, and Zimbabwe. South Africa's promotion of democracy (and, to a lesser extent, human rights), plus its own legacy of intervening to purposefully destabilize the region, leads others to be skeptical of its attempts at regional conflict management.

Alden and Vieira (2005: 1084) also note the paradox of South African economic and military dominance plus soft power in the form of culture and ideas that fails to translate into effective leadership of the region. This calls into question whether South Africa can effectively enact a *middle power* role. Bischoff (2003) suggests that in terms of industrial and military predominance, there is no question that South Africa is a middle power. What makes the controversy it whether it exercises influence, defined as "a level of diplomatic activity associated with a general degree of resourcefulness" (183). After reviewing the array of internal and external sources of ambiguity over the latter, Bischoff ultimately argues that South Africa qualifies "albeit more tenuously" for the middle power role (184). Its advocacy of the New Partnership for Africa's Development (NEPAD) places South Africa in a *mediator* role between the North and South to pursue economic development consistent with neoliberal principles. Landsberg (2005) concurs that despite its internal problems, South Africa has been able to "punch above its weight" for more than a decade after apartheid as a *middle power*. Leith and Pretorius (2009) similarly suggest that South Africa has been "punching above its weight" by playing the *middle power* role in the nuclear nonproliferation regime since 1994.

While some view pursuing a *middle power* role in a positive light, others see this as simply serving as a *regional hegemon* or more negatively as a *sub-imperialist* role designed to support the U.S. and other Western powers' interests in Africa (Bond 2004). McKinley (2004) specifically views South African foreign policy toward Zimbabwe under Mbeki as the continued enactment of a *sub-imperialist* role. Bond (2013) develops the argument further, suggesting that South Africa has played a deputy sheriff role throughout its history so that the dominant capitalist economic model prevails. This was true prior to apartheid and remains true even now that South Africa has joined the BRICS. Westhuizen (1998) argues that South Africa has emerged as a *middle power* but that it acts in its own interests, not those of the larger regional or international community, as is often imputed to middle powers. Hammill and Lee (2001) suggest that the paradox is that South Africa has been more successful at positioning itself as the kind of good international citizen expected of *middle powers* at the global level and much less successful at the regional and subregional levels. Schoeman (2000) and Serrão and Bischoff (2009) suggest that South Africa is an *emerging middle power*, recognizing a state that is emerging as a regional power with qualities and attributes that overlap with major powers at the global level as well. This particular role may itself be responsible for the perceived incoherence and inconsistency in South African foreign policy, since it the role addresses so many different audiences.

According to Alden and Soko (2005), whether South Africa was a benevolent hegemon or an exploitive power on the African continent had become a common question by the mid-2000s. They suggest that South Africa's economic and political dominance did not extend beyond its hinterland as a *regional hegemon*. South Africa and its homegrown multinational corporations had become a springboard for development in Africa in the 2000s, consistent with Mbeki's push for neoliberal economic reforms and export-oriented growth. Mbeki's "butterfly strategy" for South-South cooperation has South Africa at the head of the butterfly, with the wings stretching from Africa to North and South America and East Asia through a variety of trade agreements. As a *regional developer*, South Africa will also be at the head of regional integration and development. South Africa urged a revision of the South African Customs Union (SACU), which had previously placed it in the role of *colonizer* (1910–94) vis-à-vis Botswana, Lesotho, Namibia, and Swaziland. Instead, South Africa would become a *regional leader* of a more democratically organized multilateral institution committed to regional development. South Africa similarly pushed for a the transformation of the SADC of fourteen states in south-central Africa and along the Indian Ocean to produce opportunities for a more balanced economic cooperation and integration, though it appears that regional integration remained skewed toward South African dominance. In sum, Alden and Soko (2005: 379) suggest that South Africa's *regional hegemon* role has still not been translated into a *regional leader* role despite its ambitions and that an *African hegemon* role has also not occurred. Cooper (1998: 716) confirms that regardless of whether South Africa is a hegemon or leader, the pursuit of economic benefits is one of the driving factors behind South African foreign policy.

Ironically, Mbeki has often adopted the *anti-imperialist* role with regard to Britain's and other Western powers' perceived interference in African affairs. As part of his sense of African unity, he has strongly opposed

Western attacks on Mugabe in Zimbabwe. Since Zimbabwe is an African problem and South Africa is an *African state*, South Africa and others in the region should bear responsibility for resolving the issues with Mugabe (Lipton 2009: 337). Mbeki invoked the example of Mandela's "bullying" of Nigeria as the wrong way for Africans to deal with Africa's problems. Thus, when outsiders push for democracy and human rights, Mbeki often invokes *anti-imperialist* or *African state* roles (Barber 2005: 1095).[2] According to Neethling (2012), Zuma has continued that *anti-imperialist* role, specifically with regard to the UN-authorized actions in Libya in 2011 and the Arab Spring uprisings in Egypt. Sidiropoulos (2008) notes the *anti-imperial role* in Zuma's agenda as well as the reinforcement of *regional developer, peacemaker, peacekeeper, regional ally,* and other roles established in the post-apartheid era.

In an essay specifically devoted to identifying South African national role conceptions in operation since 1994, Landsberg and Monyae (2006) identify *example setter, mediator-integrator, regional subsystem collaborator, developer, regional protector, diplomat, peacemaker, facilitator, honest broker, bridge builder, active multilateralist,* and *faithful ally* as major roles defining the foreign policy of the country. The *example setter* role emerged quickly, as the Mandela government stressed the importance of democracy, human rights, and equality in foreign policy. This is a slightly less active version of the role than the *moral crusader* or *defender of the faith* roles identified by Alden and le Pere (2004). South Africa saw itself in various roles as a *mediator-integrator, regional sub-system collaborator,* and *developer* as it sought to restructure the SADC and promote regional integration and development, particularly under Mbeki. Indeed, the promotion of wealth and security (i.e., the *developer* and *regional protector* roles) has been essential to foreign policy (Selebi 1999; Williams 2000b).

The *diplomat* role emerged under Mandela and saw South Africa attempt to broker peace deals throughout Africa, leading Landsberg and Monyae (2006: 136) to also consider the roles of *peacemaker, facilitator,* and *honest broker* for South Africa. Selebi (1999) confirms that the diplomat role as central to many of the other roles South Africa wishes to play in the region. Southall (2006) similarly confirms the *peacemaker* and *peacekeeper* roles in a review of critical cases of South African diplomacy on the continent. The *bridge builder* role refers to South Africa's attempt to develop both South-South and North-South partnerships, particularly under Mbeki. The South-South partnerships were often targeted at specific countries—Egypt, Brazil, India, China, and Nigeria—as well as through multilateral forums like the Non-Aligned Movement. Mandela eagerly pursued the *active multilateralist* role as he sought to rejoin many of the international institutions from which South Africa was excluded during the apartheid period. Mbeki carried it forward as he sought to reform SADC and engage with the African Union and other international institutions. Finally, South Africa has pursued a *faithful ally* role with its African partners, being especially sensitive to accusations that it is really playing a *hegemonic* or *sub-imperialist* role (Landsberg and Monyae 2006: 141).[3]

This literature constantly debates what the master status or master role is for South Africa. Richard Haas (2008) identifies South Africa as a *regional power*. Habib (2009: 150) suggests that those who have described South Africa as a *pivotal state* or *regional hegemon* often conflate those terms with *hegemon*. According to Habib and Selinyane (2006: 177), "Every hegemon is a pivotal state. But it has to be more." In their understanding, hegemons must have military, economic, and other resources plus a vision for their region and the political willingness to lead. Habib and Selinyane (2006: 179) also advocate a kind of benevolent or consensual hegemon in which "a hegemon should be prepared to compromise its own dominance in respect of market share, balance of trade, and military overlordship should that be in the interests of fulfilling this vision." More important, Habib (2009: 150) suggests that South Africa began playing this role in the late 2000s, even if it did so somewhat timidly or on occasion was forced to do so by circumstance. Schoeman (2000: 49) also suggests overlap in the pivotal state, regional power (or even regional great power), and middle power roles on the way to emergence as a major power. Schraeder (2001: 230) states that South Africa is commonly considered a *regional superpower* (drawing on language used by Botha and others), adding to the somewhat confusing repertoire of roles that delineate South Africa's position vis-à-vis the regional and international systems. This mixture of roles also reflects Van Aardt's (2004) suggestion that South Africa occupies a *middle power* role globally and a *great power* role continentally.

In his analysis of the IBSA states, Stephen (2012: 293) suggests that South Africa has dual roles as a *regional power* and a *rising power*. He argues against considering South Africa or any of the other rising powers in this group as middle powers. He is skeptical that South Africa can aspire to a global power role and believes that it will instead play a regional power role with strong global diplomacy. Such rising powers may at times engage in spoiling or balancing or may be co-opted into international institutions.

Table 8.1 summarizes this narrative history of South African NRCs. The

South African role set exhibited a fair amount of consistency from independence through the beginning of the 1960s. This is not entirely surprising, given both its reduced ability to conduct foreign policy prior to the Statute of Westminster in 1931 and the fact that the main objective of South African foreign policy was to maintain the apartheid system and conduct the "diplomacy of isolation." More activity is observed after the Republic of South Africa was created in 1961 amid the massive decolonization occurring throughout Africa and the developing world. This increase in activity is also reflected in table 8.2. For South African governments intent on maintaining the apartheid system and a political and economic system in line with the capitalist West, the new black African Marxist revolutionary movements posed a great deal of threat. This led to innovations in both economic and security roles, and South Africa attempted to secure itself physically from attack and export its approach to capitalism with itself as a leader of development in the southern African region. Of course, the major break is the end of apartheid. This dramatic change led to a wholesale for-

Table 8.1. South Africa's Role Sets

1910s	*colonizer, regional hegemon*
1920s	*colonizer, regional hegemon*
1930s	*colonizer, regional hegemon*
1940s	*colonizer, regional hegemon*
1950s	*colonizer, regional hegemon*
1960s	*colonizer, patron, regional hegemon, international pariah, regional ally, regional leader, defender of the faith, regional subsystem collaborator, isolate, deputy sheriff*
1970s	*colonizer, patron, regional hegemon, international pariah, regional ally, regional developer, pivotal state, regional power, nuclear weapons state, deputy sheriff*
1980s	*colonizer, regional hegemon, international pariah, regional power, regional superpower, African state, regional developer, nuclear weapons state, deputy sheriff*
1990s	*African state, regional hegemon, defender of the faith, moral crusader, internal developer, regional developer, pivotal state, developing country, leader of the African continent, middle power, semi-peripheral state, regional leader, example setter, mediator-integrator, regional sub-system collaborator, developer, regional protector, diplomat, peacemaker, facilitator, honest broker, bridge builder, active multilateralist, faithful ally, deputy sheriff*
2000s	*African state, regional hegemon, regional superpower, regional developer, leader of the African continent, African hegemon, African great power, middle power, emerging middle power, regional leader, peacekeeper, anti-imperialist, sub-imperialist, regional power, developmental state, example setter, mediator-integrator, regional sub-system collaborator, developer, regional protector, diplomat, peacemaker, facilitator, honest broker, bridge builder, active multilateralist, faithful ally, rising power, deputy sheriff*

Table 8.2. Active-Passive Dimensions of South Africa's Role Sets

Decade	Number of Roles	Overall Activity	Low	High	Mean
1930s	2	10	5	5	5
1940s	2	10	5	5	5
1950s	2	10	5	5	5
1960s	10	33	0	5	3.3
1970s	10	36	0	5	3.6
1980s	9	29	0	5	3.2
1990s	26	72	0	5	2.8
2000s	29	100	0	5	3.4

eign policy reorientation that often appears incoherent or inconsistent. What is clear is that there has been a constant discussion of South Africa as regional power of some sort in earnest since the 1970s (and even before, by default), and this discussion continues through the post-apartheid period, even as the means of enacting the regional power role change. The debate about South Africa's position leads us to conclude that it is a kind of middle power—a regional power at home with the ability to punch above its weight globally. It does not seem like a likely candidate for major power or global power status.

Thus, we see two potential breaks, or foreign policy reorientations, in South African foreign policy role sets, once with the creation of the Republic of South Africa in 1961 and a second with the end of apartheid circa 1994. This pattern is observable with regard to the activity level associated with the role sets, as the number of roles and overall activity jump dramatically in the 1960s and again in the 1990s, though the average level of activity associated with the roles stays fairly constant in the post-1960 era. These foreign policy reorientations do not appear to be correlated with major changes in material power for South Africa. At least the second shock is more consistent with a structural model that considers both material and ideational power co-acting with agent behavior.

Militarized Interstate Disputes and South African Conflict Behavior

We explore South Africa's militarized conflict behavior over the 1950–2007 period using Poisson change-point models. If structural theories of international relations are correct, we should observe that economic growth and increases in South Africa's relative material power are associated with increases in conflict behavior. If our foreign policy approach is on target, we would expect little in the way of structural breaks in militarized or economic conflict behavior, outside of dramatic domestic reorganization (such as the end of apartheid).

Figure 8.1 displays the number of MIDs initiated or ongoing MIDs joined by South Africa between 1950 and 2007. The frequency of South Africa's military involvement appears to have changed little over the period, aside from a brief spike in the late 1980s. To systematically analyze these data, we estimate the full militarized conflict model outlined in chapter 3. We treat sub-Saharan Africa as South Africa's relevant region of analysis.[4] Neither world war is included in the model because GDP data for South Africa are only available after 1950.[5]

Table 8.3 reports the logged Bayes Factor comparisons of the marginal likelihood for each model. The model with the best fit to the data is model M_0, with zero change-points. Using Jeffrey's (1961) criterion, however, we cannot definitively separate models M_0 and M_1. That is, there is not enough evidence to state whether a model with no change-points or a model with one change-point has a better fit to the observed data. Therefore, we report the results from each model. Both M_0 and M_1 are "decisively" better fits to the observed data than models with two or more change-points.

We now identify the timing of the change-point according to M_1. Figure 8.2 displays the posterior probabilities for each temporal regime and the probability of a change-point during each year from 1950 to 2007. The top

Table 8.3. Comparison of Poisson Change-Point Models of South Africa's Militarized Conflict Behavior

	M_0	M_1	M_2	M_3	M_4	M_5
M_0	0	1.73	9.54	15.63	19.14	25.16
M_1	−1.73	0	7.82	13.91	17.42	23.43
M_2	−9.54	−7.82	0	6.09	9.6	15.62
M_3	−15.63	−13.91	−6.09	0	3.51	9.53
M_4	−19.14	−17.42	−9.6	−3.51	0	6.02
M_5	−25.16	−23.43	−15.62	−9.53	−6.02	0

Note: $\ln(BF_{ij} = m[y|M_i]/m[y|M_j])$ where BF_{ij} is the Bayes Factor comparing model M_i to a baseline model M_j, $m(y|M_i)$ is the marginal likelihood under model M_i, $(y|M_j)$ is the marginal likelihood under model M_j. Columns are M_i and rows are M_j. MCMC chains are run 20,000 times after discarding 10,000 burn-in draws.

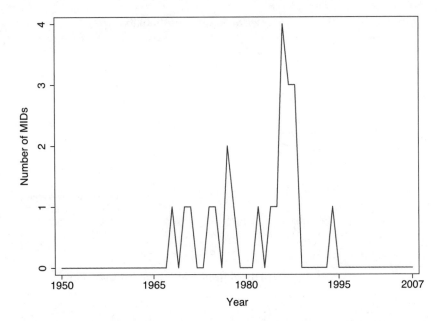

Fig. 8.1. Military Dispute Initiations and Interventions by South Africa, 1950–2007

of figure 8.2 concerns the posterior density for each temporal regime. The bar graph at the bottom of figure 8.2 reports the posterior probability densities of the change-point for each year.

Figure 8.2 indicates that the change-point occurred just prior to the formation of the Republic of South Africa, with a modal probability in 1957 and a median probability in 1960. The 95 percent probability interval, however, ranges from 1957 to 1967. The break appears to be rather gradual as, aside from the modal probability, the probabilities are rather flat over the 95 percent probability interval. The local means between the pre- and post-1960 periods are 0 and 0.489, respectively, suggesting a slightly more active foreign policy in the later era.

Table 8.4 displays the posterior parameter estimates of each endogenous variable for two models: one with no change-points and one with one change-point. The model without a change-point shows that both *Proportion of Democracies* and *Trade* are significant. *Proportion of Democracies* has a negative coefficient with greater than 95 percent confidence, while *Trade* is positive with greater than 95 percent confidence. That is, increases in the number of democracies has a pacifying effect on South African militarized

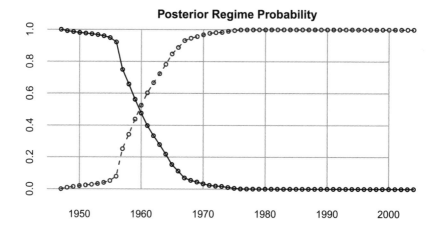

Fig. 8.2. Identifying Structural Breaks in South Africa's Militarized Conflict Behavior, 1950–2007. (*Note:* Expected modal change-point: 1960. Local means for each time regime: 0 and 0.489 militarized disputes.)

conflict, while increasing trade is associated with an *increase* in militarized conflict. *Power Ratio* appears to have no effect on militarized conflict behavior, as the mean value is within one standard deviation of 0. The model with one change-point produces similar results in the second temporal regime, but no explanatory variable is significant in the first temporal regime.

The quantitative results provide no support for structural theories. *Power Ratio* is not significant in either model. The quantitative results do identify one possible break, but *Power Ratio* is not significant in either temporal regime. In contrast, the timing of the structural break coincides with the onset of the Republic of South Africa, consistent with a foreign policy account.

South Africa Economic Conflict Behavior

We now quantitatively analyze South Africa's economic conflict behavior from 1950 to 2007. South Africa has the unique status of holding the *international pariah* role in response to its practice of apartheid. This is especially relevant in terms of economic conflict, as South Africa was the target of several rounds of multilateral economic sanctions that severely isolated the country economically. Despite (or because) of this isolation, South Africa frequently challenged the liberal international economic order (LIEO).

South Africa increased the strength of its capital controls in 1976, 1978, and 1985 in an effort to limit capital flight. The degree of South Africa's capital flight during this period exceeded that of Argentina, Brazil, and the Philippines (Smit and Mocke 1991; Boyce and Ndikumana 2001). South Africa also defaulted on its sovereign debt during major debt crises in 1985 and 1989 and again during the transition from apartheid rule in 1993. Finally, South Africa increased capital controls on foreign investment in 1996.

To explain economic conflict behavior, we estimate six probit change-

Table 8.4. Poisson Estimation of South Africa's Militarized Conflict Initiation with Zero and One Change-Point

No Break	Mean		S.D.	
Power Ratio	0.021		0.034	
Democratic Proportion	−0.189		0.065	
Trade	0.120		0.050	
Constant	−2.902		2.953	
	Pre-1960		Post-1960	
One Break	Mean	S.D.	Mean	S.D.
Power Ratio	−0.045	0.074	0.014	0.037
Democratic Proportion	0.055	1.606	−0.324	0.110
Trade	0.315	1.605	0.075	0.064
Constant	−0.287	3.233	−0.537	3.415

Note: Mean and standard deviation drawn from the posterior distribution. MCMC chains are run 20,000 times after discarding 10,000 burn-in draws. The median posterior probability of a change-point in the one-break model was 1960. Estimates of the posterior for the pre-1960 and post-1960 average over the full state space, accounting for the precision (or imprecision) of the estimated change-point.

point regression models and vary the number of change-points. We select the best-fitting model using Bayes Factor model comparisons using the economic conflict model in chapter 3. The results of the logged marginal likelihood comparisons are displayed in table 8.5. The results suggest that model M_1, with one change-point, has the best fit to the observed data.

Figure 8.3 displays the posterior probability density for each temporal regime (top) and the probability densities of the change-point (bottom) for each year between 1950 and 2007. Figure 8.3 displays a sharp structural break in 1973, with a 95 percent confidence interval between 1971 and 1973. A change-point in the early 1970s is somewhat surprising, given the larger political shocks that South Africa has experienced. The timing of the break, however, does coincide with the Durban strikes. The Durban strikes were the first action that united the working classes and began the movement for equality for the majority black population. These events also drew the attention of the world, leading to a UN resolution condemning the apartheid government and U.S. congressional hearings regarding the role of U.S. firms that interact with the South African government. The underlying rate of economic challenges increased from 0 to 0.188.

Summaries of the posterior parameter estimates for each endogenous variable are reported in table 8.6. During the first temporal regime, *Power Ratio* is negative and significant at the 95 percent level. This means that as South Africa's relative material capabilities increase, it is *less* likely to initiate an economic challenge. None of the other explanatory variables are significant predictors of economic conflict, as one standard deviation around the mean for each variable includes 0. In the second temporal regime, *Power Ratio* is no longer significant. The *Proportion of Democracies* variable, con-

Table 8.5. Comparison of Probit Change-Point Models of South Africa's Economic Conflict Behavior

	M_0	M_1	M_2	M_3	M_4	M_5
M_0	0	−8.15	1.10	2.07	5.31	19.89
M_1	8.15	0	9.25	10.22	13.46	28.04
M_2	−1.10	−9.25	0	0.98	4.21	18.79
M_3	−2.07	−10.22	−0.98	0	3.23	17.81
M_4	−5.31	−13.46	−4.21	−3.23	0	14.58
M_5	−19.89	−28.04	−18.79	−17.81	−14.58	0

Note: $\ln(BF_{ij} = m[y|M_i]/m[y|M_j])$ where BF_{ij} is the Bayes Factor comparing model M_i to a baseline model M_j, $m(y|M_i)$ is the marginal likelihood under model M_i, $(y|M_j)$ is the marginal likelihood under model M_j. Columns are M_i and rows are M_j. MCMC chains are run 20,000 times after discarding 10,000 burn-in draws.

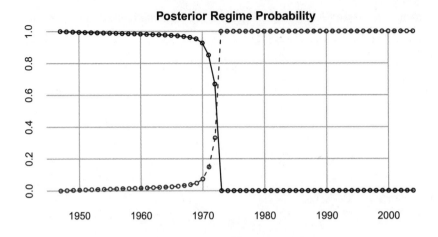

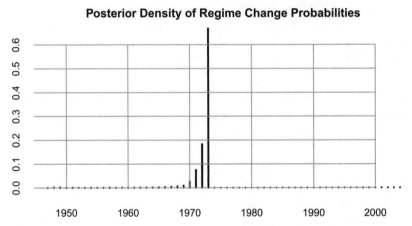

Fig. 8.3. Identifying Structural Breaks in South Africa's Economic Conflict Behavior, 1950–2007. (*Note:* Expected modal change-point: 1973. Local means for each time regime: 0 and 0.188 economic challenges.)

versely, changes from insignificant in the first temporal regime to positive in the second temporal regime with greater than 80 percent confidence. That is, as the number of democracies in sub-Saharan Africa increases, South Africa is more likely to engage in an economic challenge. *Trade* is also significant in the second regime, at the 95 percent level, after being insignificant in the first. The coefficient on *Trade* is negative, indicating that increasing integration with the world economy lowers the probability of an economic challenge.

Table 8.6. Poisson Estimation of South Africa's Economic Conflict Initiation with One Change-Point

	Pre-1973		Post-1973	
	Mean	S.D.	Mean	S.D.
Power Ratio	−0.920	0.406	0.035	0.038
GDP Growth	0.237	2.450	0.083	0.208
Democratic Proportion	0.264	2.628	0.125	0.092
Trade	0.166	3.078	−0.339	0.164
Constant	−0.014	3.172	−0.423	3.130

Note: Mean and standard deviation drawn from the posterior distribution. MCMC chains are run 20,000 times after discarding 10,000 burn-in draws. The median posterior probability of a break in the model was 1973. Estimates of the posterior for the pre-1973 and post-1973 average over the full state space, accounting for the precision (or imprecision) of the estimated change-point.

The quantitative results for economic conflict offer little support for structural theories. The outcome for *Power Ratio* runs in contrast to structural expectations, and the one identified structural break occurs as South Africa's relative power in the region is actually on the decline. In contrast, the structural break coincides with the Durban strikes, an important domestic event that precipitated the beginning of the movement that would eventually end apartheid, and increased scrutiny on the government by foreign powers. This account is more consistent with our foreign policy account.

Conclusion

Ironically, of the five BRICS we have analyzed, South Africa is the least likely candidate for a rising power and the one with the most dramatic changes in identity and conflict behavior. As a new, independent state, South Africa clearly shifted from earlier NRCs to those that would begin to predominate in the postcolonial period. This shift was also reflected in South Africa's militarized conflict. While state identity expressed through NRCs shifted again at the end of apartheid, we did not observe a similar change in militarized conflict behavior. Oddly, the only shift in economic conflict behavior came in 1973—not a time predicted in the foreign policy literature but one that can be explained by reference to the Durban riots. Altogether, this suggests that neither identity nor conflict behavior changed as a result of South Africa's purported rise.

What do we see for South Africa's future? Debate will likely continue about who South Africa is, and the answer will depend on the regional and global context. Is South Africa a regional hegemon or leader? What is its proper region—southern Africa or Africa more generally? Is South Africa an African great power? What is South Africa's role on the global stage—an emerging or rising power, or perhaps a solid, middle power like Canada or South Korea. All of these roles imply some sort of special position for South Africa in the region and the world, though accurately capturing the country's identity may prove difficult. Domestic politics is clearly at play in the articulation of the state's NRCs, as are pressures from abroad. International actors clearly want to socialize South Africa into some type of preeminent role vis-à-vis its neighbors and likely a role that helps facilitate the LIEO and African security. It is unlikely that we will see much in the way of militarized or economic conflict. In fact, increased trade between South Africa and its neighbors seems to facilitate peace. Future efforts at integrating trade in the region should be a force for peace, even though regional partners may view such efforts as subordination.

CHAPTER 9

Conclusion: Toward a Better Understanding of Emerging Powers

Our project in this book was to explore the phenomenon of emerging or rising powers. Much has been made of this phenomenon in recent years. It is hard to escape the analysis of the activities of this group of states by the media, pundits, and policymakers, even as some of these states are more active than others in conducting foreign policy. The analysis of rising powers has also begun to generate a great deal of scholarship. Our goal was to develop an approach to analyze what these states say about themselves in terms of their identity—an answer to the "Who are we?" question—as well as to figure out a way to analyze their conflict behavior. In analyzing words and deeds, we wanted to be particularly sensitive to dramatic changes over time given the way that rising powers are described in both popular and scholarly discourse. The foreign policy revisionism and international conflict associated with the rising powers of the past is well sewn into the fabric of existing international relations theory. But it seemed to us that existing IR theory might not be adequate, with its foundations in structural materialist and decidedly realist approaches.

We developed a theoretical framework that encompasses existing knowledge about material competition in the international system. To this horizontal dimension of politics, we added a vertical dimension by taking into account socialization processes that govern ideational components of interstate interaction, including identity construction. While materialist theories of competition tend to be mechanistic in expecting that rising power produces conflict, our incorporation of ideational factors and socialization adds the possibility that agents influence events. Decisions about political revisionism are, after all, decisions made by agents reacting to and shaping structural forces. We brought together theorizing about structure at the international level, which makes us very interested as a discipline in emerging powers, with theorizing about agents at the foreign policy level, which helps us to understand their actual behavior.

Structural materialist theories that emphasize competition almost always expect that increased power should produce conflict behavior. Rising power should also produce foreign policy orientations and identities that are more aggressive and status-seeking over time to match the growth in power. Our more nuanced approach, which considers both material competition and ideational socialization, suggested that we would be unlikely to see shifts in behavior and identity matching power in any lockstep way. Instead, we suggested that a variety of domestic and international factors may work to shift foreign policy orientations, and dramatic changes in power may not be the only one. If anything, we may see socialization and domestic political processes working to smooth out rough changes, so that identity and behavior appear more evolutionary.

We focused our empirical inquiry on the BRICS. While there are many potential candidates for analysis as rising powers, the BRICS seems to have occupied a special place in the discourse of the media, policymakers, and academics alike. Classification is a critical part of social science, and in this case, we have noted the many problems associated with conceptualizing and operationalizing rising powers. The popular operationalization of emerging powers as the BRICS is a convenient solution, though it may not be entirely analytically defensible. Each of the BRICS is a somewhat problematic fit to the concept of a rising power, but we see this project as the beginning of a more systematic way of analyzing foreign policy change associated with rising powers. Each substantive chapter in this volume has described and analyzed the identities of BRICS states using NRCs as a conceptualization of state identity as well as both militarized and economic conflict behavior. In this final chapter, we draw together this case-by-case analysis to make some comparisons and reach some conclusions about our inquiry into the rising powers phenomenon.

NRCs and Identity

Our theoretical model of state master statuses described in the first chapter and visualized in figure 2.1 demonstrates our expectations for the roles associated with emerging powers. On balance, they should have more achieved than ascribed roles. They should have a growing number of roles compared to minor members of the system. These roles should also be on balance increasingly active compared to passive roles that do not require much involvement or effort in the international system. What do we see across the BRICS?

Most of the roles found in the role sets for the BRICS seem to reflect achievement rather than ascription. By the time states achieve a master status of emerging power, we would expect them to be primarily choosing the roles they wish to occupy. Although this is what we would expect theoretically, it is possible that our methodology of relying on the foreign policy histories of states may bias reported roles to favor those that states seek of their own accord. There are certainly some examples where regional power or regional leader roles are ascribed to states, such as Brazil, though even in this case we find some contention over that role. We also have examples, such as China, where other states are attempting to altercast states into roles. This means that other states attempt to alter the environment or enact their own roles that require the other to adopt a certain role.

Holsti (1970: 284) found support for his hypothesis that "the more active or involved a state is in international or regional affairs, the more national role conceptions its leaders will perceive." He found that all the major powers had five or more NRCs in the time period under consideration (1965–67). The highest number in his sample was eight (United States and United Arab Republic), followed by the USSR and China with seven, and so on. The general numbers of NRCs that we have identified in this book are relatively consistent with those from Holsti's sample in the 1960s. However, all of our states show increases in the number of roles over time to numbers that Holsti might find staggering. Figure 9.1 shows the number of roles in the BRICS role sets over time. A general upward trend is evident, despite some ups and downs for individual states across the 20th century. This is consistent with what we might expect for rising powers that are becoming more involved in the world. Surprisingly, South Africa achieves the highest number of roles at twenty-nine by the 2000s. Equally astonishingly, China has the fewest by the 2000s at nine. If structural materialist theories (and even Holsti's realist-inspired analysis of NRCs) were correct, identities should be a by-product of increased power. More power should produce more roles. This is obviously not the case. In several of our BRICS states, the search for identity is more prominent in times where states may be uncertain of their material capabilities, such as Russia in the 1990s after the end of the Cold War and South

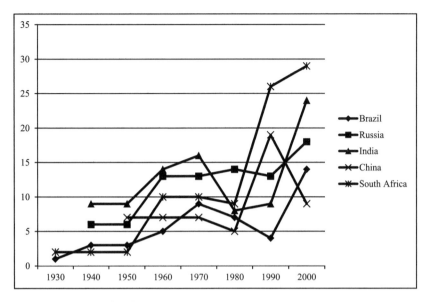

Fig. 9.1. Numbers of Roles across Time

Africa after apartheid. The proliferation of roles may therefore reflect increased domestic contention over the appropriate NRCs to reflect state identity, which our foreign policy orientation would expect.

We also analyzed the activity associated with roles in the role sets of the BRICS. Holsti (1970: 287) used his scale of activity-passivity to rank states, once again finding that the major powers occupy the top group, with the most active overall scores. Activity and passivity refer to the level of commitments and functions in the external environment. Figure 9.2 shows an overall increase in the level of activity of NRCs contained within the BRICS role sets over time, as we would expect of rising powers. More involvement and more complex interactions in the international and regional systems certainly should produce more active roles for rising powers. Yet once again, the overall activity levels do not reflect the distribution of power among such states. South Africa's role set contains the highest overall level of activity by the 2000s, followed by India, Russia, Brazil, and China with the lowest. This is probably not what a purely structural materialist account of international politics (or Holsti's realist-inspired account) would expect.

Holsti suggests further that we might compare such measures of activity and passivity to other kinds of data, such as alliance commitments, patterns

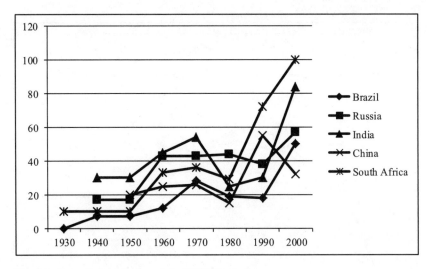

Fig. 9.2. Overall Activity Levels in BRICS Role Sets

of trade, participation in international organizations, and the size of military forces. It is instructive that he suggests a comparison to these kinds of "hard data" in his terms but does not necessarily suggest using them to predict behavior. As we argue earlier in the book, NRCs are patterns of congealed behavior, and using behavior to predict behavior at any one point in time is problematic. If we compare the role set overall activity data with the militarized data displayed in the various figures throughout the substantive chapters, we do not find any obvious correlation. This is reinforced if we move away from the overall level to the median level of activity in the role sets.

We should be careful about putting too much weight on the overall scores for the role sets, since some of them reflect contention and a search for identity that means that not all of the roles are actively enacted at the same time. Instead, it may make more sense to examine the average levels of activity associated with the NRCs in each role set. Figure 9.3 shows that most of the BRICS states have clustered around the midpoint of the scale (3) for most of the 20th century. This suggests that these states are indeed at least moderately active in the international system for most of their histories but have not become dramatically more active on the whole as they move into their purported rising period.

Overall, we do not find that state identity, at least as measured by NRCs,

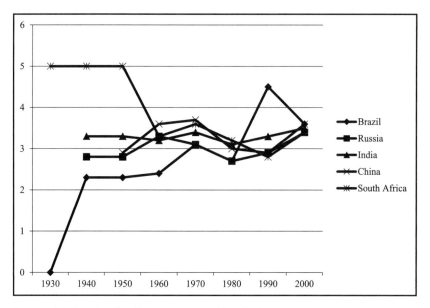

Fig. 9.3. Median Levels of Activity in BRICS Role Sets

moves in lockstep with changes in power. We find a few cases where role sets change in connection with traditional demarcations in the foreign policy histories of states, such as post-apartheid South Africa and post–Cold War Russia. In most cases, we see role sets evolving relatively slowly over time through a process of adding and dropping roles to a core set of beliefs about the identity of a state. Wholesale foreign policy revisionism is rare for most states most of the time, including these rising powers. Most of the discussion of roles for each BRICS state reflects the fact that domestic politics is driving the selection of NRCs. Domestic politics also filters international pressures in the selection of NRCs.

When it comes to considering these states as rising powers, their roles reflect this identity over time. Most of these states are considered regional powers or regional leaders fairly early in the period under consideration here. By the 2000s, most are considering themselves emerging or rising powers, major powers, or even great powers. Is this a result of increased capabilities? In part, but these identities build on earlier identities that reflect preeminence in a region or, in the case of Russia, previous historical great power status.

Militarized and Economic Conflict Behavior

We quantitatively analyzed militarized and economic conflict behavior using a change-point model. The model allows us to estimate parameters as well as examine whether there are structural breaks—or changes in the effect of a variable—related to conflict behavior. If structural theories are correct, we would expect to find that countries experience structural breaks in their behavior consistent with when they identify as an emerging power in the international system. We would also expect that increases in power within a region would be associated with increases in conflict behavior. In contrast, if our foreign policy approach is correct, we would expect a smoother, more evolutionary process of behavior change, or structural breaks that coincide with domestic transformations.

We summarize the results of the change-point models of militarized and economic behavior for each of the BRICS in tables 9.1 and 9.2. Each table reports the number of identified change-points, the year with the modal posterior probability density of the change-point, variables identified as having a significant effect (and their direction), and the net effect of material power. The latter variable is isolated because if structural theories are correct, we would expect to find that increases in material power are positively related to conflict.

Table 9.1 shows that dramatic changes in militarized conflict behavior are rare across the BRICS: only Russia and perhaps South Africa show any

Table 9.1. Summary of Militarized Conflict Behavior Results

Country	# of Change-Points (Timing)	Significant Variables (effect)	Net Effect of Material Power
Brazil	0	Power Ratio (−), Power Ratio Squared (+), Trade (−), World War II (+)	Negative, decreasingly in strength
Russia	1 (1936)	1st regime: Trade (−), World War I (+) 2nd regime: Trade (−), Proportion Democratic (+)	None
India	0		None
China	0	Power Ratio Squared (−), Neighbor Conflict (+), Proportion Democratic (+), Trade (−), World War I (+)	Negative
South Africa	0/1 (1957)	Proportion Democratic (−), Trade (+)	None

evidence of undergoing a structural break in their underlying militarized conflict behavior. Moreover, the timing of the change-points appears to be more closely associated with domestic factors than changes related to either state's role as an emerging power. Russia experienced a change-point in 1936, but this is more likely attributed to the lasting policy legacy of Stalin following his consolidation of power (the Great Purge) rather than a change in the USSR's place in the international order. South Africa may have also experienced a structural break—we were unable to definitively select between models with zero or one change-point—but the timing of the break is more likely attributed to the formation of the Republic of South Africa and a truly independent foreign policy from Great Britain than to South Africa's status as an emerging power. In contrast, Brazil, India, and China did not experience structural breaks in their militarized conflict behavior.

Moreover, there is little evidence that increases in material capabilities are, on their own, associated with more assertive foreign policies. In the two cases (Brazil and China) where *Power Ratio* is a significant predictor of conflict, it exerts a *negative* effect. In the other three cases, *Power Ratio* does not appear to be significantly related to conflict. Taken together, these results suggest that structural theories do a poor job of accounting for the militarized conflict behavior of emerging powers. Instead, the relative stability of foreign policy behavior, with changes emerging from domestic transformations, indicates that our foreign policy theoretic approach provides greater explanatory power.

Table 9.2 demonstrates that BRICS experience far greater volatility in their economic conflict behavior than in their militarized conflict behavior. Brazil, for example, experienced two change-points in economic conflict behavior during the 1980s. Russia appears to have had a structural break in 1991, while South African economic policy changed in 1973. Neither China nor India, however, experienced a change in their underlying foreign policy process. While both experience tremendous changes in the level of trade and economic engagement with the rest of the world between 1960 and the present, the effect associated with each incremental increase does not appear to have changed.

The change-points associated with Brazil occur during the 1980s, hardly a time of growing Brazilian power. Rather, the 1980s were a time of financial crisis, and Brazil underwent dramatic domestic upheaval, transitioning from military rule to democratic governance. Similarly, Russian economic conflictual behavior changed at the end of the Cold War, an event driven primarily by dramatic domestic change and a period of uncertainty regarding its future international roles rather than a period of growing economic strength. Finally, the change-point in South Africa occurred at a point of relative stability in terms of international economic strength but coincided with domestic events such as the Durban strikes.

In addition, we find that *Power Ratio* appears to exert either no influence or a negative influence on economic conflict behavior in the BRICS. In Brazil, Russia, and China, *Power Ratio* has no effect on economic conflict. In India, increases in *Power Ratio* are associated with a pacifying effect on economic conflict. Finally, *Power Ratio* has a negative influence on South African economic conflict behavior in the first temporal regime, but has no significant effect on economic conflict behavior in the second temporal regime. In sum, increases in material power apparently do not make emerging powers more conflictual in their economic behavior. This result runs in contrast to the expectation of structural theories of international relations. Instead, domestic factors seem to provide a better explanation of changes in economic conflict behavior, consistent with foreign policy theories.

If changes in international material power do not explain militarized and economic conflict behavior, what does? And what does this tell us about future conflict? In terms of military behavior, it seems that even emerging powers have relatively stable conflict predictors, as there are few identified change-points. Three of the variables appeared to be significant predictors of militarized conflict in the case of more than one state: *Trade*, *Proportion Democratic*, and date of entry into *World War I*. In terms of eco-

Table 9.2. Summary of Economic Conflict Behavior Results

Country	# of Change-Points (Timing)	Significant Variables	Net Effect of Material Power
Brazil	2 (1983, 1984)	1st regime: Trade (−) 2nd regime: Proportion Democratic (+) 3rd regime: Proportion Democratic (−)	None
Russia	1 (1991)	1st regime: Proportion Democratic (−) 2nd regime: Trade (−)	None
India	0	Power Ratio (−), GDP Growth (+), Trade (−)	Negative
China	0		
South Africa	1 (1973)	1st regime: Power Ratio (−) 2nd regime: Democratic Proportion (−), Trade (−)	Negative, then none

nomic conflict behavior, the foreign policies of emerging powers appear to be much more volatile, but this volatility likely stems from domestic changes rather than changes in relative material capabilities.

For Brazil, Russia, and China, *Trade* appears to be exert a significant pacifying effect on militarized conflict behavior. For these states, continued integration into the global economy appears to restrain their behavior, while decreases in the level of integration may make them more belligerent. These results are consistent with the expectations of the capitalist peace literature. In the cases of India and South Africa, however, this explanation does not appear to hold. For India, increased integration into the global economy has no effect on militarized conflict behavior, while for South Africa, increased reliance on trade is associated with an *increase* in militarized conflict.

The *Proportion of Democracies* in a state's neighborhood is associated with increases in militarized conflict for the two states that were autocratic for the largest portion of the years under review, Russia and China. This suggests that both of those states identify distinct policy dissimilarities with neighboring states as they democratize. In contrast, South Africa becomes less likely to engage in militarized conflict as the *Proportion of Democracies* increases around them. Neither Brazil nor India appears to be influenced by their region's degree of democratization.

In terms of future behavior, our results suggest that integrating emerging powers into the global economy is the best way to constrain their militarized conflict. In contrast, democratization of a region may provoke violent responses from autocratic emerging powers. This does not mean, of course, that existing powers should suppress nascent democratization movements in states surrounding emerging powers. A propensity for militarized conflict, however, should not be a surprise, as such movements may be viewed as threats to the influence of emerging powers within their home regions. On balance, trade incentives may be a useful policy tool to offset the potential animosity of an emerging power should its neighbors democratize.

For economic conflict, *Trade* and the *Proportion of Democracies* within a region again are the only variables that appear to exert a significant influence in more than two cases during any temporal regime. In four of the BRICS—Brazil (first regime), Russia (second regime), India, and South Africa (second regime)—*Trade* is associated with a negative and significant impact on economic conflict behavior. That is, increased integration leads to decreases in economic conflict. In the case of China, *Trade* does not appear to exert a significant influence. On balance, it appears that trade at best reduces the likelihood of economic conflict and at worst has no effect on economic conflict for emerging powers.

The effect of the *Proportion of Democracies* in an emerging power's region has more mixed results. The coefficient for *Proportion of Democracies* in Brazil, for example, changes from insignificant in the first regime (1929–83), positive in the second regime (1983–84), and negative in the third regime (1984–2007). That is, increases in the number of Brazil's democratic neighbors changes from having no effect to an increase in the likelihood of economic conflict to a decrease in the likelihood of economic conflict. Similar variability is seen in Russia: the coefficient in positive in the first regime (1929–91), and insignificant in the second regime (1991–2007). This means that as the number of democracies increases, Russia is more likely to engage in economic conflict until 1991, after which the proportion of democracies has no impact on its likelihood of economic conflict. South Africa also experiences change in the effect of the *Proportion of Democracies* on its economic conflict behavior, changing from an insignificant effect during the first regime (1950–74) to a negative effect during the second regime (1974–2007). Finally, the *Proportion of Democracies* has an insignificant effect on economic conflict for India and China.

In terms of future expectations, it appears that integration in the global economy decreases or at worst has no effect on an emerging power's propensity for economic conflict. Taken together with the similar results for militarized conflict, it seems that economic engagement is the best policy tool to reduce the potential for observed conflict of any kind with emerging powers. This does not mean, of course, that there will be no tension between emerging powers and existing great powers. Rather, instances of observed conflict seem less likely when states are closely linked through the international economy.

Our theory and modeling techniques identify factors that influence conflict behavior and permit these to change over time. This means that within a given temporal regime, we can predict expected conflict behavior. The theory and modeling techniques do not, however, necessarily tell us *when* change-points will take place and *when* the effect of predictors will change. That is, our theory provides less insight for predicting when change-points will occur than for identifying such changes. Yet our model does help us rule out changes in relative material capabilities as a key cause of changes in foreign policy behavior; rather, it points to domestic factors as the primary drivers of change-points and their accompanying foreign policy reorientations. This alone is a significant theoretical advancement, as it points to agency rather than merely structure as a significant factor in the behavior of emerging states. For scholars and policymakers, this means that increases in power capabilities do not necessarily lead to more assertive foreign policies; that the actions of states are not deterministic, as structural accounts of rising powers imply; and that foreign policy tools can be used to ensure peaceful relations between major and emerging powers in both the security and economic dimensions.

Theoretical and Methodological Challenges

Preexisting IR theory is somewhat inadequate in explaining the current crop of rising powers. Most of the structural realist theories of great power turnover and war are probably best left to the explanation of the historical cases for which they were created. The main drawback to these theories was an almost complete focus on material competition in the international system. This zero-sum competition when applied to the rise and fall of great powers leads rather quickly to an expectation that all rising powers are a potential threat to system stability, with an almost exclusive focus on security and war. In the 1990s, we had the Japan threat in the U.S. policy discourse, because everyone assumed that Japan was a rising power that would challenge U.S. hegemony in a major war (notwithstanding the constitutional restrictions on Japanese military involvement at the time). Yet primarily for domestic political and economic reasons, that challenge never materialized. By the 2000s, U.S. pundits had moved on to the China threat, also assuming that increased power would compel China to engage in a hostile bid for global leadership. We are equally skeptical that this challenge will match existing structural materialist theories' expectations for the future.

We believe that the current international system now has a thicker social aspect that means that we can talk about socialization pressures on states in addition to traditional concerns about competition. Socialization is not a new feature of the international system (see, e.g., Thies 2013), but the transformation of the system in the post–World War II era means that there are more avenues for socialization to occur via international organizations (governmental and nongovernmental), interactions between state and nonstate actors, and the ever-present global media (Keohane and Nye 1977; Mansbach and Vasquez 1981; Rosenau 1990). We revisited some earlier work on the interaction of socialization and competition to generate some theoretical expectations about an emerging or rising power master status. This model also expected that role transitions could be associated with conflict.

The problem with this theoretical framework is that while it helps us to understand identities and behaviors associated with rising powers, it has the opposite problem of the older structural materialist theories. Those theories predicted that conflict (and associated identity change) would come at some point, though not all gave very specific predictions about when. Our theoretical framework expected more evolutionary change, though we cannot rule out that dramatic changes may occur and we cannot predict exactly when they would. We think what we have observed thus far with rising powers is more consistent with our theoretical approach, but structural materialist theories may not yet have had their day in the sun— that is, power shifts have not yet been dramatic enough to cause a structural break in behavior and identities.

We may also be looking at the wrong states. We adopted the BRICS group as our operationalization of the rising powers concept because it is so familiar now in popular and scholarly circles. But it is an odd collection of states that in many ways contains more differences than similarities. Even on strictly military capabilities, Russia's power has declined precipitously in both absolute and relative terms since the end of the Cold War according to standard measures. It might make more sense to interpret Russia's behavior in recent years through the older argument about imperial overstretch rather than through the rising powers frame of reference (Kennedy 1987). China dwarfs the rest of these states economically, though even its unparalleled economic growth has suffered recently with stock market volatility and the government's seeming inability to manage the economy. South Africa has seen virtually no change in its capabilities over time and is increasingly losing the stage it had as a moral leader under the initial post-apartheid presidency. What about Germany and Japan? Germany is increasingly called on to lead the European Union through the Greek crisis and now the refugee crisis emanating from the Syrian civil war. Japan has recently revised its constitution to allow for the overseas deployment of military personnel for collective self-defense. Both have more capabilities according to standard measures than France or the United Kingdom, each of which continue to act militarily and diplomatically as if they are great powers in accordance with their victor status at the end of World War II. Both Germany and Japan are large economies with functional militaries, but are not often discussed as great powers as a consequence of their histories.

Our choice to focus on the foreign policy histories of states as documented by scholars may also introduce problems in the analysis. Though none of these problems are crippling, as chapter 3 discusses, there are known drawbacks to this approach. Future research might employ one of the alternatives, such as coding leader speeches or newspaper articles for roles as a comparison to our secondary source materials method. Our Bayesian change-point modeling approach is also ideal for identifying structural breaks in a data-generating process, but we must still identify the variables that we believe predict behavior generally. Given that we are predicting counts of militarized and economic conflict using a monadic approach, we were relying on our own judgment, since standard models usually look solely at onset or incidence of conflict within a dyadic framework. Future work may refine the statistical approach to modeling such conflict for the BRICS.

We have also demonstrated that identities and behavior are not directly related to each other. We conceptualized our NRCs as congealed behavior. Roles reflect both structural positions and the kinds of actor it is possible to be in a society. Thus, roles are largely functional and are related to routine behavioral expectations. Yet comparisons of our role sets for the numbers of roles, overall role activity, and even average level of NRC activity do not appear to correlate with periods of increased militarized or economic conflict. More work needs to be done to examine the connection between identity and behavior, but our findings call into question the knee-jerk constructivist IR belief that behavior is endogenous to identity. Our multimethod approach incorporating qualitative and quantitative analysis is a first step toward better grasping this relationship, but future work may uncover better combinations of methods to get at the same problem.

While we are cognizant of the inherent limitations of any research design, including our own, we believe that our combination of theory and methods has allowed us to assess whether the BRICS are likely to engage in foreign policy revisionism leading to economic and militarized conflict behavior. Our tentative answer is no, at least not in what we see in terms of identities and behavior thus far. While some notable changes have occurred in identities and behaviors for the BRICS, there appears to be nothing particularly noteworthy associated with the period captured by the designation

rising power. The BRICS may continue their development bank and summits, and scholars, policymakers, and pundits may continue to refer to
them as rising powers, but we have shown that generally speaking, there is
no reason to fear them as a group. Individual BRICS certainly may begin to
act as they think a rising power or great power should act, but this may be
mostly symbolic. Indeed, Goldman Sachs, the same firm responsible for the
BRIC acronym, announced in November 2015 that it was closing its BRIC
fund, which had lost 88 percent of its assets since its 2010 peak (a decline
from $842 million to $98 million). For the foreseeable future, both the architecture of international security and the LIEO are still dominated by the
United States and its supporters. Violations of the economic and security
order will be sanctioned, such as Russia over its involvement in Ukraine,
but direct conflict with the United States seems unlikely. Instead, accommodation through changes in the economic and security order are likely,
leading many (but not all) of these purported potential revisionist powers
to become satisfied status quo regional or great powers.

NOTES

Chapter 1

1. See Carranza 2016 for a nice review of the material and ideational component of joining the "great power club" according to the main international relations theories. This piece also includes a good discussion of whether nuclear weapons are an important part of becoming a great power, a question that recurs in several of our substantive chapters: all of the BRICS pursued such weapons at some point, although Brazil and South Africa have renounced their programs.

2. But see also Hurrell's (2013: 220) important critique, which describes the development of the idea of emerging powers against the backdrop of modernization theory and great power politics—what he terms as the "bricolage . . . that has been taking place within each of the emerging states and through which old and new ideas and policies are melded together in ways that are working against these states becoming simply absorbable within some expanded version of a liberal Greater West." Wansleben's (2013) genealogy shows how the BRIC concept was created to encourage investment in large emerging economies that provided safe, long-term returns.

3. Realists like Schweller (2011) suggest that while these emerging powers may have come of age in a pacific time (as a consequence of many of the liberal factors noted earlier), they will return to a state of conflict in the future. He notes that emerging powers are often seen as spoilers, supporters, or shirkers. Spoilers produce great power conflict, supporters produce great power concert, and emerging powers that play all three roles, including shirkers, produce what he calls "time's entropy"—a dysfunctional world on autopilot that leads to an erosion of international order that must eventually be resolved through war.

Chapter 2

1. This is reflected in the Routledge book series Role Theory and International Relations, which has already published Walker, Malici, and Shafer 2010; Thies 2013; Walker 2013; Below 2014; Harnisch, Bersick, and Gottwald 2015.

2. Parts of this chapter are reproduced from Thies 2015a.

3. On a global sample of states from 1960 to 1999, Thies, Chyzh, and Nieman (2016) find support for each of these mechanisms as applied to state-building efforts.

4. Holsti (1970: 286) develops a scale of activity-passivity in national role conceptions that ranges from 0 to 5 (low to high). At the high end, scoring 5, are the roles of bastion of revolution-liberator, regional leader, regional protector and defender of the peace. Scoring 4 are the roles of active independent, liberator supporter, anti-imperialist agent, balancer, and antirevisionist/Zionist/communist agent. Scoring 3 are the roles of defender of the faith, mediator-integrator, regional-subsystem collaborator, and developer. Scoring 2 are the roles of faithful ally and independent. Scoring 1 are the roles of bridge and example. Finally, scoring 0 are the roles of internal developer, isolate, and protectee. This scale will be used to indicate which role conceptions require a greater deal of foreign policy activity in a given time period.

5. See Thies 2003 on the confusion between socialization as process versus socialization as outcome that often pervades the literature.

6. The literature on status attribution (Larson and Shevchenko 2010; Volgy et al. 2011; Paul, Larson, and Wohlforth 2014) does not problematize status in the same way. Rather, it simply assumes states crave higher-level status and explores the dynamics that unfold as a result. This literature tends to ignore the auxiliary roles to which we look for evidence of changes in identity and conflict/cooperative propensities.

7. Cf. Larson and Shevchenko's (2010) strategies of social mobility, social competition, and social creativity in dealing with status inconsistency.

8. We assume that a repertoire of roles, or role set, is equivalent to a state's identity. Wendt (1999) describes four levels of identity: personal or corporate, type, role, and collective. Corporate identities are presocial and represent the intrinsic features of an agent that give it actorness over space and time. Type identities represent categories into which actors might be sorted based on shared characteristics. Roles are the types of actors it is possible to be or positions within a social hierarchy. Roles are differentiated from types in that every role requires a counterrole; thus, roles are inherently social. Collective identities involve a merger of ego and alter. We argue that the role set is a reasonable representation of state identity. Moreover, roles represent a relational aspect of identity, which ties together nicely with our dyadic analysis of conflict.

Chapter 3

1. This section draws on Thies 2016.

2. In the original scale, those NRCs at the high end scoring 5 are the roles of bastion of revolution-liberator, regional leader, regional protector and defender of the Peace. Scoring 4 are the roles of active independent, liberator supporter, anti-imperialist agent, balancer, and anti-revisionist/Zionist/communist agent. Scoring

3 are the roles of defender of the faith, mediator-integrator, regional-subsystem collaborator, and developer. Scoring 2 are the roles of faithful ally and independent. Scoring 1 are the roles of bridge and example. Finally, scoring 0 are the roles of internal developer, isolate and protectee.

3. This is stated more formally as Bayes's Law, $P(\theta|Data) = (P[\theta]P[Data|\theta]/P[Data])$, where θ is an unknown parameter and $Data$ are the observed data. The posterior probability ($\theta|Data$) is proportional to the product of the prior probability $P(\theta)$ and the likelihood function $P(Data|\theta)$. Since $P(Data)$ has already been observed, it has a probability of 1 and is treated as a normalizing constant (Gill 2009: 17).

Though the underlying epistemological debate between Frequentist and Bayesian practitioners is not the focus here, maximum likelihood inference shares with the Bayesian approach a common interpretation of observed data and parameter estimates (King 1989: 21–30; Kmenta 1997: 178; Gill 1999, 2009). In fact, if the prior probability is assigned a uniform distribution, the results of both maximum likelihood and Bayesian estimation are identical (Gelman and Hill 2007: 392; see also Gill 1999, 2009: 62). If an informed prior is employed, the relative weight of the prior probability on the posterior decreases as the number of observations in the data increases. For an introduction to Bayesian statistics and inference, see Gelman et al. 1995 and Gill 2009.

4. Explanatory variables that exert temporally dependent effects are considered "weakly exogenous." For an in-depth discussion of the different types of exogeneity, see Engle, Henry, and Richards 1983; Granato 1991.

5. The Bayes Factor is used to compare the fit of two models to observed data.

6. See Chib 1998 for a more technical description of the estimator. See Park 2010 for a thorough discussion of the estimator and an application to political science.

7. A nonergodic Markov process does not return to a previous temporal regime (Gill 2006: 415).

8. As opposed to traditional Monte Carlo chains, which are independent draws of a probability distribution, MCMCs generate draws that are mildly dependent (since the next movement of the Markov chain is conditional on its current position). Gill (2009: 343–44) notes that the "basic principle is that once this chain has run sufficiently long enough it will find its way to the desired posterior distribution of interest and we can summarize this distribution by letting the chain wander around, thus producing summary statistics from recorded values." The posterior values for the explanatory variables provided by these summary statistics give point estimates and probability intervals.

9. In the case of a sharp (within a single time period) break that occurred with complete certainty, one could achieve equivalent results by using the time period as a binary variable, interacted with each other variable in the model (assuming, of course, that the timing of the break is precisely known). Unlike the current approach, an interaction with a binary time regime variable would not generate any measures of uncertainty.

10. The number of change-points in the economic equations is dependent on the number of economic conflict events. We estimate five militarized conflict models for India and South Africa because data is available for shorter time frames than for Brazil, Russia, and China: 1947–2007 for India and 1950–2007 for South Africa.

11. We use diffuse, weakly informed priors rather than noninformative, uniformly distributed priors on the parameter estimates to facilitate calculation of marginal likelihoods (Chib 1995).

12. A MID occurs when "the threat, display or use of military force short of war by one member state is explicitly directed towards the government, official representatives, official forces, property, or territory of another state" (Jones, Bremer, and Singer 1996: 168).

13. The posterior sampling distribution of a Poisson with covariates does not adhere to a known conditional distribution. Frühwirth-Schnatter and Wagner (2006) developed a technique taking the logarithm of time between successive events to transform the Poisson regression into linear regression with log exponential (1) errors. See Park 2010 for an application of this technique to U.S. conflict data.

14. While not as readily apparent a challenge to the LIEO as the other two indicators, financial openness is extremely important to the United States (Caprio and Summers 1993; Wade 2002). For example, even in the immediate aftermath of the Mexican peso crisis, the Senate Foreign Relations Committee on South Asia extensively questioned undersecretary of commerce Jeffrey Garten about his failure to open the Indian financial system to U.S. firms (Bhagwati 1998: 11).

15. See Park (2011b) for more detail of this approach with an application to the Bank of England's monetary policy during the interwar period.

16. We focus on changes in policy rather than attempting to identify a priori what level of regulation constitutes a challenge to the LIEO.

17. We do not include *Power Ratio Squared* in the economic conflict model. While a potential target may preemptively change its policies and behavior to avoid militarized interaction with a rising power, given the construction of the economic conflict dependent variable, such actions are implausible. The U.S. government, for example, is unlikely to surrender private U.S. firms to a rising state in an effort to head off an economic challenge.

18. Tomz and Wright (2007, 2010) nevertheless find that poor economic performance is surprisingly weakly related to asset expropriation and sovereign loan default, suggesting that sovereign theft is a political rather than an economic decision (see also Reinhart and Rogoff 2009).

19. Das, Papioannou, and Trebesch (2012) find that debt, on average, makes a state *less* likely to default because of incentives for both creditors and debtors to restructure debt and because of debtors' desire for future credit access.

Chapter 4

1. Vigevani and Oliveira (2007) argue that the Cardoso administration attempted to replace "autonomy through distance" with "autonomy through integration."

2. Lafer (2000: 223) argues that autonomy and development have been the dominant themes in Brazilian foreign policy since the 1930s.

3. See Selcher 1985; Thies 2001b, 2008 for more on the rival role in Latin America.

4. See Ricúpero 1995 for a discussion of Brazilian foreign policy along both the axis of relative equality among partners and the axis of asymmetrical relations that informs Alden and Vieira 2005. Lafer (2000) also draws on these axes to help explain the origins of contemporary Brazilian identity. Burges (2005) suggests that Lula's foreign policy, while demonstrating continuity with the past, also attempted a psychological transformation in its underpinnings demonstrating *auto-estima* (self-confidence) in the pursuit of South-South relationships that overcome traditional North-South dependencies, both economic and psychological.

5. See also Bertazzo 2010 on Brazil's leadership in regional security.

6. See Prys 2010 on the "achievement-expectations gap" in classifying regional powers.

7. Brazil entered World War I in 1917 and World War II in 1942.

8. Country codes between 100 and 200 are treated as "South America." *Power Ratio Squared* is divided by ten to scale the coefficient.

9. We also analyze models that only include Brazil's primary rival, Argentina, in the *Power Ratio* measure. This alternative specification has no significant impact on the results.

10. *Power Ratio Squared* is scaled by 1/10.

11. We do not include GDP Growth in Brazil's economic conflict equation because its inclusion produces fitted probabilities that are numerically 0 or 1.

Chapter 5

1. See Cantir and Kaarbo (2012, 2016) on role contestation within democratic states.

2. See Aksenyonok 2008: 71 on the junior partner role.

3. See Kassianova 2001 for a similar discussion grounded broadly in domestic identity construction; Chafetz 1996 for one grounded in role theory; Light 2003.

4. Thies (2001a, 2013) considers master statuses as roles that are salient in every situation. It is not clear from Thibault and Lévesque (1997) that they intend for these statuses to occupy that position, but they are another form of role nonetheless. As Linton (1936: 113) notes, roles are statuses that are put into action.

5. See Light 2003 for a similar discussion of roles emanating from these major policy statements.

6. The states often seek approval for their roles from Russia, the primary external actor in the region. However, this did not prevent Turkmenistan from adopting the role of permanent neutral in 1994. Kazakhstan and Uzbekistan have forged a rival role relationship since independence. Kazakhstan also seeks Russia's approval in its bid for the regional hegemon role, while that status was granted informally to Uzbekistan during the Soviet era.

7. This means that we compare Russia's relative military capabilities to the entire state system rather than to just one region. Restricting Russia's region to Europe (using country codes 200–399) does not change the substantive results. Nor does comparing Russia's power ratio vis-à-vis its rivals, such as the United States, Germany, Japan, and China.

8. There is a spike of approximately 8% in the probability that the break occurred in 1947.

9. The period was named after the Nikolai Yezhov, head of the secret police.

10. *World War I* and *World War II* are included in both time periods because parameter estimates of the posterior for the pre-1936 and post-1936 average over the full state space, accounting for the precision (or imprecision) of the estimated change-point.

11. Armenia and Kyrgyzstan, for example, are to be compensated by Russia for the penalties they will incur for running afoul of World Trade Organization bylaws after joining the European Economic Union (Matlack 2014).

Chapter 6

1. See Mohan 2009 for a challenge to the "Nehruvian consensus" that there was uniform agreement on Nehru's vision of Indian foreign policy.

2. See Levi 1964 for an analysis of the nonaligned role during the Chinese invasion of India in 1962.

3. We treat all countries with country codes between 700 and 899 as "Asia" for the purposes of calculating the *Power Ratio* measures. We also estimate models where *Power Ratio* is calculated with only India's primary rivals, China and Pakistan. These alternative model specifications produced no substantive changes in the results. *Power Ratio Squared* is divided by 100 to scale the coefficient.

4. Indian troops fought with British forces in both wars, even contributing the largest volunteer army in history to the World War II effort.

Chapter 7

1. See Thies 2010; Harnisch 2011; Thies and Breuning 2012 for recent overviews of foreign policy role theory.

2. See Ng-Quinn 1993 for an application of role theory to China's premodern identity. See Blanchard and Lin 2013 for a review of identity during the 1911 revolution.

3. Altercasting refers to attempting to place a person in a particular role through words and behaviors (Thies 2010).

4. See Shambaugh (2004–5) for a recent overview of Chinese regional engagement strategies.

5. See Thies 2015b for an analysis of the U.S.-Chinese role relationship as regional protector-protectee during the Open Door period at the turn of the 20th century.

6. See Carlson 2011 for a review of the literature on Chinese nationalism and national identity that is careful to point out the dangers of assuming a single, over-arching, coherent Chinese national identity. See Shih and Jiwu 2013 on China's civilizational identity.

7. See Glaser and Medeiros 2007 for an analysis of the origin of the concept of peaceful rise and its replacement with peaceful development.

8. See also Medeiros and Fravel 2003 on the *victim* and *great power* roles.

9. See Paul 2014 for an overview of strategies employed by the United States and other states to manage China's rise, including the umbrella strategy of hedging and its components of diplomatic engagement, soft balancing, and limited hard balancing. This general approach constitutes a wait-and-see take on managing rising powers.

10. China formally entered World War I in 1917 and World War II in 1941.

11. We treat all countries with country codes between 700 and 899 as "Asia." We also estimate models where *Power Ratio* is calculated only with China's rivals, Russia and Japan. These alternative model specifications produced no substantive changes in the results. *Power Ratio Squared* is divided by 100 to scale the coefficient.

12. The model with the second-best fit (with one change-point) predicts a break in 1950, immediately after the Communist Party came to power.

13. We run only three models since there are only two events.

Chapter 8

1. Both the Status of the Union Act (1934) and Royal Executive Functions and Seals Act (1934) confirmed South Africa's status as a sovereign state. See Dugard et al. 2005: 19 for a legal interpretation of South Africa's sovereignty and independence from the United Kingdom.

2. See Cornelissen 2008 for an interesting analysis of South Africa's competition for sports megaevents, such as the 2010 FIFA world football finals, that demonstrates a strong strain of pan-Africanism and their use to elevate the global status of the state as well as to serve domestic political goals. See Ndlovu 2010 for a similar analysis of the use of sports as cultural diplomacy in South Africa.

3. See Nathan 2005 for an overview of the Mandela and Mbeki foreign policies that stresses the same kinds of consistencies despite the often repeated claim that foreign policy was incoherent and inconsistent in both administrations.

4. We treat all countries with country codes between 400 and 599 as "Africa" for the purposes of calculating the *Power Ratio* measure. We do not include a squared term or *Neighbor Conflict*, since doing so produces fitted probabilities that are numerically 0 or 1. There are actually no cases of *Neighbor Conflict* in the data, consistent with the "African Peace" of interstate wars (Lemke 2002: 163–94). Africa differs from other regions in that many states gain independence and enter the international system during the period under review. Our operationalization of power— the Correlates of War project's composite index of national capabilities—is sensitive to state entry (Ray and Singer 1973; Kadera and Sorokin 2004). Given the large

volume of entries, rather than calculating South Africa's share of total power in the sub-Saharan system, we calculate South Africa's average bilateral power share. As was previously the case, the variable ranges from 0 to 1, where .5 is parity and 1 is perfect preponderance.

5. South Africa, technically a dominion with equal status to Britain, entered World War II as a British ally in 1939.

REFERENCES

Abraham, Itty. 2007. The Future of Indian Foreign Policy. *Economic and Political Weekly* 42 (42): 4209–12.

Acharya, Amitav. 2014. Power Shift or Paradigm Shift? China's Rise and Asia's Emerging Security Order. *International Studies Quarterly* 58:158–73.

Aguiar, Mark, and Gita Gopinath. 2006. Defaultable Debt, Interest Rates and the Current Account. *Journal of International Economics* 69 (1): 64–83.

Alden, Chris, and Garth Le Pere. 2004. South Africa's Post-Apartheid Foreign Policy: From Reconciliation to Ambiguity? *Review of African Political Economy* 100:283–97.

Alden, Chris, and Mills Soko. South Africa's Economic Relations with Africa: Hegemony and Its Discontents. *Journal of Modern African Studies* 43 (3): 367–92.

Alden, Chris, and Marco Antonio Vieira. 2005. The New Diplomacy of the South: South Africa, Brazil, India, and Trilateralism. *Third World Quarterly* 26 (7): 1077–95.

Aksenyonok, Alexander. 2008. Paradigm Change in Russian Foreign Policy: The Five-Day War as a Watershed. *Russia in Global Affairs* 6 (4): 66–76.

Alexandroff, Alan S., and Andrew F. Cooper, eds. 2010. *Rising States, Rising Institutions: Challenges for Global Governance*. Baltimore: Brookings Institution Press.

Allen, Vernon L., and Evert Van de Vliert. 1984. A Role Theoretical Perspective on Transitional Processes. In Vernon L. Allen and Evert Van de Vliert, eds., *Role Transitions: Explorations and Explanations*. New York: Plenum.

Anderson, Walter. 2001. Recent Trends in Indian Foreign Policy. *Asian Survey* 41 (5): 765–76.

Apeldoorn, Bastiaan van, Naná de Graaf, and Henk Overbeek. 2012. The Rebound of the Capitalist State: The Rearticulation of the State-Capital Nexus in the Global Crisis. *Globalizations* 9 (4): 467–70.

Appadorai, A. 1960. On Understanding Indian Foreign Policy. *International Relations* 2:69–79.

Armijo, Leslie Elliott. 2007. The BRICS Countries (Brazil, Russia, India, and China) as an Analytical Category: Mirage or Insight. *Asian Perspective* 31 (4): 7–42.

Armijo, Leslie Elliott, Laurissa Mühlich, and Daniel C. Tirone. 2014. The Systemic

Financial Importance of Emerging Powers. *Journal of Policy Modeling* 36 (1): 67–88.

Atanassova-Cornelis, Elena. 2012. Chinese Nation-Building and Foreign Policy: Japan and the U.S. as the Significant "Others" in National Identity Construction. *East Asia* 29:95–108.

Atzili, Boaz. 2012. *Good Fences, Bad Neighbors: Border Fixity and International Conflict.* Chicago: University of Chicago Press.

Ayoob, Mohammed. 1987. Southeast Asia in Indian Foreign Policy: Some Preliminary Observations. *Contemporary Southeast Asia* 9 (1): 1–11.

Baltazzo, Juliana. 2010. New Regionalism and Leadership in Brazilian Security and Defense Policy. *Security and Defense Studies Review* 10:91–106.

Baranovsky, Vladimir, and Sergey Utkin. 2012. Europe as Seen from Russia. *Perspectives* 20 (2): 63–82.

Barber, James. 2005. The New South Africa's Foreign Policy: Principles and Practice. *International Affairs* 81 (5): 1079–96.

Barbieri, Katherine, Omar M. G. Keshk, and Brian M. Pollins. 2008. *Correlates of War Project Trade Data Set Codebook.* Version 2.0. http://correlatesofwar.org

Barbieri, Katherine, Omar M. G. Keshk, and Brian M. Pollins. 2009. Trading Data: Evaluating our Assumptions and Coding Rules. *Conflict Management and Peace Science* 26 (5): 471–91.

Barbosa, Rubens A. 2001. A View from Brazil. *Washington Quarterly* 24 (2): 149–57.

Barnett, Michael. 1999. Culture, Strategy and Foreign Policy Change: Israel's Road to Oslo. *European Journal of International Relations* 5 (1): 5–36.

Barry, William D., Jacqueline H. R. DeMerritt, and Justin Esarey. 2010. Testing for Interaction in Binary Logit and Probit Models: Is a Product Term Essential? *American Journal of Political Science* 54 (1): 248–66.

Barton, William P. 1950. Indian Foreign Policy. *Australian Quarterly* 22 (4): 25–34.

Beck, Nathaniel, and Simon Jackman. 1998. Beyond Linearity by Default: Generalized Additive Models. *American Journal of Political Science* 42:596–627.

Below, Amy. 2014. *Environmental Politics and Foreign Policy Decision Making in Latin America: Ratifying the Kyoto Protocol.* New York: Routledge.

Bengtsson, Rikard, and Ole Elgström. 2012. Conflicting Role Conceptions? The European Union in Global Politics. *Foreign Policy Analysis* 8 (1): 93–108.

Beylerian, Onnig, and Christophe Canivet. 1997. China: Role Conceptions after the Cold War. In Pierre LePrestre, ed., *Role Quests in the Post–Cold War Era: Foreign Policies in Transition.* Montreal: McGill-Queen's University Press.

Bezerra, Paul, Jacob Cramer, Megan Hauser, Jennifer L. Miller, and Thomas J. Volgy. 2015. Going for the Gold versus Distributing the Green: Foreign Policy Substitutability and Complementarity in Status Enhancement Strategies. *Foreign Policy Analysis* 11 (3): 253–72.

Bhagwati, Jagdish. 1998. The Capital Myth: The Difference between Trade in Widgets and Dollars. *Foreign Affairs* 1:7–12.

Bischoff, Paul-Henri. 2003. External and Domestic Sources of Foreign Policy

Ambiguity: South African Foreign Policy and the Projection of Pluralist Middle Power. *Politikon: South African Journal of Political Studies* 30 (10): 183–201.

Blanchard, Jean-Marc F., and Kun-Chin Lin. 2013. Contemplating Chinese Foreign Policy: Approaches to the Use of Historical Analysis. *Pacific Focus: Inha Journal of International Studies* 28 (2): 145–69.

Bond, Patrick. 2004. The ANC's "Left Turn" and South African Sub-Imperialism. *Review of African Political Economy* 31 (102): 599–616.

Bond, Patrick. 2013. Sub-Imperialism as Lubricant of Neoliberalism: South African "Deputy Sheriff" Duty within BRICS. *Third World Quarterly* 34 (2): 251–70.

Boughton, James M. 2001. *Silent Revolution: The International Monetary Fund, 1979–1989.* Washington, DC: International Monetary Fund.

Boyce, James K., and Léonce Ndikumana. 2001. Is Africa a Net Creditor? New Estimates of Capital Flight from Severely Indebted Sub-Saharan African Countries, 1970–96. *Journal of Development Studies* 38 (2): 27–56.

Brands, Hal. 2011. Evaluating Brazilian Grand Strategy under Lula. *Comparative Strategy* 30 (1): 28–49.

Braumoeller, Bear F. 2012. *The Great Powers and the International System: Systemic Theory in Empirical Perspective.* Cambridge: Cambridge University Press.

Bremer, Stuart A. 1992. Dangerous Dyads: Conditions Affecting the Likelihood of Interstate War, 1816–1965. *Journal of Conflict Resolution* 36 (2): 309–41.

Bremmer, Ian. 2009. State Capitalism and the Crisis. *McKinsey Quarterly*, July. http://www.mckinsey.com/industries/public-sector/our-insights/state-capitalism-and-the-crisis

Breslin, Shaun. 2009. Understanding China's Regional Rise: Interpretations, Identities, and Implications. *International Affairs* 85 (4): 817–35.

Breslin, Shaun. 2010. China's Emerging Global Role: Dissatisfied Responsible Great Power. *Politics* 30 (S1): 52–62.

Brewster, David. 2010. An Indian Sphere of Influence in the Indian Ocean? *Security Challenges* 6 (3): 1–20.

Brittingham, Michael Alan. 2007. The "Role" of Nationalism in Chinese Foreign Policy: A Reactive Model of Nationalism and Conflict. *Journal of Chinese Political Science* 12 (2): 147–66.

Brooke, Jim. 1981. Dateline Brazil: Southern Superpower. *Foreign Policy* 44:167–80.

Brummer, Klaus, and Cameron G. Thies. 2015. The Contested Selection of National Role Conceptions. *Foreign Policy Analysis* 11 (3): 273–93.

Brütsch, Christian, and Mihaela Papa. 2013. Deconstructing the BRICS: Bargaining, Coalition, Imagined Community, or Geopolitical Fad? *Chinese Journal of International Politics* 6:299–327.

Burges, Sean. 2005. Auto-Estima in Brazil: The Logic of Lula's South-South Foreign Policy. *International Journal* 60:1133–51.

Burges, Sean. 2006. Without Sticks or Carrots: Brazilian Leadership in South America during the Cardoso Era, 1992–2003. *Bulletin of Latin American Research* 25 (1): 23–42.

Burges, Sean. 2008. Consensual Hegemony: Theorizing Brazilian Foreign Policy after the Cold War. *International Relations* 22 (1): 65–84.

Buzan, Barry. 1991. *People, States, and Fear: An Agenda for International Security Studies in a Post–Cold War Era.* 2nd ed. Boulder, CO: Lynne Rienner.

Buzan, Barry, and Michael Cox. 2013. China and the US: Comparable Cases of "Peaceful Rise"? *Chinese Journal of International Politics* 6:109–32.

Buzan, Barry, and Ole Waever. 2003. *Regions and Powers: The Structure of International Security.* Cambridge: Cambridge University Press.

Calder, Kent E. 2006. China and Japan's Simmering Rivalry. *Foreign Affairs* 85 (2): 129–39.

Cantir, Cristian, and Juliet Kaarbo. 2012. Contested Roles and Domestic Politics: Reflections on Role Theory in Foreign Policy Analysis and IR Theory. *Foreign Policy Analysis* 8 (1): 5–24.

Cantir, Cristian, and Juliet Kaarbo, eds. 2016. *Domestic Role Contestation, Foreign Policy, and International Relations.* New York: Routledge.

Caprio, Gerard, Jr., and Lawrence H. Summers. 1993. *Finance and Its Reform.* Washington, DC: World Bank.

Carmody, Padraig R., and Francis Y. Owusu. 2007. Competing Hegemons? Chinese versus American Geo-Economic Strategies in Africa. *Political Geography* 26 (5): 504–24.

Carlin, Bradley P., and Siddhartha Chib. 1995. Bayesian Model Choice via Markov Chain Monte Carlo Methods. *Journal of the Royal Statistical Society: Series B (Methodological)* 57 (3): 473–84.

Carlsnaes, Walter. 1993. On Analysing the Dynamics of Foreign Policy Change: A Critique and Reconceptualization. *Conflict and Cooperation* 28 (1): 5–30.

Carlson, Allen. 2011. It Should Not Only Be about Nationalism: China's Pluralistic Nationalism and Its Implications for Chinese Foreign Relations. *International Studies* 48 (3–4): 223–36.

Carranza, Mario E. 2016. Rising Regional Powers and International Relations Theories: Comparing Brazil and India's Foreign Security Policies and the Search for Great-Power Status. *Foreign Policy Analysis.* http://dx.doi.org/10.1111/fpa.12065

Chafetz, Glenn. 1996–97. The Struggle for a National Identity in Post-Soviet Russia. *Political Science Quarterly* 111 (4): 661–88.

Chafetz, Glenn, Hillel Abramson, and Suzette Grillot. 1996. Role Theory and Foreign Policy: Belarussian and Ukrainian Compliance with the Nuclear Nonproliferation Regime. *Political Psychology* 17 (4): 727–57.

Chase, Robert S., Emily B. Hill, and Paul Kennedy. 1996. Pivotal States and U.S. Strategy. *Foreign Affairs* 75 (1): 33–51.

Chib, Siddhartha. 1995. Marginal Likelihood from the Gibbs Output. *Journal of the American Statistical Association* 90 (432): 1313–21.

Chib, Siddhartha. 1996. Calculating Posterior Distributions and Modal Estimates in Markov Mixture Models. *Journal of Econometrics* 75:79–97.

Chib, Siddhartha. 1998. Estimations and Comparison of Multiple Change-Point Models. *Journal of Econometrics* 86:221–41.

Chib, Siddhartha, and Edward Greenberg. 1996. Markov Chain Monte Carlo Simulation Methods in Econometrics. *Economic Theory* 12:409–31.

Chiba, Daina, Carla Martinez Machain, and William Reed. 2014. Major Powers and Militarized Conflict. *Journal of Conflict Resolution* 58 (6): 976–1002.

Chinn, Menzie D., and Hiro Ito. 2008. A New Measure of Financial Openness. *Journal of Comparative Policy Analysis* 10 (3): 309–22.

Chiriyankandath, James. 2004. Realigning India: Indian Foreign Policy after the Cold War. *Round Table: The Commonwealth Journal of International Affairs* 93:199–211.

Christensen, Steen. 2013. Brazil's Foreign Policy Priorities. *Third World Quarterly* 34 (2): 271–86.

Cooper, Andrew F. 1998. The Multiple Faces of South African Foreign Policy. *International Journal* 53 (4): 705–32.

Cooper, Andrew F., and Daniel Flemes. 2013. Foreign Policy Strategies of Emerging Powers in a Multipolar World: An Introductory Review. *Third World Quarterly* 34 (6): 943–62.

Cornelissen, Scarlett. 2008. Scripting the Nation: Sport, Mega-Events, Foreign Policy, and State-Building in Post-Apartheid South Africa. *Sport in Society* 11 (4): 481–93.

Crocker, Chester A. 1980. South Africa: Strategy for Change. *Foreign Affairs* 59 (2): 323–51.

Cummings, Sally. 2001. Happier Bedfellows? Russia and Central Asia under Putin. *Asian Affairs* 32 (2): 142–52.

Das, Udaibir S., Michael G. Papioannou, and Christoph Trebesch. 2012. *Sovereign Debt Restructurings, 1950–2010: Literature Survey, Data, and Stylized Facts*. Washington, DC: International Monetary Fund.

Davies, Robert. 1985. *South African Strategy towards Mozambique in the Post-Nkomati Period: A Critical Analysis of the Effects and Implications*. Uppsala: Scandinavian Institute of African Studies, Uppsala University.

Davies, Robert, and Dan O'Meara. 1985. Total Strategy in Southern Africa: An Analysis of South African Regional Policy since 1978. *Journal of Southern African Studies* 11 (2): 183–211.

Deng, Yong. 2008. *China's Struggle for Status: The Realignment of International Relations*. New York: Cambridge University Press.

Dittmer, Lowell, and Samuel S. Kim. 1993. In Search of a Theory of National Identity. In Lowell Dittmer and Samuel S. Kim, eds., *China's Quest for National Identity*. Ithaca: Cornell University Press.

Doran, Charles F. 1991. *Systems in Crisis: New Imperatives of High Politics at Century's End*. New York: Cambridge University Press.

Dreyer, June T. 2006. Sino-Japanese Rivalry and Its Implications for Developing Nations. *Asian Survey* 46 (4): 538–57.

Dugard, John, Bethlehem, Daniel L., and Mas Du Plessis. 2005. *International Law: A South African Perspective*. 3rd ed. Lansdowne: Juta and Company.

Eaton, Jonathan, and Mark Gersovitz. 1984. A Theory of Expropriation and Deviations from Perfect Capital Mobility. *Economic Journal* 373:16–40.

Egreteau, Renaud. 2012. The China-India Rivalry Reconceptualized. *Asian Journal of Political Science* 29 (1): 1–22.

Engle, Robert F., David F. Henry, and Jean-François Richard. 1983. Exogeneity. *Econometrica* 51 (2): 277–304.

Elman, Colin. 1996. Horses for Courses: Why *Not* Neorealist Theories of Foreign Policy? *Security Studies* 6 (1): 7–53.

Engstrom, Par. 2012. Brazilian Foreign Policy and Human Rights: Change and Continuity under Dilma. *Critical Sociology* 38 (6): 835–49.

Erdman, Howard L. 1966. The Foreign Policy Views of the Indian Right. *Pacific Affairs* 39 (1–2): 5–18.

Evans, Graham. 1996. South Africa in Remission: The Foreign Policy of an Altered State. *Journal of Modern African Studies* 34 (2): 249–69.

Evans, Graham. 1999. South Africa's Foreign Policy after Mandela: Mbeki and His Concept of an African Renaissance. *Round Table: The Commonwealth Journal of International Affairs* 88 (352): 621–28.

Fearon, James D., and David D. Laitin. 2008. Integrating Qualitative and Quantitative Methods. In Janet M. Box-Steffensmeier, Henry E. Brady, and David Collier, eds., *The Oxford Handbook of Political Methodology*. Oxford: Oxford University Press.

Flemes, Daniel, ed. 2010. *Regional Leadership in the Global System: Ideas, Interests and Strategies of Regional Powers*. Farnham: Ashgate.

Flemes, Daniel, and Leslie Wehner. 2012. *Drivers of Strategic Contestation in South America*. GIGA Working Paper, No. 207. Hamburg: German Institute of Global and Area Studies.

Flemes, Daniel, and Thorsten Wojczewski. 2010. *Contested Leadership in International Relations: Power Politics in South America, South Asia, and Sub-Saharan Africa*. GIGA Working Paper, No. 121. Hamburg: German Institute of Global and Area Studies.

Fontera, Richard M. 1960. Anti-Colonialism as a Basic Indian Foreign Policy. *Western Political Quarterly* 13 (2): 421–32.

Foot, Rosemary. 2006. Chinese Strategies in a U.S.-Hegemonic Global Order: Accommodating and Hedging. *International Affairs* 82 (1): 77–94.

Fordham, Benjamin O. 2011. Who Wants to Be a Major Power? *Journal of Peace Research* 48 (5): 587–603.

Forsberg, Tuomas. 2014. Status Conflicts between Russia and the West: Perceptions and Emotional Biases. *Communist and Post-Communist Studies* 47:323–31.

Fourcade, Marion. 2013. The Material and Symbolic Construction of the BRICs: Reflections Inspired by the RIPE Special Issue. *Review of International Political Economy* 20 (2): 256–67.

Fravel, M. Taylor. 2008. Power Shifts and Escalation: Explaining China's Use of Force in Territorial Disputes. *International Security* 32 (3): 44–83.

Fravel, M. Taylor. 2010. International Relations Theory and China's Rise: Assessing China's Potential for Territorial Expansion. *International Studies Review* 12:505–32.

Friedberg, Aaron L. 2005. The Future of U.S.-China Relations: Is Conflict Inevitable? *International Security* 30 (2): 7–45.

Frühwirth-Schnatter, Sylvia, and Helga Wagner. 2006. Auxiliary Mixture Sampling for Parameter-Driven Models of Time Series of Small Counts with Applications to State Space Modelling. *Biometrika* 93 (4): 827–41.

Gartzke, Erik. 2007. The Capitalist Peace. *American Journal of Political Science* 51 (1): 166–91.

Gartzke, Erik, and J. Joseph Hewitt. 2010. International Crises and the Capitalist Peace. *International Interactions* 36 (2): 115–45.

Garver, John W. 1996. Sino-Indian Rapprochement and the Sino-Pakistan Entente. *Political Science Quarterly* 111 (2): 323–47.

Garver, John W. 2002. The Security Dilemma in Sino-Indian Relations. *India Review* 1 (4): 1–38.

Gaskarth, Jamie, ed. 2015. *Rising Powers, Global Governance, and Global Ethics.* London: Routledge.

Geldenhuys, Deon. 1981. *Some Foreign Policy Implications of South Africa's "Total National Strategy," with Particular Reference to the "12-Point Plan."* Johannesburg: South African Institute for International Affairs.

Gelman, Andrew, John B. Carlin, Hal S. Stern, and Donald B. Rubin. 1995. *Bayesian Data Analysis.* Boca Raton, FL: Chapman and Hall/CRC Press.

Gelman, Andrew, and Jennifer Hill. 2007. *Data Analysis Using Regression and Multilevel/Hierarchical Models.* New York: Cambridge University Press.

Ghosh, Partha S., and Rajaram Panda. 1983. Domestic Support for Mrs. Gandhi's Afghan Policy: The Soviet Factor in Indian Politics. *Asian Survey* 23 (3): 261–79.

Giacalone, Rita. 2012. Latin American Foreign Policy Analysis: External Influences and Internal Circumstances. *Foreign Policy Analysis* 8:335–53.

Gill, Jeff. 1999. The Insignificance of Null Hypothesis Testing. *Political Research Quarterly* 52 (3): 647–74.

Gill, Jeff. 2006. *Essential Mathematics for Political and Social Research.* Cambridge: Cambridge University Press.

Gill, Jeff. 2009. *Bayesian Methods: A Social and Behavior Sciences Approach.* 2nd ed. Boca Raton, FL: Chapman and Hall/CRC Press.

Gilpin, Robert. 1981. *War and Change in World Politics.* New York: Cambridge University Press.

Glaser, Bonnie S., and Evan S. Medeiros. 2007. The Changing Ecology of Foreign Policy-Making in China: The Ascension and Demise of the Theory of "Peaceful Rise." *China Quarterly* 190:291–310.

Glosny, Michael A. 2010. China and the BRICs: A Real (but Limited) Partnership in a Unipolar World. *Polity* 42 (1): 100–129.

Goldmann, Kjell. 1988. *Change and Stability in Foreign Policy: The Problems and Possibilities of Détente.* Princeton: Princeton University Press.

Goldstein, Joshua. 1988. *Long Cycles: Prosperity and War in the Modern Age.* New Haven: Yale University Press.

Granato, Jim. 1991. An Agenda for Econometric Model Building. *Political Analysis* 3 (1): 123–54.

Gunter, Frank R. 2004. Capital Flight from China: 1984–2001. *China Economic Review* 15:63–85.

Gustavsson, Jakob. 1999. How Should We Study Foreign Policy Change? *Conflict and Cooperation* 34 (1): 73–95.

Haas, Richard N. 2008. The Age of Nonpolarity: What Will Follow U.S. Dominance. *Foreign Affairs* 87 (3): 44–56.

Habib, Adam. 2009. South Africa's Foreign Policy: Hegemonic Aspiration, Neoliberal Orientation, and Global Transformation. *South African Journal of International Affairs* 16 (2): 143–59.

Habib, Adam, and N. Selinyane. 2006. Constraining the Unconstrained: Civil Society and South Africa's Hegemonic Obligations in Africa. In W. Carlsnaes and P. Nel, eds., *In Full Flight: South African Foreign Policy after Apartheid*. Midrand: Institute for Global Dialogue.

Hajzler, Christopher. 2012. Expropriation of Foreign Direct Investments: Sectoral Patterns from 1993 to 2006. *Review of World Economy* 148:119–49.

Hakim, Peter. 2002. Two Ways to Go Global. *Foreign Affairs* 81 (1): 148–62.

Hamill, James, and Donna Lee. 2001. A Middle Power Paradox? South African Diplomacy in the Post-Apartheid Era. *International Relations* 15 (4): 33–59.

Hansel, Mischa, and Miriam Möller. 2015. Indian Foreign Policy and International Humanitarian Norms: A Role-Theoretical Analysis. *Asian Politics and Policy* 7 (1): 79–104.

Harnisch, Sebastian. 2001. Change and Continuity in Post-Unification German Foreign Policy. *German Politics* 10 (1): 35–60.

Harnisch, Sebastian. 2012. Conceptualizing the Minefield: Role Theory and Foreign Policy Learning. *Foreign Policy Analysis* 8 (1): 47–69.

Harnisch, Sebastian, Sebastian Bersick, and Jörn-Carsten Gottwald. 2015. *China's International Roles: Challenging or Supporting International Order*. New York: Routledge.

Harnisch, Sebastian, Cornelia Frank, and Hanns W. Maull. 2011. *Role Theory in International Relations: Approaches and Analyses*. London: Routledge.

Hart, Andrew F., and Bruce D. Jones. 2010. How Do Rising Powers Rise? *Survival: Global Politics and Strategy* 52 (6): 63–88.

Hermann, Charles F. 1990. Changing Course: When Governments Choose to Redirect Foreign Policy. *International Studies Quarterly* 34:3–21.

Hermann, Margaret G. 1987. Assessing the Foreign Policy Role Orientations of Sub-Saharan African Leaders. In Stephen G. Walker, ed., *Role Theory and Foreign Policy Analysis*. Durham, NC: Duke University Press.

Hirschmann, David. 1979. Changes in Lesotho's Policy towards South Africa. *African Affairs* 78 (311): 177–96.

Holsti, K. J. 1970. National Role Conceptions in the Study of Foreign Policy. *International Studies Quarterly* 14 (3): 233–309.

Holsti, K. J. 1982. *Why Nations Realign: Foreign Policy Restructuring in the Postwar World*. London: Allen and Unwin.

Hurrell, Andrew. 2006. Hegemony, Liberalism, and Global Order: What Space for Would-Be Great Powers? *International Affairs* 82 (1): 1–19.

Hurrell, Andrew. 2010. Brazil and the New Global Order. *Current History* 109 (724): 60–66.

Hurrell, Andrew. 2013. Narratives of Emergence: Rising Powers and the End of the Third World. *Brazilian Journal of Political Economy* 33 (2): 203–21.

Hussain, Karki. 1962. China's Image of India's Foreign Policy of Non-Alignment. *Indian Journal of Political Science* 23 (1): 240–51.

Ivanov, Igor. 2001. The New Russian Identity: Innovation and Continuity in Russian Foreign Policy. *Washington Quarterly* 24 (3): 5–13.

Jayaramu, P. S. 1991. Trends in World Politics and the Challenges to Indian Foreign Policy. *Indian Journal of Political Science* 52 (2): 185–94.

Jeffrey, Harold. 1961. *Theory of Probability*. New York: Oxford University Press.

Jones, Daniel M., Stuart A. Bremer, and J. David Singer. 1996. Militarized Interstate Disputes, 1816–1992: Rationale, Coding Rules, and Empirical Patterns. *Conflict Management and Peace Science* 15 (2): 163–212.

Jordaan, Eduard. 2003. The Concept of a Middle Power in International Relations: Distinguishing between Emerging and Traditional Middle Powers. *Politikon: South African Journal of Political Studies* 30 (1): 165–81.

Kacowicz, Arie M. 1998. *Zones of Peace in the Third World: South America and West Africa in Comparative Perspective*. Albany: SUNY Press.

Kadera, Kelly M. 2001. *The Power-Conflict Story: A Dynamic Model of Interstate Rivalry*. Ann Arbor: University of Michigan Press.

Kadera, Kelly M., Mark J. C. Crescenzi, and Megan L. Shannon. 2003. Democratic Survival, Peace, and War in the International System. *American Journal of Political Science* 47 (2): 234–47.

Kadera, Kelly M., and Gerald L. Sorokin. 2004. Measuring National Power. *International Interactions* 30 (3): 211–30.

Kahler, Miles. 2013. Rising Powers and Global Governance: Negotiating Change in a Resilient Status Quo. *International Affairs* 89 (3): 711–29.

Kapur, Ashok. 1971. Strategic Choices in Indian Foreign Policy. *International Journal* 27:448–68.

Kapur, Ashok. 1985. Indian Foreign Policy. *Round Table: The Commonwealth Journal of International Affairs* 74:230–39.

Kapur, Ashok. 1988. The Indian Subcontinent: The Contemporary Structure of Power and the Development of Power Relations. *Asian Survey* 28 (7): 693–710.

Karunakaran, K. P. 1979. A New Perspective on Indian Foreign Policy. *Indian Journal of Political Science* 40 (1): 26–39.

Kass, Robert E., and Adrian E. Raftery. 1995. Bayes Factor. *Journal of the American Statistical Association* 90 (430): 773–95.

Kassianova, Alla. 2001. Russia: Still Open to the West? Evolution of the State Identity in the Foreign Policy and Security Discourse. *Europe-Asia Studies* 53 (6): 821–39.

Keenleyside, T. A. 1982. Nationalist Indian Attitudes towards Asia: A Troublesome Legacy for Post-Independence Indian Foreign Policy. *Pacific Affairs* 55 (2): 210–30.

Keller, Edmond J. 1997. Rethinking African Regional Security. In David A. Lake and Patrick M. Morgan, eds., *Regional Orders: Building Security in a New World*. University Park: Pennsylvania State University Press.

Kennedy, Paul. 1987. *The Rise and Fall of the Great Powers*. New York: Vintage.

Keohane, Robert O., and Joseph S. Nye. 1977. *Power and Interdependence: World Politics in Transition*. Boston: Little, Brown.

Kindleberger, Charles P. 1973. *The World in Depression, 1929–1939*. Berkeley: University of California Press.

King, Gary. 1989. *Unifying Political Methodology*. Ann Arbor: University of Michigan Press.

Kleistra, Yvonne, and Igor Mayer. 2001. Stability and Flux in Foreign Affairs: Modelling Policy and Organizational Change. *Conflict and Cooperation* 36 (1): 381–414.

Klotz, Audie. 2000. Migration after Apartheid: Deracialising South African Foreign Policy. *Third World Quarterly* 21 (5): 831–47.

Kmenta, Jan. 1997. *Elements of Econometrics*. 2nd ed. Ann Arbor: University of Michigan Press.

Korbin, Stephen J. 1984. Expropriation as an Attempt to Control Foreign Firms in LCDs: Trends from 1960 to 1979. *International Studies Quarterly* 28 (3): 329–48.

Kripalani, Acharya J. B. 1959. For Principled Neutrality: A New Appraisal of Indian Foreign Policy. *Foreign Affairs* 38 (1): 46–60.

Lafer, Celso. 2000. Brazilian International Identity and Foreign Policy: Past, Present, and Future. *Daedalus* 129 (2): 207–38.

Laïdi, Zaki. 2012. BRICS: Sovereignty, Power, and Weakness. *International Politics* 49 (5): 614–32.

Lake, David A. 1993. Leadership, Hegemony, and the International Economy: Naked Emperor or Tattered Monarch with Potential. *International Studies Quarterly* 37:459–89.

Lake, David A. 2009. *Hierarchy in International Relations*. Ithaca: Cornell University Press.

Lake, David A., and Patrick M. Morgan, eds. 1997. *Regional Orders: Building Security in a New World*. University Park: Pennsylvania State University Press.

Landry, David M. 1974. Brazil's New Regional and Global Roles. *World Affairs* 137 (1): 23–37.

Landsberg, Chris. 2005. Toward a Developmental Foreign Policy? Challenges for South Africa's Diplomacy in the Second Decade of Liberation. *Social Research* 72 (3): 723–56.

Landsberg, Chris, and David Monyae. 2006. South Africa's Foreign Policy: Carving a Global Niche. *South African Journal of International Affairs* 13 (2): 131–45.

Larson, Deborah Welch, and Alexei Shevchenko. 2003. Shortcut to Greatness: The New Thinking and the Revolution in Soviet Foreign Policy. *International Organization* 57 (1): 77–109.

Larson, Deborah Welch, and Alexei Shevchenko. 2010. Status Seekers: Chinese and Russian Responses to U.S. Primacy. *International Security* 34 (4): 63–95.

Larson, Deborah Welch, and Alexei Shevchenko. 2014. Russia Says No: Power, Status, and Emotions in Foreign Policy. *Communist and Post-Communist Studies* 47:269–79.

Lavrov, Sergei. 2006. The Rise of Asia, and the Eastern Vector of Russia's Foreign Policy. *Russia in Global Affairs* 4 (3): 68–80.

Lee, Hoon, and Sara McLaughlin Mitchell. 2012. Foreign Direct Investment and Territorial Disputes. *Journal of Conflict Resolution* 56 (4): 675–703.

Leith, Rian, and Joelien Pretorius. 2009. Eroding the Middle Ground: The Shift in Foreign Policy Underpinning South African Nuclear Diplomacy. *Politikon: South African Journal of Political Studies* 36 (3): 345–61.

Lemke, Douglas. 2002. *Regions of War and Peace*. Cambridge: Cambridge University Press.

Levi, Werner. 1964. Indian Neutralism Reconsidered. *Pacific Affairs* 37 (2): 137–47.

Levy, Jack S. 2008. Power Transition Theory and the Rise of China. In Robert S. Ross and Zhu Feng, eds., *China's Ascent: Power, Security, and the Future of International Politics*. Ithaca: Cornell University Press.

Levy, Jack S., and William R. Thompson. 2010. Balancing on Land and at Sea. *International Security* 35 (1): 7–43.

Li, Xiaoting. 2013. The Taming of the Red Dragon: The Militarized Worldview and China's Use of Force, 1949–2001. *Foreign Policy Analysis* 9:387–407.

Liberman, Peter. 2001. The Rise and Fall of the South African Bomb. *International Security* 26 (2): 45–86.

Lieberman, Evan. 2005. Nested Analysis as a Mixed-Method Strategy for Comparative Research. *American Political Science Review* 99 (3): 435–52.

Light, Margot. 1996. Foreign Policy Thinking. In Neil Malcolm, Alex Pravda, Roy Allison, and Margot Light, eds., *Internal Factors in Russian Foreign Policy*. Oxford: Oxford University Press, for the Royal Institute of International Affairs.

Light, Margot. 2003. In Search of an Identity: Russian Foreign Policy and the End of Ideology. *Journal of Communist Studies and Transition Politics* 19 (3): 42–59.

Lima, Maria Regina Soares de, and Mônica Hirst. 2006. Brazil as an Intermediate State and Regional Power: Action, Choice, and Responsibilities. *International Affairs* 82 (1): 21–40.

Linton, Ralph. 1936. *The Study of Man*. New York: Appleton-Century.

Lipton, Merle. 2009. Understanding South Africa's Foreign Policy: The Perplexing Case of Zimbabwe. *South African Journal of International Affairs* 16 (3): 331–46.

Lo, Bobo. 2002. *Russian Foreign Policy in the Post-Soviet Era: Reality, Illusion, and Mythmaking*. London: Palgrave Macmillan.

Lo, Bobo. 2004. The Long Sunset of Strategic Partnership: Russia's Evolving China Policy. *International Affairs* 80 (2): 295–309.

Lukin, Vladimir P. 1992. Our Security Predicament. *Foreign Policy* 88:57–75.

Lustick, Ian S. 1996. History, Historiography, and Political Science: Multiple Historical Records and the Problem of Selection Bias. *American Political Science Review* 90:605–18.

MacFarlane, Neil. 2006. The "R" in BRICs: Is Russia an Emerging Power? *International Affairs* 82 (1): 41–57.

Mack, Doris L., and Robert T. Mack Jr. 1957. Indian Foreign Policy since Independence. *Australian Outlook* 11 (1): 23–32.

Maddison, Angus. 2003. *The World Economy: Historical Statistics*. Paris: OECD.

Madsen, Richard. 1995. *China and the American Dream: A Moral Inquiry*. Berkeley: University of California Press.

Makarychev, Andrey S. Rebranding Russia: Norms, Politics and Power. In Nathalie Tocci, ed., *Who Is a Normative Foreign Policy Actor? The European Union and Its Global Partners*. Brussels: Centre for European Policy Studies.

Malamud, Andrés. 2011. A Leader without Followers? The Growing Divergence between the Regional and Global Performance of Brazilian Foreign Policy. *Latin American Politics and Society* 53 (3): 1–24.

Malik, J. Mohan. 1991. India's Response to the Gulf Crisis: Implications for Indian Foreign Policy. *Asian Survey* 31 (9): 847–61.

Malik, J. Mohan. 1994. Indian Rivalry in Myanmar: Implications for Regional Security. *Contemporary Southeast Asia* 16 (2): 137–56.

Mandela, Nelson. 1993. South African Foreign Policy. *Foreign Affairs* 72 (5): 86–97.

Mankoff, Jeffrey. 2007. Russia and the West: Taking the Longer View. *Washington Quarterly* 30 (2): 123–35.

Mansbach, Richard W., and John A. Vasquez. 1981. *In Search of Theory: A New Paradigm for Global Politics*. New York: Columbia University Press.

Mares, David R. 1997. Regional Conflict Management in Latin America: Power Complemented by Diplomacy. In David A. Lake and Patrick M. Morgan, eds., *Regional Orders: Building Security in a New World*. University Park: Pennsylvania State University Press.

Mares, David R. 2001. *Violent Peace: Militarized Interstate Bargaining in Latin America*. New York: Columbia University Press.

Marrese, Michael, and Jan Vanous. 1983. *Soviet Subsidization of CMEA Trade with Eastern Europe*. Berkeley: University of California Press.

Marshall, Monty G., and Keith Jaggers. 2008. Polity IV Project: Political Regime Characteristics and Transitions, 1800–2007. Version p4v2008e (Computer File).

Martin, Andrew D., Kevin M. Quinn, and Jong Hee Park. 2008. MCMCpack, Version 1.0-1. http://mcmcpack.wustl.edu/

Matlack, Carol. 2014. Putin's Eurasian Union Looks Like a Bad Deal, Even for Russia. *Bloomberg Businessweek*, May 29.

McCourt, David M. 2014. *Britain and World Power since 1945*. Ann Arbor: University of Michigan Press.

McGowan, Pat, and F. Ahwireng-Obeng. 1998. Partner or Hegemon? South Africa in Africa, Part 2. *Journal of Contemporary African Studies* 16 (2): 165–95.

McGowan, Pat, and M. O'Leary. 1975. Methods and Data for the Comparative Analysis of Foreign Policy. In C. Kegley Jr., G. Raymond, R. Rood, and K. Skinner, eds., *International Events and Comparative Analysis of Foreign Policy*. Columbia: University of South Carolina Press.

McKinley, Dale T. 2004. South African Policy towards Zimbabwe under Mbeki. *Review of African Political Economy* 31 (100): 357–64.

Medeiros, Evan, and Taylor Fravel. China's New Diplomacy. *Foreign Affairs* 82 (6): 22–35.

Mendras, Marie. 1997. Towards a Post-Imperial Identity. In Vladimir Baranovsky, ed., *Russia and Europe: The Emerging Security Agenda.* Oxford: Oxford University Press.

Metz, Steven. The Mozambique National Resistance and South African Foreign Policy. *African Affairs* 85 (341): 491–507.

Meyer, John W., John Boli, George M. Thomas, and Francisco O. Ramirez. 1997. World Society and the Nation State. *American Journal of Sociology* 103 (1): 144–81.

Mielniczuk, Fabiano. 2013. BRICS in the Contemporary World: Changing Identities, Converging Interests. *Third World Quarterly* 34 (6): 1075–90.

Miller, Benjamin. 2007. *States, Nations, and the Great Powers: The Sources of Regional War and Peace.* Cambridge: Cambridge University Press.

Miller, Jennifer L., Jacob Cramer, Thomas J. Volgy, Paul Bezerra, Megan Hauser, and Christina Sciabarra. 2015. Norms, Behavioral Compliance, and Status Attribution in International Politics. *International Interactions* 41:779–804.

Mitchell, Sara McLaughlin, Scott Gates, and Håvard Hegre. 1999. Evolution in Democracy-War Dynamics. *Journal of Conflict Resolution* 43 (6): 771–92.

Mochizuki, Mike, and Deepa M. Ollapally. 2011. Identity and Asian Powers: What Does It Mean for International Relations of Asia and Beyond? *International Studies* 48 (3–4): 197–99.

Modelski, George. 1987. *Long Cycles in World Politics.* Seattle: University of Washington Press.

Mohan, C. Raja. 2006. India and the Balance of Power. *Foreign Affairs* 85 (4): 17–32.

Mohan, C. Raja. 2009. The Re-Making of Indian Foreign Policy: Ending the Marginalization of International Relations Community. *International Studies* 46 (1–2): 147–63.

Moore, Gregory J. 2016. The Power of "Sacred Commitments": Chinese Interests in Taiwan. *Foreign Policy Analysis* 12 (2): 214–35.

Mousseau, Michael. 2003. The Nexus of Market Society, Liberal Preferences, and Democratic Peace: Interdisciplinary Theory and Evidence. *International Studies Quarterly* 47 (4): 483–510.

Mousseau, Michael. 2009. The Social Market Roots of Democratic Peace. *International Security* 33 (4): 52–86.

Mueller, John. 1989. *Retreat from Doomsday: The Obsolescence of Major War.* New York: Basic Books.

Mukherjee, Rohan, and David M. Malone. 2011. Indian Foreign Policy and Contemporary Security Challenges. *International Affairs* 87 (1): 87–104.

Narang, Vipin, and Paul Staniland. 2012. Institutions and Worldviews in Indian Foreign and Security Policy. *India Review* 11 (2): 76–94.

Narayanan, K. R. 1972. New Perspectives in Indian Foreign Policy. *Round Table: The Commonwealth Journal of International Affairs* 62:453–64.

Nathan, Laurie. 2005. Consistencies and Inconsistencies on South African Foreign Policy. *International Affairs* 81 (2): 361–72.

Nau, Henry, and Richard Fontaine. 2012. *India as a Global Power: Contending Worldviews from India.* Policy Report, Sigur Center for Asian Studies, George Washington University, Washington, DC.

Nau, Henry, and Cory Welt. 2013. *How Russia Sees the World: Domestic Foreign Policy Debates.* Policy Report, Sigur Center for Asian Studies' Rising Powers Initiative and the Institute for European, Russian, and Eurasian Studies, George Washington University, Washington, DC.

Ndlovu, Sifiso Mxolisi. 2010. Sports and Cultural Diplomacy: The 2010 FIFA World Cup in South Africa's Foreign Policy. *Soccer and Society* 11 (1–2): 144–53.

Neethling, Theo. 2012 Reflections on Norm Dynamics: South African Foreign Policy and the No-Fly Zone over Libya. *South African Journal of International Affairs* 19 (1): 25–42.

Nel, Philip. 2010. Redistribution *and* Recognition: What Emerging Regional Powers Want. *Review of International Studies* 36 (4): 951–74.

Nel, Philip, Ian Taylor, and Janis Van der Westhuizen. 2000. Multilateralism in South Africa's Foreign Policy: The Search for a Critical Rationale. *Global Governance* 6 (1): 43–60.

Nel, Philip, Ian Taylor, and Janis Van der Westhuizen. 2001. *South Africa's Multilateral Diplomacy and Global Change: The Limits of Reformism.* Aldershot: Ashgate.

Ng-Quinn, Michael. 1993. National Identity in Premodern China: Formation and Role Enactment. In Lowell Dittmer and Samuel S. Kim, eds., *China's Quest for National Identity.* Ithaca: Cornell University Press.

Nieman, Mark David. 2013. "The Return on Social Bonds: The Effect of Social Contracts on International Conflict and Economics." Ph.D. diss., University of Iowa.

Nieman, Mark David. 2016a. Moments in Time: Temporal Patterns in the Effect of Democracy and Trade on Conflict. *Conflict Management and Peace Science* 33 (3): 273–93.

Nieman, Mark David. 2016b. The Return on Social Bonds: Social Hierarchy and International Conflict. *Journal of Peace Research* 53 (5): 665–79.

Nolte, Detlef. 2010. How to Compare Regional Powers: Analytical Concepts and Research Topics. *Review of International Studies* 36 (4): 881–901.

Oblath, Gabot, and David Tarr. 1991. *The Terms-of-Trade Effects from the Elimination of State Trading in Soviet-Hungarian Trade.* Washington, DC: World Bank.

Odgaard, Leselotte. 2013. Peaceful Coexistence Strategy and China's Diplomatic Power. *Chinese Journal of International Politics* 6:233–72.

Ollapally, Deepa M. 2011. India: The Ambivalent Power in Asia. *International Studies* 48 (3–4): 201–22.

Ollapally, Deepa M. 2014. China and India: Economic Ties and Strategic Rivalry. *Orbis* 58 (3): 342–57.

Ollapally, Deepa M., and Rajesh Rajagopalan. 2011. The Pragmatic Challenge to Indian Foreign Policy. *Washington Quarterly* 34 (2): 145–62.

O'Neill, Jim. 2001. *Building Better Global Economic BRICs.* Goldman Sachs, Global Economics Paper No. 66, London.

Organski, A. F. K. 1958. *World Politics*. New York: Alfred A. Knopf.

Organski, A. F. K., and Jacek Kugler. 1980. *The War Ledger*. Chicago: University of Chicago Press.

Palmer, Glenn, Vito D'Orazio, Michael Kenwick, and Matthew Lane. 2015. The MID4 Data Set: Procedures, Coding Rules, and Description. *Conflict Management and Peace Science* 32:222–42.

Pant, Harsh V. 2008. Indian Foreign and Security Policy: Beyond Nuclear Weapons. *Brown Journal of World Affairs* 15 (2): 225–38.

Pant, Harsh V. 2009. India in the Indian Ocean: Growing Mismatch between Ambitions and Capabilities. *Pacific Affairs* 82 (2): 279–97.

Pant, Harsh V. 2013. The BRIC Fallacy. *Washington Quarterly* 36 (3): 91–105.

Park, Jinsoo. 2013. Political Rivals and Regional Leaders: Dual Identities and Sino-Japanese Relations within East Asian Cooperation. *Chinese Journal of International Politics* 6:85–107.

Park, Jong Hee. 2010. Structural Change in U.S. Presidents' Use of Force. *American Journal of Political Science* 54 (3): 766–82.

Park, Jong Hee. 2011a. Analyzing Preference Changes Using Hidden Markov Item Response Theory Models. In Galin Jones, Steve Brooks, Andrew Gelman, and Xiao-Li Meng, eds., *Handbook of Markov Chain Monte Carlos: Methods and Applications*. Boca Raton, FL: Chapman and Hall/CRC.

Park, Jong Hee. 2011b. Changepoint Analysis of Binary and Ordinal Probit Models: An Application to Bank Rate Policy under the Interwar Gold Standard. *Political Analysis* 19 (2): 188–204.

Paul, T. V., Deborah Welch Larson, and William C. Wohlforth, eds. 2014. *Status in World Politics*. Cambridge: Cambridge University Press.

Peterson, Timothy M., and Cameron G. Thies. 2012. Beyond Ricardo: The Link between Intraindustry Trade and Peace. *British Journal of Political Science* 42 (4): 747–67.

Petersson, Bo. 1998. *National Self-Images among Russian Regional Politicians*. CFE Working Paper, Centre for European Studies, Lund University.

Polachek, Solomon W. 1980. Conflict and Trade. *Journal of Conflict Resolution* 24 (1): 55–78.

Power, Paul F. 1964. Indian Foreign Policy: The Age of Nehru. *Review of Politics* 26 (2): 257–86.

Priestland, David. 2009. *The Red Flag: A History of Communism*. New York: Grove Press.

Prys, Miriam. 2010. Hegemony, Domination, Detachment: Differences in Regional Powerhood. *International Studies Review* 12:479–504.

R Development Core Team. 2010. *R: A Language and Environment for Statistical Computing*. Vienna: R Foundation for Statistical Computing. http://www.R-project.org

Rahr, Alexander. 2007. Germany and Russia: A Special Relationship. *Washington Quarterly* 30 (2): 137–45.

Raknerud, Arvid, and Håvard Hegre. 1997. The Hazard of War: Reassessing the Evidence of the Democratic Peace. *Journal of Peace Research* 34:385–404.

Rasler, Karen A., and William R. Thompson. 2005. Systemic Theories of Conflict. In Sara McLaughlin Mitchell, Paul F. Diehl, and James D. Morrow, eds., *Guide to the Scientific Study of International Process*. Malden, MA: Wiley-Blackwell.

Ray, James Lee, and J. David Singer. 1973. Measuring the Concentration of Power in the International System. *Sociological Methods and Research* 1 (4): 403–37.

Reinhard, Carmen, and Kenneth Rogoff. 2009. *This Time Is Different: Eight Centuries of Financial Folly*. Princeton: Princeton University Press.

Richardson, Courtney J. 2011. A Responsible Power? China and the U.N. Peacekeeping Regime. *International Peacekeeping* 18 (3): 286–97.

Ricúpero, Rubens. 1995. *Visions of Brazil*. Rio de Janeiro: Record.

Roberts, Cynthia. 2010. Russia's BRICs Diplomacy: Rising Outsider with Dreams of an Insider. *Polity* 42 (1): 38–73.

Rodrik, Dani. 1992. *Making Sense of the Soviet Trade Shock in Eastern Europe: A Framework and Some Estimates*. Cambridge, MA: National Bureau of Economic Research.

Rodrik, Dani. 1994. Foreign Trade in Eastern Europe's Transition: Early Results. In Olivier Jean Blanchard, Kenneth A. Froot, and Jeffrey D. Sachs, eds., *The Transition in Eastern Europe*, vol. 2, *Restructuring*. Chicago: University of Chicago Press.

Roeder, Phillip J. 1997. From Hierarchy to Hegemony: The Post-Soviet Security Complex. In David A. Lake and Patrick M. Morgan, eds., *Regional Orders: Building Security in a New World*. University Park: Pennsylvania State University Press.

Rosati, Dariusz K. 1994. The Impact of the Soviet Trade Shock on Central and East European Economies. *Empirica* 21 (1): 55–82.

Rosati, Jerel A., Martin W. Sampson III, and Joe D. Hagan 1994. The Study of Change in Foreign Policy. In Jerel A. Rosati, Joe D. Hagan, and Martin W. Sampson III, eds., *Foreign Policy Restructuring: How Governments Respond to Foreign Policy Change*. Columbia: University of South Carolina Press.

Rosecrance, Richard. 1986. *The Rise of the Trading State: Commerce and Conquest in the Modern World*. New York: Basic Books.

Rosenau, James. 1981. *The Study of Political Adaptation*. London: F. Pinter.

Rosenau, James. 1990. *Turbulence in World Politics: A Theory of Change and Continuity*. Princeton: Princeton University Press.

Rosenn, Keith S. 1974–75. Expropriation in Argentina and Brazil: Theory and Practice. *Virginia Journal of International Law* 15 (2): 277–318.

Ross, Robert S., and Zhu Feng, eds. 2008. *China's Ascent: Power, Security, and the Future of International Politics*. Ithaca: Cornell University Press.

Rozman, Gilbert. 1999. China's Quest for Great Power Identity. *Orbis* 43 (3): 383–402.

Russell, Roberto, and Juan Gabriel Tokatlian. 2003. From Antagonistic Autonomy to Relational Autonomy: A Theoretical Reflection from the Southern Cone. *Latin American Politics and Society* 45 (1): 1–24.

Schoeman, Maxi. 2000. South Africa as an Emerging Middle Power. *African Security Review* 9 (3): 47–58.

Schraeder, Peter J. 2001. South Africa's Foreign Policy: From International Pariah to Leader of the African Renaissance. *Round Table: The Commonwealth Journal of International Affairs* 90 (359): 229–43.

Schweller, Randall L. 1997. *Deadly Imbalances: Tripolarity and Hitler's Strategy of World Conquest*. New York: Columbia University Press.

Schweller, Randall L. 2011. Emerging Powers in an Age of Disorder. *Global Governance* 17:285–97.

Scott, David. 2006. India's "Grand Strategy" for the Indian Ocean: Mahanian Visions. *Asia-Pacific Review* 13 (2): 97–129.

Seabra, Pedro. 2012. Brazil's Upward Spiral: From Aspiring Player to Global Ambitions. In N. Tsifakis, ed., *International Politics in Times of Change*. Athens: Konstantinos Karamanlis Institute for Democracy.

Selcher, Wayne A. 1985. Brazilian-Argentine Relations in the 1980s: From Wary Rivalry to Friendly Competition. *Journal of Interamerican Studies and World Affairs* 27 (2): 25–53.

Selebi, Jackie. 1999. South African Foreign Policy: Setting New Goals and Strategies. *South African Journal of International Affairs* 6 (2): 207–16.

Serrão, Olivier, and Paul-Henri Bischoff. 2009. Foreign Policy Ambiguity on the Part of an Emergent Middle Power: South African Foreign Policy through Other Lenses. *Politikon: South African Journal of Political Studies* 36 (3): 363–80.

Shambaugh, David. 2004–5. China Engages Asia: Reshaping the Regional Order. *International Security* 29 (3): 64–99.

Shambaugh, David. 2012. *China as a Global Power: Understanding Beijing's Competing Identities*. Policy Report, Sigur Center for Asian Studies, George Washington University, Washington, DC.

Sharma, Ruchir. 2012. Broken BRICs: Why the Rest Stopped Rising. *Foreign Affairs* 91 (2): 2–7.

Shih, Chih-Yu. 1993. *China's Just World: The Morality of Chinese Foreign Policy*. Boulder, CO: Lynne Rienner.

Shih, Chih-Yu, and Yin Jiwu. 2013. Between Core National Interest and a Harmonious World: Reconciling Self-Role Conceptions in Chinese Foreign Policy. *Chinese Journal of International Politics* 6:59–84.

Shirk, Susan. 1997. Asia-Pacific Regional Security: Balance of Power or Concert of Powers? In David A. Lake and Patrick M. Morgan, eds., *Regional Orders: Building Security in a New World*. University Park: Pennsylvania State University Press.

Sidiropoulos, Elizabeth. 2008. South African Foreign Policy in the Post-Mbeki Period. *South African Journal of International Affairs* 15 (2): 107–20.

Singer, J. David, Stuart Bremer, and John Stuckey. 1972. Capability Distribution, Uncertainty, and Major Power War, 1820–1965. In Bruce Russett, ed., *Peace, War, and Numbers*. Beverly Hills, CA: Sage.

Singh, Baljit. 1965. Pundits and Panchsheela: Indian Intellectuals and Their Foreign Policy. *Background* 9 (2): 127–36.

Singh, Jaswant. 1998. Against Nuclear Apartheid. *Foreign Affairs* 77 (5): 41–52.

Skidmore, David. 1994. Explaining State Responses to International Change. In Jerel A. Rosati, Joe D. Hagan, and Martin W. Sampson III, eds., *Foreign Policy Restructuring: How Governments Respond to Foreign Policy Change*. Columbia: University of South Carolina Press.

Smit, B. W., and B. A. Mocke. 1991. Capital Flight from South Africa: Magnitudes and Causes. *South African Journal of Economics* 59 (2): 101–17.

Smith, Hanna. 2005. What Can Multipolarity and Multilateralism Tell Us about Russian Foreign Policy Interests? In Hanna Smith, ed., *Russia and Its Foreign Policy*. Helsinki: Aleksanteri Institute.

Sotero, Paulo. 2010. Brazil's Rising Ambition in a Shifting Global Balance of Power. *Politics* 30 (S1): 71–81.

Southall, Roger. 2006. Introduction: South Africa, an African Peacemaker? In Roger Southall, ed., *South Africa's Role in Conflict Resolution and Peacemaking in Africa*. Cape Town: Human Sciences Research Council Press.

Sprout, Harold, and Margaret Sprout. 1965. *The Ecological Perspective on Human Relations with Special Reference to International Politics*. Westport, CT: Greenwood Press.

Sridharan, Kripa. 1996. Parliamentary Opposition and Indian Foreign Policy. *Asian Journal of Political Science* 4 (2): 15–31.

Srivastava, G. P. 1960. Second Thoughts on Indian Foreign Policy. *Indian Journal of Political Science* 21 (2): 143–53.

Stephen, Matthew D. 2012. Rising Regional Powers and International Institutions: The Foreign Policy Orientations of India, Brazil, and South Africa. *Global Society* 26 (3): 289–309.

Stephen, Matthew D. 2014. Rising Powers, Global Capitalism, and Liberal Global Governance: A Historical Materialist Account of the BRICs Challenge. *European Journal of International Relations* 20 (4): 912–38.

Stewart-Ingersoll, Robert, and Derrick Frazier. 2010. India as a Regional Power: Identifying the Impact of Roles and Foreign Policy Orientation on the South Asian Security Order. *Asian Security* 6 (1): 51–73.

Stewart-Ingersoll, Robert, and Derrick Frazier. 2012. *Regional Powers and Security Orders: A Theoretical Framework*. London: Routledge.

Stryker, Sheldon, and Anne Statham. 1985. Symbolic Interaction and Role Theory. In Gardner Lindzey and Elliot Aronson, eds., *Handbook of Social Psychology*, 3rd ed. New York: Random House.

Stuenkel, Oliver, 2013. The Financial Crisis, Contested Legitimacy, and the Genesis of Intra-BRICs Cooperation. *Global Governance* 19:611–30.

Sutter, Robert. 2014. China and America: The Great Divergence? *Orbis* 58 (3): 358–77.

Tanham, George. 1992. Indian Strategic Culture. *Washington Quarterly* 15 (1): 129–42.

Thibault, Jean-François, and Jacques Lévesque. 1997. The Soviet Union/Russia: Which Past for Which Future? In Philippe Le Prestre, ed., *Role Quests in the Post–Cold War Era: Foreign Policies in Transition*. Montreal: McGill-Queen's University Press.

Thies, Cameron G. 2001a. A Social Psychological Approach to Enduring Rivalries. *Political Psychology* 22 (4): 693–725.

Thies, Cameron G. 2001b. Territorial Nationalism in Spatial Rivalries: An Institutionalist Account of the Argentine-Chilean Rivalry. *International Interactions* 27 (4): 399–431.

Thies, Cameron G. 2002. A Pragmatic Guide to Qualitative Historical Analysis in the Study of International Relations. *International Studies Perspectives* 3 (4): 351–72.

Thies, Cameron G. 2003. Sense and Sensibility in the Study of State Socialization: A Reply to Kai Alderson. *Review of International Studies* 29 (4): 543–50.

Thies, Cameron G. 2008. The Construction of a Latin American Interstate Culture of Rivalry. *International Interactions* 34 (3): 231–57.

Thies, Cameron G. 2009. National Design and State Building in Sub-Saharan Africa. *World Politics* 61 (4): 623–69.

Thies, Cameron G. 2010a. Role Theory and Foreign Policy. In Robert A. Denemark, ed., *The International Studies Encyclopedia*, vol. 10, 6335–56. West Sussex, UK: Wiley-Blackwell.

Thies, Cameron G. 2010b. State Socialization and Structural Realism. *Security Studies* 19 (4): 689–717.

Thies, Cameron G. 2012. International Socialization Processes v. Israeli National Role Conceptions: Can Role Theory Integrate IR Theory and Foreign Policy Analysis? *Foreign Policy Analysis* 8 (1): 25–46.

Thies, Cameron G. 2013. *The United States, Israel, and the Search for International Order: Socializing States.* New York: Routledge.

Thies, Cameron G. 2015a. China's Rise and the Socialization of Rising Powers. *Chinese Journal of International Politics* 8 (3): 281–300.

Thies, Cameron G. 2015b. The United States and China: Altercast Roles and Changing Power in the Twentieth Century. In Sebastian Harnisch, ed., *China's International Roles: Challenging or Supporting International Order?* New York: Routledge.

Thies, Cameron G. 2016. Role Theory and Foreign Policy Analysis in Latin America. *Foreign Policy Analysis.* https://doi.org/10.1111/fpa.12072

Thies, Cameron G., and Marijke Breuning. 2012. Integrating Foreign Policy Analysis and International Relations through Role Theory. *Foreign Policy Analysis* 8 (1): 1–4.

Thies, Cameron G., Olga Chyzh, and Mark David Nieman. 2016. The Spatial Dimensions of State Fiscal Capacity: The Mechanisms of International Influence on Domestic Extractive Efforts. *Political Science Research and Methods* 4 (1): 5–26.

Thomas, Raju G. C. 1980. Continuity and Change under the Janata Government. *Pacific Affairs* 53 (2): 223–44.

Thomas, Raju G. C. 1981. Relationships in Southern Asia: Differences in the Indian and American Perspectives. *Asian Survey* 21 (7): 689–709.

Thompson, William R. 1995. Principal Rivalries. *Journal of Conflict Resolution* 39 (2): 195–223.

Tocci, Nathalie, with Ian Manners. 2008. Comparing Normativity in Foreign Policy: China, India, the EU, the US and Russia. In Nathalie Tocci, ed., *Who Is a Normative Foreign Policy Actor? The European Union and Its Global Partners.* Brussels: Centre for European Policy Studies.

Tomz, Michael, and Mark L. J. Wright. 2007. Do Countries Default in "Bad Times"? *Journal of the European Economic Association* 5 (2–3): 352–60.

Tomz, Michael, and Mark L. J. Wright. 2010. Sovereign Theft: Theory and Evidence about Sovereign Default and Expropriations. In William Hogan and Federico Sturzenegger, eds., *The Natural Resources Trap: Private Investment without Public Commitment.* Cambridge, MA: MIT Press.

Trenin, Dmitri. 2009. Reimagining Moscow's Foreign Policy. *Foreign Affairs* 88 (6): 64–78.

Tsygankov, Andrei P. 1997. From International Institutionalism to Revolutionary Expansionism: The Foreign Policy Discourse of Contemporary Russia. *Mershon International Studies Review* 41 (2): 247–68.

Tudoroiu, Theodor. 2012. Conceptualizing BRICS: OPEC as a Mirror. *Asian Journal of Political Science* 20 (1): 23–45.

Valdez, Jonathan C. 1993. *Internationalism and the Ideology of Soviet Influence in Eastern Europe.* New York: Cambridge University Press.

Vigevani, Tullo, and Gabriel Cepaluni. 2007. Lula's Foreign Policy and the Quest for Autonomy through Diversification. *Third World Quarterly* 28 (7): 1309–26.

Vigevani, Tullo, and Marcelo Fernandes de Oliveira. 2007. Brazilian Foreign Policy in the Cardoso Era: The Search for Autonomy through Integration. *Latin American Perspectives* 34 (5): 58–80.

Volgy, Thomas J., Renato Corbetta, Keith A. Grant, and Ryan G. Baird, eds. 2011. *Major Powers and the Quest for Status in International Politics: Global and Regional Perspectives.* New York: Palgrave Macmillan.

Volgy, Thomas J., and John E. Schwarz. 1994. Foreign Policy Restructuring and the Myriad Webs of Restraint. In Jerel A. Rosati, Joe D. Hagan, and Martin W. Sampson III, eds., *Foreign Policy Restructuring: How Governments Respond to Foreign Policy Change.* Columbia: University of South Carolina Press.

Wade, Robert Hunter. 2002. US Hegemony and the World Bank: The Fight over People and Ideas. *Review of International Political Economy* 9 (2): 201–29.

Walker, Stephen G. 1981. The Correspondence between Foreign Policy Rhetoric and Behavior: Insights from Role Theory and Exchange Theory. *Behavioral Science* 26:272–81.

Walker, Stephen G. 1992. Symbolic Interactionism and International Politics: Role Theory's Contribution to International Organization. In Martha Cottam and Chih-Yu Shih, eds., *Contending Dramas: A Cognitive Approach to International Organizations.* New York: Praeger.

Walker, Stephen G. 2013. *Role Theory and the Cognitive Architecture of British Appeasement Decisions.* New York: Routledge.

Walker, Stephen G., Akan Malici, and Mark Shafer. 2010. *Rethinking Foreign Policy Analysis: States, Leaders, and the Microfoundations of Behavioral International Relations.* New York: Routledge.

Walker, Stephen G., and Sheldon W. Simon. 1987. Role Sets and Foreign Policy Analysis in Southeast Asia. In *Role Theory and Foreign Policy Analysis*, edited by Stephen G. Walker. Durham, NC: Duke University Press.

Waltz, Kenneth N. 1979. *Theory of International Politics*. Boston: McGraw-Hill.

Wansleben, Leon. 2013. Dreaming with BRICs: Innovating the Classificatory Regimes of International Finance. *Journal of Cultural Economy* 6 (4): 453–71.

Wehner, Leslie. 2015. Role Expectations as Foreign Policy: South American Secondary Powers' Expectations of Brazil as a Regional Power. *Foreign Policy Analysis* 11 (4): 435–55.

Wehner, Leslie, and Cameron G. Thies. 2014. Role Theory, Narratives, and Interpretation: The Domestic Contestation of Roles. *International Studies Review* 16:411–36.

Welch, David A. 2005. *Painful Choices: A Theory of Foreign Policy Change*. Princeton: Princeton University Press.

Wendt, Alexander. 1999. *Social Theory of International Politics*. Cambridge: Cambridge University Press.

Westhuizen, Janis Van Der. 1998. South Africa's Emergence as a Middle Power. *Third World Quarterly* 19 (3): 435–56.

Williams, Rocky. 2000a. From Peacekeeping to Peacebuilding? South African Policy and Practice in Peace Missions. *International Peacekeeping* 7 (3): 84–104.

Williams, Rocky. 2000b. South African Foreign Policy: Getting Critical. *Politikon: South African Journal of Political Studies* 27 (1): 73–91.

Wimmer, Andreas, and Brian Min. 2006. From Empire to Nation-State: Explaining Wars in the Modern World, 1816–2001. *American Sociological Review* 71 (6): 867–97.

Wish, Naomi Bailin. 1980. Foreign Policy Makers and Their National Role Conceptions. *International Studies Quarterly* 24:532–54.

Wolf, Reinhard. 2011. Respect and Disrespect in International Politics: The Significance of Status Recognition. *International Theory* 3 (1): 105–42.

Wolf, Reinhard. 2014. Rising Powers, Status Ambitions, and the Need to Reassure: What China Could Learn from Imperial Germany's Failures. *Chinese Journal of International Politics* 7 (2): 185–219.

Wolfers, Arnold. 1962. *Discord and Collaboration*. Baltimore: Johns Hopkins University Press.

Wood, Glynn L., and Daniel Vaagenes. 1984. Indian Defense Policy: A New Phase? *Asian Survey* 24 (7): 721–35.

Xiaoyu, Pu. 2012. Socialisation as a Two-Way Process: Emerging Powers and the Diffusion of International Norms. *Chinese Journal of International Politics* 5:341–67.

Yuan, Jing-Dong. 2007. The Dragon and the Elephant: Chinese Indian Relations in the 21st Century. *Washington Quarterly* 30 (3): 131–44.

Zaman, Rashed Uz. 2006. Kautilya: The Indian Strategic Thinker and Indian Strategic Culture. *Comparative Strategy* 25 (3): 231–47.

Zinkin, Taya. 1955. Indian Foreign Policy: An Interpretation of Attitudes. *World Politics* 7 (2): 179–208.

INDEX